Toddler Adoption

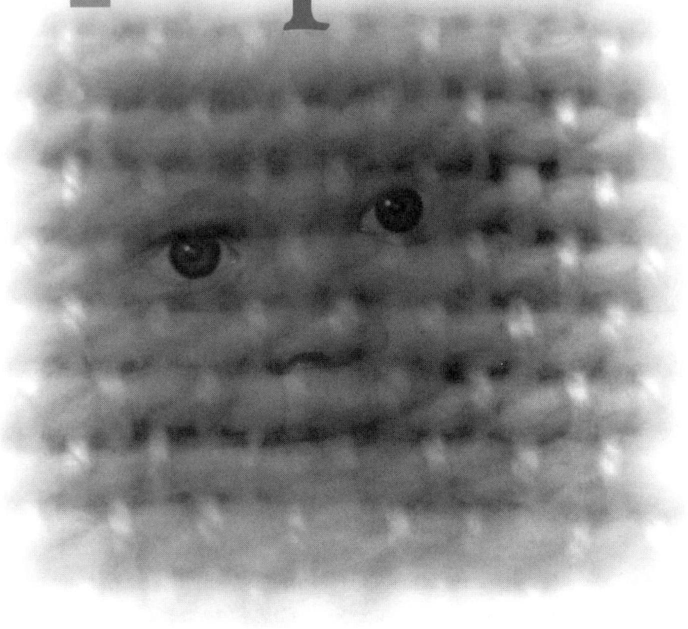

The Weaver's Craft

Mary Hopkins-Best

Perspectives Press
Indianapolis, IN

Perspectives Press
P.O. Box 90318
Indianapolis, IN 46290-0318
U.S.A.
(317)872-3055
http://www.perspectivespress.com

Book design by Wade Smola, T-Square Design, Fort Wayne, IN

Manufactured in the United States of America

Hardcover ISBN 0-944934-17-X
Paperback ISBN 0-944934-21-8

The author gratefully acknowledges reprint permission for the poems appearing in this book:

"Song of the Waiting Mother" by Christine Futia, first appeared in *Roots & Wings* magazine, Fall, 1989, and is reprinted here with the permission of the author.

"My Angry Son" is reprinted here with the permission of the author Grace Sandness from her book *The Loving River* (Dayton, MN: Balance Beam Press, 1983).

"Love will Grow" is reprinted here with the permission of the author Grace Sandness from her book *Commitment, The Reality of Adoption* (Dayton, MN: Balance Beam Press, 1983).

Library of Congress Cataloging in Publication Data:

Hopkins-Best, Mary
Toddler adoption : the weaver's craft / Mary Hopkins-Best.
p. cm.
Includes bibliographical references (p.) and index.
Hardcover, ISBN 0-944934-17-X
Paperback, ISBN 0-944934-21-8
1. Adoption—United States. 2. Toddlers—United States—Family relationships. 3. Toddlers—United States—Psychology. 4. Toddlers—Care—United States. I. Title
HV875.55.H66 1997
362.7'34—dc21 97-5617
CIP

Dedication

To my parents, Arlene and Gene Hopkins, who taught
me that Love is patient and kind and is not jealous.

To my husband, Richard, who showed me that
Love does not seek its own and rejoices in the truth.

To my daughter, Natalie, who made me understand that
You can have all the knowledge but without love are nothing.

And to my son Gustavo, who taught me that
Love endures all things, believes all things, hopes all things.

Love never ends.

Acknowledgments

Our toddler adoption would not have happened without the gentle guidance and support of Marilyn Smith, our social worker from HOPE Adoption and Family Services, Inc. Thank you Marilyn, for helping us discover for ourselves what we needed to do.

This book would not have been possible without the many families who generously contributed information about their own toddler adoptions. Thank you from the bottom of my heart.

My gratitude to Nancy Spoolstra, Ed Biggerstaff, and Jon Bell, who both provided invaluable feedback on earlier drafts of this book. Patricia Irwin Johnston, my publisher, has been a friend and guide throughout the development of this book. As she said, "The book has been a journey in itself." This book is complete because of the contributions of many, but I owe a special debt of gratitude to my editor, Cynthia Peck. Her personal insight as an adoptive toddler parent, and her professional expertise as an author and editor made the final draft a reality.

And finally, thank you to the woman who gave life to our son, and named him Gustavo, a name which means "brave and strong." Without her, neither my family as it is, nor this book, would exist. Mathilde, I pray you know that our son is not only still brave and strong, but that he is also healthy, happy, and loved beyond measure.

Mary Hopkins-Best
November, 1996

Table of Contents

The Weaver's Craft

by Richard Best

Threads of many colors,
the subtle and the bold.
Threads that form a pattern
of origins untold.

Threads for strength,
some spun from strife,
some rough, some smooth,
the threads of life.

Often fibers that bring strength
cut, cause pain and sorrow.
The weaver's craft to understand
that beauty waits the morrow.

Fibers torn
to be mended.
Fibers new
to be tended.

Joined with strands
that came before,
by loving hands
and hearts and lore.

One pattern formed
from beginnings rent.
Merged with another
through love, not descent.

Unique patterns
from the start,
harmonized
by the weaver's art.

The weaver's craft
to mend, then blend...
to form new patterns
that join and transcend.

CHAPTER One

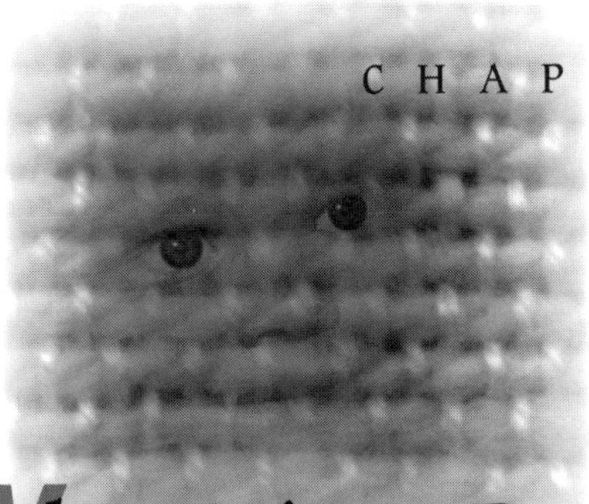

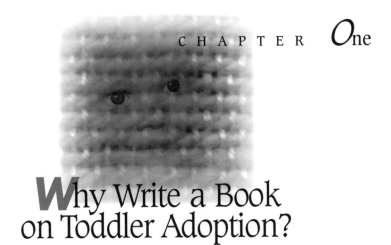

Why Write a Book on Toddler Adoption?

We reach many crossroads and destinations as we journey through life. As I huddled with my husband and daughter at the edge of a dusty cobblestone street in Cuzco, Peru, waiting for the little boy who would soon be our son, I marveled at how far—in so many ways—we had come for this child. In the six years since the birth of our daughter, grief and loss and new hope had forged and strengthened us. We had endured three frustrating years of infertility tests and treatment before changing our direction as we sought to expand our family. One crossroad. When we turned to domestic adoption, we were quickly chosen by a sincere young birth mother to parent her child—only to have her decide to parent her baby herself. Another crossroad. Unable to face the empty bassinet and the devastating possibility of another failed adoption, we explored the possibilities in international adoption. Surely there was a child in the world, perhaps a preschool aged child who had been abandoned or neglected, who might need us to be his parents! And so, here we were, sitting on a curb in Cuzco, anxiously peering down the road and watching for some sign of the pick-up truck that had delivered us to our hotel just two hours earlier.

Suddenly, there it was, bouncing up the street toward us. Time stood still. People piled out of the truck. All I could see was a solemn little boy wearing the corduroy outfit we'd lovingly selected for his "homecoming." The attorney handed my son to me, and our lives were changed forever. We reach many destinations as we travel, but the journey never ends. For our family, a new journey was beginning.

When eighteen-month-old Gustavo entered our lives, we were filled with excitement, awe, and a certain sort of naive self-confidence. We were, after all, "experienced" parents of one child born to us. Nonetheless, my own professional background in child development alerted me to issues that I knew might affect the adjustment of an internationally adopted toddler. Early deprivation, lack of nurture and stimulation, malnutrition, and a host of other problems related to neglect can have a profound effect on an infant's subsequent growth and development. My husband and I knew this as we began to look at the possibility of adopting a toddler, and we turned both to research and to the professionals to guide us with our decision. To our surprise, we found virtually nothing in the adoption literature that specifically addressed our questions.

Taking this as a "good omen" of sorts, we chose to pursue the adoption of Gustavo, whose brief biography indicated a history of neglect and lack of consistent caregivers. We understood, in a limited way, that he would have some special needs, but we did not fully grasp the extent of the challenges that lay ahead. What we were to learn could fill a book, and so it has. *Toddler Adoption* is written for prospective parents considering the adoption of a child between twelve and thirty-six months old, as well as for parents who have already adopted and now may be seeking explanations for problems their children may be experiencing. The stories of families are woven with the facts of child development to produce a book about the extraordinary challenges and rewards inherent in toddler adoption.

Why Adopt A Toddler?

Years ago, a toddler who became available for adoption was apt to become an adolescent who was *still* available for adoption. Families choosing adoption chose infants—the younger, the better. Some of this has changed in the nineties. Faced with fewer infants available for adoption, some prospective adopters are reconsidering their options. Other prospective adopters choose older children for different reasons. Some choose to adopt a toddler with the hope of avoiding the demanding, dependent, and expensive "baby" stage. Unfortunately, these prospective parents may be making a good choice for all the wrong reasons.

It is tempting to believe that a toddler who has experienced institutional care, neglect, or early abuse will soon thrive with proper love and behavior management from his dedicated new parents. Physical, cognitive, and emotional delays, however, are not "loved away." Overcoming previous trauma, bonding with the new family, and adapting to a new lifestyle are not quick or easy processes. Many children who *do* become strongly attached to their new families continue for many years to be sensitive to stress in their lives—reverting to their own hard-earned survival tactics in times of real or perceived crisis.

Gustavo bounded into our life as a bundle of contradictions. There was little doubt that our family was uncommonly enriched by Gustavo's adoption, but our parenting skills were seriously tested by his unique needs. While we anticipated a variety of developmental delays, we were not always prepared for the way in which these delays unfolded. Our greatest concern, however, was Gustavo's reluctance to form a growing and trusting bond to us despite our best efforts to be loving, supportive, and trustworthy. The techniques that had worked so well with his sister were ineffective with our new son. Without a growing bond of attachment to us, his new family, we felt that Gustavo's ability to catch up to his peers could be severely compromised.

When we scoured the adoption literature for answers, we found information about similar issues in older children, but the recommended parenting strategies weren't always appropriate for a toddler.

We reached out to friends who had adopted and to friends who were parenting toddlers adopted as infants only to find that their interests and concerns were very different from ours. We needed assistance and reassurance from others who understood both the tremendous joys and the disturbing frustrations we were experiencing. It was a lonely and discouraging time.

It was not until we found families whose children had arrived as toddlers that we began to see a pattern emerge that validated our own concerns. More than anything else, sharing and comparing stories with these families helped us understand the issues unique to adoption at this developmental stage. We could see that many toddlers who had experienced neglect, institutional care, and disrupted placements initially displayed developmental delays and did not automatically attach to their adoptive parents. Those toddlers who had enjoyed a healthy and stable caregiver relationship seemed to have fewer attachment difficulties but needed to be supported in their grief over the loss of those early relationships. Finally, the toddlers who had enjoyed a healthy early attachment, who were appropriately prepared for their adoption, and whose new parents were able to assume the new caregiving role gradually made the smoothest transitions and experienced the fewest obvious developmental delays. Unfortunately, most toddlers who are available for adoption have not enjoyed consistent parenting, nor are they gradually transitioned into their new families. Therefore, most toddler adoptions involve significant losses and unique challenges.

Looking back now, what we discovered seems so obvious. At the time, however, we could only feel the intense relief that comes from identifying some of the "givens" and some of the solutions—and realizing that group knowledge is a powerful ally.

What's So Special about Toddler Adoption?

If the stories we were hearing were to be believed, then it appeared that adopting a toddler poses challenges that are substantially different from those in adopting an infant or older child. It follows, then, that a successful toddler adoption requires both special attention by adoption professionals and special strategies for adoptive parents. Failure to recognize the unique issues involved in helping a toddler make a smooth transition to a permanent family may lead to the assumption that the developmental regression, attachment delays, and behavior problems that often accompany the move are due to inadequate skills or commitment on the part of the adoptive parents.

All aspects of a toddler's development are affected by the combination of early life experiences, changes in living environment, or changes in caregivers. Yet, a child of this age is neither cognitively nor linguistically able to participate in the typical adoption preparations often used with older children that will help him prepare for the transition. Adoption simply represents another mysterious life change in a series of confusing changes in environment, food, schedules, expectations, and caregivers. At the precise age when he is beginning to organize his world so that it makes sense and can be acted *upon*, events beyond his control prevent him from doing so. It is no wonder that the single most important developmental task of his first year of life—learning to *trust*—is undermined or eroded.

To understand that a toddler's ability to attach to his new parents can be severely compromised allows parents to approach their youngster in a way designed to meet his special needs. Traditional parenting strategies which rely on a child's desire to please and to be close to her parent (such as time-out) rarely work. Separation and withholding approval simply reinforce such a child's poor self-concept and inhibit attachment. And of course, physical retaliation only serves to set up a power struggle in which the adult has the initial overwhelming advantage.

A child who is adopted as a toddler needs parents who understand both his developmental needs and the effect of his early life experiences on that development. The adults who are involved in his adoption plan need to identify appropriate strategies that will help him prepare for the move to his adoptive family. And adoptive parents need help understanding how regression, grief, anger and attachment play a role in the behavior of their new toddler and they need assistance in ministering to their child's needs. The purpose of this book is to explore these very issues.

A Word about the Families in this Book

I have supplemented our son's story with information from other parents of adopted toddlers. Parents of twenty-six children adopted as toddlers graciously completed an extensive questionnaire about their adoption experience. To these I have added anecdotal information gleaned from conversations with thirty more families of adopted toddlers. These families came to the project from a number of sources. Some contacted me after reading an article that I had written on bonding with a toddler which appeared in a national adoption magazine. Others provided information after attending one of my workshops on the topic. Still others were referred by friends.

Families included those who had adopted domestically or internationally within three months to fifteen years of the time the data was reported. Some of their children had no discernible physical, mental, or behavioral special needs while others were diagnosed with serious mental health and other disabling conditions. See the Appendix for a more complete description of demographic information about the families.

The questionnaire used to gather information about toddler adoption covered a range of topics including the status of their child prior to adoption; their reason for adopting a toddler; first reactions; transition strategies; characteristic behaviors of their child before, during and after adoption; parenting strategies; support systems; advice for others contemplating the adoption of a toddler; and parental satisfaction. A number of families provided available supporting documentation such as psychological reports, school achievement records, and medical information. Finally, I was able to talk to and observe approximately half of the children for whom I had data.

The responses of families ranged across the continuum from "easier than expected," to "extremely challenging," suggesting that the respondents were not a biased group. The behaviors parents described were consistent both for children who had enjoyed a healthy prior attachment and those who had not been attached and/or had experienced frequent disruptions, lending validity and generalizability to the observations. While the stories that parents have shared may not represent all toddler adoptions, they do echo a common theme worth exploring and understanding.

The Audience for this Book

While this book is primarily written for parents, I hope that it will be helpful also to professionals who work with families whose lives may be touched by toddler adoption. The family who makes an informed adoption decision tends to be the most satisfied with the outcome. The frank discussion of the special issues involved in toddler adoption should help with this process. Realistic expectations enhance a positive experience.

Adoption social workers involved with prospective parents have an obligation from the very start to portray toddler adoption realistically. A toddler's unique developmental needs must be acknowledged and presented to prospective parents as being different from those of infants and older children. To fail to do so out of fear of jeopardizing a possible placement of an available child is unfair to all parties involved and could have disastrous results. I have talked to a number of adoptive parents of toddlers who have told me, frankly, that they were reluctant to share with social workers, family, or friends the problems they were experiencing in the placement for fear that their adoption would be jeopardized or that their parenting competence would be questioned. This can be avoided if parents know the issues and have realistic expectations from the very start.

Finally, this book can be a reference tool for a variety of other professionals who may work with and help families formed through toddler adoption—teachers, family therapists, support providers—as well as anyone else who would benefit from insight about the possible relationship between childrens' ongoing special needs and their adoption during toddlerhood.

After reading *Toddler Adoption*, some may conclude that they are not ready for the challenge of adopting a child who may experience significant developmental delays, intense grief reactions, and/or attachment difficulties. It is far better to reach that conclusion during the adoption planning process than to risk a disrupted placement later on. Other readers may choose to put the idea of adopting a toddler on hold for a while. For those who are ready, however, the information contained on these pages can be empowering. Knowing the work that must be done and the challenge that lies ahead will enable parents to be involved at every step of their journey. Knowing the right questions to ask is as important as knowing the answers.

As important as I hope this book will be for these audiences, *Toddler Adoption* was written, too, for those who are already parenting children who arrived home at this critical stage in their development. Regardless of the children's ages now, I think this book will help adoptive parents understand *now* some of the problems for which they had no easy answers at the time. I have found from my own personal experience and my conversations with many other parents of adopted toddlers the tremendous sense of relief just in knowing others who understand what you are experiencing. Given the silence and misconceptions that abound, too many families who might benefit from peer and professional support are needlessly bearing their concerns alone. Sometimes we need permission to share our stories—especially when they meet with blank stares or criticism on the first telling. It is my hope that this book will grant that permission to those who need it. Beyond camaraderie, though, I hope that readers will find specific strategies that they, like the families described in this book, can use effectively to integrate their new toddler into their families as well as into their hearts.

While there are many adult audiences for this book, it is children for whom this book has ultimately been written—children unable to tell their own stories. If the information contained herein helps the transition and adoption of even one toddler, it will have served a valuable purpose. If my son were to speak for himself and all the other children who came to their families as toddlers, he might tell you this:

> *Please learn as much as you can about me before you decide to be my mom or dad, so you won't be surprised about me. Don't think of me as a helpless infant, even though I may not*

yet be able to do all the things most kids my age can do. Don't treat me as if I'm older than I really am just because I act as if I don't need you to take care of me, however. When I push you away is when I need you to hold me and tell me that you will never let me go. I had to learn to do many things for myself before you came into my life, and it's hard for me to learn to depend on you as much as I should. Please recognize and help me with my special needs, but remember that I am still a lot more like other kids than I am different. See me first as your child, not as your adopted child or a child with special needs.

Sometimes I feel really sad and really mad. Don't pretend that I don't have these feelings, and don't get discouraged when I take out my strong feelings on you. Most of the time I am not really mad at you, but you're the one who's here now and the one I can safely show my feelings to. I know in my heart that you didn't do anything to hurt me, but I get all mixed up.

My memories of other moms and other places where I've lived are all in my mind, but they're stored in pictures, sounds, feelings, and even smells. I don't have the words to talk about these things. I can't figure out why that other mom disappeared, and I'm worried that you might go away, too. I often have to test you because it's hard for me to believe that you won't leave me, too. In fact, it's pretty scary for me to love you and trust you, so I might have to test your love the most when you start to be important to me.

Sometimes I just want to curl up in a ball and be a little baby again so someone will take care of me. Other times I want to do everything by myself and I feel like running away from you. Please be patient. We have a long time together. After all, the really worthwhile things in life usually aren't very easy and they don't happen overnight."

CHAPTER *Two*

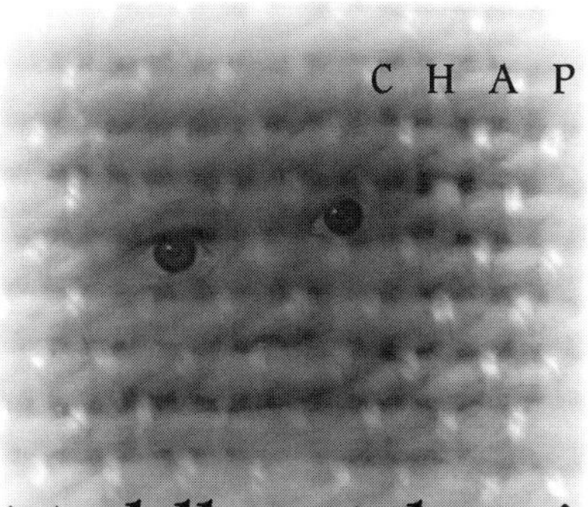

Is Toddler Adoption for You?

Tom and Sherry accepted a referral for birth siblings, ages one and three, because they wanted to avoid the expense and hassle of going through the adoption process twice. They preferred the idea of parenting children from infancy, but reasoned that getting two children at the same time was worth the trade-off.

Why do prospective adoptive parents choose a toddler? Is a three-year-old just part of a package deal that includes an infant? Does age preclude some adoptive parents from other choices? Are people requesting the oldest possible baby so they can have the experience of parenting a young child—but not have the burden of four or five years of costly daycare?

There appears to be a difference between families who deliberately *choose* to adopt a toddler and those who accept the placement of a toddler for other reasons. Parental age, financial and work considerations, the reality of what children are available, program requirements, waiting times, and a host of other factors often figure into a family's final decision regarding the child they hope to adopt. Yet, those parents who come to their decision as the result of a careful *refining* process increase the probability of a successful experience.

The most satisfied toddler adopters turn out to be those who believe completely in the *rightness* of their decision. They have come to toddler adoption with an understanding of the gains and losses that exist *on both sides,* and as a result, are better prepared to embrace the rewards and challenges that lay ahead.

Everyone has his own reasons for wanting to parent. Some people want to create the opportunity for their children to experience the type of childhood they experienced. Others want a child to carry on the family name or even a family business. Regardless of the motives, many people feel some sense of loss when the decision to parent is fulfilled through adoption. Adoption itself involves losses of its own: control, privacy, and normalcy. While infertile individuals have to deal with the loss of their ability to give birth, all adoptive parents need to deal with the loss of their genetic connection to their child. These losses need to be dealt with before considering parenting through adoption.

Some prospective parents are attracted to toddler adoption because they know that the availability of healthy infants is limited. They may believe that by being flexible and agreeing to the placement of an "older" child—a toddler—their chances of finding a child will be greater. Others who do not meet the eligibility criteria established by some agencies or countries for a healthy infant may look to a toddler adoption simply because they have been told that is the only child for whom they will be considered. The adoption of an older child usually qualifies as a "special needs" adoption. Many adoption specialists such as Holly Van Gulden and Lisa Bartels-Rabb consider *any child* over the age of one to be an "older child", but for reasons other than his age, such a child should also be viewed as a child with special needs.

In a sense, *every* adoption is a "special needs" adoption. As part of the preparation process, therefore, it is important for people to examine carefully their own needs, motivation, and resources before undertaking the adoption of a toddler or *any* child. In her book, *Adopting after Infertility*, Pat Johnston describes a helpful process for developing an adoption plan:

1. Personal reflection about adoption's losses and your feelings about them.
2. Sharing your discoveries about yourself with your partner.
3. Discussing ways to blend your separate needs and wishes in order to select a consensus or compromise course of action.
4. Gathering information about the options you find of interest.
5. Inventorying personal resources—time, money, emotional energy and physical capacity.
6. Building a detailed plan for pursuing that course of action—developing strategies, assigning tasks.
7. Pursuing the course of action.
8. Evaluating and adjusting the plan as needed.

This is a process that can be useful for preferential adoptors and single adoptors as well as couples dealing with primary or secondary infertility. Prospective adoptive parents who are single will of course, want to adapt this process to meet their individual needs. For example, they could discuss the results of their personal reflection with a trusted friend or family member.

Building on the idea that proper preparation is an essential element of healthy and successful adoptions, Margi Miller and Nancy Ward, from Children's Home Society of Minnesota, developed an excellent workbook titled *With Eyes Wide Open: A Workbook for Parents Adopting International Children Over Age One.* This workbook is designed to help prospective parents with the decision and preparation to adopt a child over the age of one. It would be an excellent accompaniment to this book.

This chapter is organized to help parents develop their adoption plan, examine the reasons why they might consider toddler adoption and understand the challenges and losses associated with such a decision. Chapters three through nine are specifically directed toward the needs of parents who have already begun the process or who have already adopted a toddler. Reading these chapters may also assist prospective parents through the process of deciding whether toddler adoption is for them. While reading about the children who become available for adoption, their preparation and transition, normal toddler development, the grieving toddler, attachment issues, and behavior management, prospective parents can try to envision themselves as adoptive moms or dads in the situations described. If the fantasy begins to lose its appeal, perhaps this is *not* what a prospective parent really wants to do!

Why Are Toddlers Available?

In our own country, eager parents who set out to adopt a healthy toddler with no emotional, physical, or cognitive delays may find this easier said than done. Such a child may not even exist. Unfortunately, most of the children who are available for adoption have spent time—often years—in foster care before a court orders the termination of the custodial rights of the birth parents. The fact is that even those toddlers whose birthparents are known to have mental, physical, or cognitive disabilities, or those who are known to have experienced severe neglect or other abuse, or those who have a diagnosed disability themselves, are frequently placed with relative ease—often with their foster families—not with the eager prospective parents just embarking on their search for a child.

While the foster care route to adoption may seem logical and even attractive, prospective adoptive parents are unwise to enter into a foster care agreement with the assumption that they will be able to adopt the child placed in their care. Any foster placement prior to court ordered termination of parental rights and assignment of guardianship to the foster parents involves a legal and emotional risk. One mother described her attempts to adopt the two-year-old for whom she had provided foster care since early infancy. After a draining and expensive six month court battle, the child was returned to the birthmother. Her experience is not an uncommon one.

Although none of the families who completed questionnaires for this book successfully adopted a toddler following foster care, it is still a possibility. Two families shared their experiences in foster parenting from toddlerhood the children they hoped to adopt. In one family, two boys, placed at ages one and three, are now four and six years of age. In the second family, eight-year-old Michael has lived with his foster parents since age two. None of these children have yet achieved the permanency of family, but their foster families remain hopeful. A third woman fostered her child of eighteen months from the age of four weeks and fully expected to adopt her eventually. She was unprepared—and completely devastated—when the toddler she considered to be her daughter was suddenly returned to her birth parents.

The international picture regarding the availability of toddlers for adoption is somewhat different. Instead of being removed from their families by a social service system, these toddlers more often come into care due to poverty or societal prejudice involving the circumstances of their birth. Many have medical needs that cannot be met by their family or in their homeland. Some are abandoned by their families in order to better meet the needs of other birth children. Some are abandoned because of gender. In many countries, the adoption process is lengthy because adoption is simply not a priority or is the target of criticism, and children reach the age of one or more before they are legally available for adoption even though they were relinquished or abandoned at birth. A number of countries that previously allowed a relatively short turn-around time between referral, placement, and adoption have now established procedures that significantly delay the process. Many toddlers adopted internationally have spent their first year(s) of life in one or more institutions. Most of these children demonstrate developmental delays and attachment problems related to neglect. Still, there *are* toddlers available for placement. If toddler adoption is right for you, preparation and persistence should help you to locate a child with a minimal amount of restriction and delay.

How Do You Find Out about Available Toddlers?

There is no single or best resource for toddler adoption. All of the families with whom I have had contact who have adopted a toddler domestically have worked through public agencies. Most of the children were identified through "Waiting Children" listings. Families adopting toddlers internationally have utilized public agencies, private agencies, facilitators, and direct parent-initiated adoption. Some international toddler adoptions began as infant referrals, but due to prolonged legal procedures or other delays, the child was a toddler by the time of placement. However, people who make a deliberate toddler adoption plan will not want to count on an infant aging up to toddlerhood during a lengthy adoption process. Deliberate toddler adopters will want to search for a child who can come home as soon as possible.

Public (county and state) agencies are likely to be responsible for placing toddlers whose birthparents' rights to guardianship were involuntarily terminated because of high risk factors to the child such as drug exposure, neglect or other forms of abuse. Typically, these children and their families have been involved with social services for quite some time before legal termination of parental rights.

Information about toddlers who are waiting for a placement is available through local, state, and national sources. There are adoption exchanges at each level that can act as a matching service or facilitator for registered children and families. These agencies exchange information with other state or national listing services about the children awaiting placement. Agencies often actively recruit parents through a variety of means, including updated photo listing books sent to public agencies, parent support groups, and libraries; newsletters; television specials such as "Wednesday's Child"; the Internet and World Wide Web; or newspaper features. Many private and public agencies utilize these exchange services. For a good place to start to gather information about U.S. waiting children, contact the National Adoption Center at 1-800-TO-ADOPT (1500 Walnut St., Suite 701, Philadelphia, PA 19102).

Many agencies involved with international adoption also have information about toddlers who are waiting for families and will gladly discuss such a placement. Since most families request very young infants, toddlers can become difficult to place as they "age out" in orphanages abroad. Social workers can match prospective parents with another family who has adopted a toddler, so they will gain good insight into what may lie ahead. Adoptive Families of America (2309 Como Ave., St. Paul, MN, 55108)) is an excellent source of information on agencies and support groups throughout the United States. The AFA bimonthly publication *Adoptive Families* includes information about waiting children, including toddlers, in each issue, although most of those featured have some additional special need besides their age.

Deliberate Toddler Adoption.

I suspect it is safe to say that few of us who adopted toddlers woke up one day with a clear vision that toddler adoption was our golden route to parenthood. Nor was toddler adoption the first option most of us considered. For this reason, time taken to work through an adoption plan is time well-taken. People who choose to parent because they want to satisfy a need to nurture another human life are likely to be well-equipped for parenting by any route. At a workshop conducted for adoptive and foster parents in Hayward, Wisconsin, in June, 1995, Vera Fahlberg emphasized that the job description for parenting is to create an environment that encourages a child to achieve his or her full potential. People who can envision themselves creating a nurturing environment for *any* child, should consider whether they could create that special environment for a toddler-age child.

People may have very different motivations for adopting a toddler. The best case scenario, I believe, is the "deliberate toddler adoption"—one in which the decision to adopt a toddler is the result of a careful refining process. First, parenting through adoption is carefully considered; then, adoption of children with special needs is contemplated, and finally, adoption of a toddler is consciously chosen as the preferred plan of action.

Families may decide deliberately to adopt a toddler for a variety of reasons, including anticipated life style, their own ages when they begin parenting, personalities and preferences, belief systems, age range of children already in the family, previous experiences with children, and observation of others who have succeeded, to name but a few. For several families contributing to the data for this book, an earlier positive parenting experience was the deciding factor in choosing toddler adoption. Four of the families reported being so satisfied with their first toddler adoption that they continued adopting children in that age range. Interestingly, three of the four families had not initially intended their first child to be a toddler. However, delays in the adoption process resulted in their child maturing to the toddler age while they negotiated the adoption. Based on the success of those first adoptions, each family felt up to the challenge of adopting a second toddler. The fourth family made deliberate plans to adopt their first and second toddlers. They anticipated the challenges associated with parenting a child who had been neglected and had experienced multiple caregivers because they were experienced adoptive and foster parents of older children with similar challenges. Yet while they anticipated the challenges associated with their toddler's attachment problems, they said they had not considered the impact of adopting two toddlers within one year. They expected that the two toddlers would quickly bond to each other and be more interested in attaching to Mom and Dad. Instead, the older toddler actually experienced a major setback in attachment to his older siblings and parents after the arrival of the new younger sibling.

Another couple reported being strongly influenced to choose toddler adoption because they had friends who had successfully adopted three toddlers. They observed their friends, and pictured themselves being in a similar situation. This couple carefully considered their resources and decided that they did not have the needed financial and emotional reserves to pursue open infant adoption, and feared that they would have difficulty handling the potential losses such as a birthmother's change of heart associated with open adoption. They also believed that their ages (early forties) would not be attractive to most birth parents. Two couples and a single parent decided that their ages and personalities were best suited to parenting toddlers. All of these parents believed that, even though the difference in age between infant and toddler was relatively small, there would be less "older parent stigma" associated with a toddler adoption.

The reasoning of parents as they worked through their options varied in depth and sophistication, but virtually all who made a *deliberate* plan to adopt a toddler also claimed to feel more in control of their adoption plan. Some parents were motivated by the mistaken assumption that a toddler would be less physically taxing than an infant. While they were surprised to learn how exhausting it was to chase after their toddler-on-the-run, they were not overwhelmed at the error in their thinking. One mother reasoned that her personality was better suited to toddler adoption because she had never been attracted by the physical helplessness of an infant. A single mother analyzed her lifestyle and reasoned that her activities and interests better complemented the needs of a toddler than those of an infant. She enjoyed outdoor activities such as camping and swimming, going to plays, eating out, and being generally physically active, and reasoned that a toddler would be able to immediately join her in many of those activities.

Two families were motivated to adopt older children because they believed in adopting waiting children rather than competing for healthy infants. In both cases, however, these families wanted to maintain the age order of children already in the family, so they chose waiting toddlers. In each case, the *deliberation* in their adoption plans contributed to their overall success and satisfaction.

Still, the majority of adoptive parents who provided information for this book did not initially set out to adopt a toddler. Most, like my family, considered other options before deciding on a toddler. An important step in that process for us was to find an agency with a philosophy and mission that fit our values. Perhaps it was fortuitous that the very agencies specializing in "healthy domestic infant adoptions" which we rejected because of what we felt were arbitrary acceptance standards would not have accepted us because we did not meet their age or religion requirements. We weeded out other agencies because placement was tentative (pending a birthmother's signed surrender) waiting lists were extremely long, or the adoption options were limited. We were fortunate to find an agency committed to empowering families to develop their own adoption plans, assisting families with unusual adoption plans, and serving a diverse client population.

Our failed open adoption caused us to reconsider infant adoption. The competitive process of domestic healthy infant adoptions bothered us. It was our feeling that the rightful role of the birth parent in the selection process and the tremendous over supply of hopeful adoptive parents has resulted in the Adoption Olympics. The reality is that there are not enough healthy domestic infants to meet the adoption demand. We didn't want to join the ranks of prospective parents trying earnestly to attract birth parents with the nicest home, most loving family, best future, slickest portfolio, most perks, and all-around most American family. With the encouragement of our social worker, we finally came to the realization that because of our family stability, parenting experience, experience with children with special needs, and motivations for parenting, we were good candidates for adoption of a special needs child. Another very important factor in our decision was that my husband and I both love the toddler stage of development. We find the toddler's emerging sense of personhood, developing language skills, and rapid physical development a source of constant wonder and amusement. These considerations eventually led us to our decision to pursue international toddler adoption.

When parents make an informed and deliberate toddler adoption plan, the unique issues associated with toddler adoption are acknowledged and considered realistically. David Kirk, author of *Shared Fate: A Theory and Method of Adoptive Relationships*, emphasizes the need for all adoptive families to accept the differences between genetically related and adoptive families. He stresses that while adoptive families are more *similar* to genetically related families than they are different, there are unique differences that must be acknowledged, dealt with, and appreciated. Likewise, families formed through toddler adoption are more like genetically related families and other adoptive families than they are *different*, but there are significant differences, nonetheless. Appreciation of those differences is one of the first realities most parents of adoptive toddlers experience.

A new toddler adoptive dad lamented, "He isn't at all like my birth son was at age two," while another mom commented, "I can't talk about our problems with the other members of our waiting-for-adoption support group. They're worrying about their babies' lactose intolerance while we're dealing with a raging three-year-old. We don't seem to have much in common anymore." The toddler adopters whom I know have had to deal with a variety of special needs. Some have had to convince social workers and foster parents of the need for their children to be prepared for adoption. Others had to advocate for a transition process that allowed them to gradually assume the caregiver role. Many have needed to support their children through the grieving process, and most needed to use specific attachment strategies with their new children. Most parents also found it necessary to use special behavior management approaches and specific strategies to help their children catch up developmentally with their peers.

People who are happy with their choice to adopt a toddler view parenting as a privilege rather than a right, and see toddlers as filled with potential. They recognize that there are no guarantees in parenting, and are prepared to respond as needed to a variety of potential outcomes. Well informed deliberate toddler adopters realize that the act of adoption is just the beginning of a life long process of family development.

Unfortunately there are some people whose reasons for choosing toddler adoption are misguided from the start. Primary among these are those who are motivated by pity or a sense of duty, neither of which is healthy for the child or the parents. An adoptive father called me recently to ask my advice about the lack of attachment behaviors displayed by his adopted children. The following is a verbatim transcript of his opening comments. "Well, I know you're interested in how children do who were adopted as toddlers, so I thought you'd want to know that it just doesn't work. We adopted three kids as toddlers after raising three of our own because we thought it was our duty to do something about all these kids without decent homes. Well, you just can't take those types of kids and put them in a good home. They just can't fit in. Our own kids never gave us the problems these adopted ones have. What you really need is some type of military institution for them because that's all they'll respond to."

Apparently, he and his wife chose toddler adoption because it made them feel self righteous, not because they were committed to their children's needs. During my many years preparing teachers of children with special needs, I have had to redirect a number of prospective candidates who were motivated by a similar pity for children with disabilities. Pity devalues the object of the pity and allows the perpetrator to maintain a sense of superiority and self-righteousness.

Interestingly, all adoptive parents, but especially those of us who did not adopt healthy Caucasian infants, occasionally encounter people who assume we were motivated to adopt our children out of a sense of pity. "Oh, you must be such special people to take a child that nobody else wanted," or " It's a good thing there are people who will take care of these very troubled children," and "What a lucky little boy." These comments only perpetuate the myth of adoption as a second-rate (or third or fourth rate) route to parenting. Sometimes ignoring such comments is the best tactic. Other times we try to educate people with responses such as, "We are so fortunate to have the opportunity to parent Gustavo. We are all so fortunate to have found each other. We needed each other to be a family." My favorite response to comments about how grateful my lucky son will be in the future is, "Yes, I lie awake at night envisioning the day my teenage children will announce how grateful they are that we are their parents."

There are other equally misguided motivations for choosing to adopt a toddler. One prospective adoptive parent told me that he liked the idea of adopting a child whose birth parent's rights to parent had been terminated involuntarily because, "If a kid has been legally taken away from his parents you wouldn't have to worry about birthparents changing their minds or showing up again." Ouch.

Other parents deliberately chose toddler adoption because they thought that would be a way to avoid all the "messy stuff" associated with the care of infants, such as making formula and changing diapers. The reality is that toddlers are masters of their own special messes. Their toileting accidents are bigger, they have a penchant for emptying cupboards and coloring on walls, and they can decorate the entire kitchen with thrown food.

Many prospective adoptive parents assume that by adopting a toddler they will get to skip the part about getting up in the middle of the night. Wrong again. The adjustment of toddlers to their new surroundings and families often requires as much night-parenting as day-parenting at a time when they can be far from reasonable.

One dad told me that he had chosen to adopt a mobile three-year-old because he didn't want to have to carry a younger child. If he was physically incapable of carrying a child and intended to implement other strategies to achieve the physical contact needed for a healthy attachment, I would have thought this was a well-informed decision. However, as I watched this father and his daughter interact, I realized that he avoided *all* physical contact with his daughter. When she tried to crawl unto his lap, he put her down saying, "You're too big a girl to sit on laps." Unfortunately, Dad was motivated to adopt a toddler because he simply wanted to avoid *any* physical contact!

I was talking recently with another couple who had adopted an institutionalized three-year-old from the Ukraine. I asked them about their daughter, and Dad replied, "Well, she isn't at all affectionate like most kids her age, but then we're not very demonstrative either so we seem to be a good match." It's hard to imagine that parents could be motivated to adopt a toddler so they could maintain physical and emotional distance. The long-term prognosis for these situations is poor, and sadly, these people are probably perpetuating the type of parenting they experienced as children.

Toddler Adoption by Default.

Another route to toddler adoption is what I refer to as "toddler adoption by default." This occurs when parents receive an infant referral, but so much time elapses between the referral and the placement that the child is a toddler by the time he arrives home. The positive aspect of this situation is that parents typically have a long-term investment in the adoption, so that even though they may be initially startled by how much their child has grown in the elapsed time since referral, they are strongly committed to the child and the adoption. Some parents whom I've talked to, however, expressed strong disappointment that the infant that had been referred to them was gone, and in her place was a toddler with a very distinct personality and unique set of needs. I call this "time warping" the child: continuing to envision the child at the age at which they were initially referred, rather than adjusting the vision to match the developing child. This is most likely to happen when parents continue to fixate on an infant photo, or when they don't receive updated photos and descriptions as the child grows.

A wonderful activity for parents who are waiting for the placement of a referred child is to read as much as they can about each stage of development their child is progressing through as they wait. In addition to being better prepared to parent their child after placement, this will contribute to their sense of connection to their absent child.

Sometimes parents imagine that they are adopting a "big infant" when they adopt a child who is between the ages of one and three. Prospective parents may be motivated to deny the differences associated with toddlers if they really have their hearts set on an infant but believe that they are unable to do so for one reason or another. These folks may convince themselves, with the encouragement of well-meaning friends or professionals, that toddlers are just large-sized infants. This denial that toddler adoption is different from infant adoption may happen for a number of reasons. People may subconsciously believe that infant adoption is better. They may not be able to accept the loss of the opportunity to parent a child during infancy. They may have a poor understanding of child development, or they may be very naive and uninformed. Some toddler adopters have shared with me that there was a little voice in their head that warned them that toddler adoption would be different, but that they chose not to trust their own intuition when they were assured by friends and professionals that toddlers were still very malleable. In *Adopting after Infertility*, Pat Johnston points out that people who have become victimized by their infertility may illogically reason that if their reproductive systems aren't working, then maybe they shouldn't trust their judgment, either. People reeling from having been rejected to adopt a healthy infant may also be particularly vulnerable to suggestion.

Interestingly, in some cases parents acknowledge the uniqueness of toddler adoption when social workers do not. One mother was very chagrined at being chastised by her social worker when she and her husband selected toddler adoption. When informed of their plan, the social worker retorted, "Well, I thought we had agreed on a special needs adoption." In spite of Mom and Dad's assurance and acceptance that their new son *would* have special needs, the social worker continued to deny those needs until she was forced, through confrontation with the child, to acknowledge his attachment difficulties.

When parents or professionals assume that toddler adoption is essentially the same as infant adoption, they are abdicating their responsibility to make an informed and deliberate adoption plan. Unfortunately, some parents don't find out until after placement that toddler adoption is a very different undertaking than infant adoption.

Parents who have raised birth or adopted children since infancy may be especially prone to want to deny the uniqueness of toddler adoption. In our own case, we overestimated the advantage of our previous toddler-parenting experience as a help in understanding and responding to Gustavo's needs. Our prior parenting experience was an advantage in terms of figuring out strategies that would foster Gustavo's cognitive, language, and physical development, but we soon discovered that the assumptions we had about attachment and behavior management that were based on our prior experience were of no help at all! When those tried-and-true strategies that worked so well with other children fail miserably with the newly adopted toddler, it's human nature for parents to either blame themselves, or think something is terribly wrong with their child. However, people who are willing to adjust or perhaps even totally overhaul their parenting techniques are good candidates for toddler adoption. When parenting a child from infancy, there is much more opportunity to influence his development than when starting at age one, two, or three. People who can accept the fact that their parenting strategies will be focused more on supporting, than on molding, are wonderful candidates for toddler adoption.

People who believe in their hearts and minds that toddler adoption is inferior to infant adoption or procreation will want to consider a different route to parenting. A very satisfied new adoptive toddler mom cautioned, "Don't adopt a toddler as a concession because you can't get any other child. Spend time with toddlers and let yourself fall in love with that stage of development." On the other end of the continuum, two parents described how they actively sought, but could not locate, infants with particular disabilities, and subsequently accepted toddlers who had the disability they were seeking. In both of these cases, the parents prepared extensively for their children's' physical/medical needs, but felt quite unprepared for the toddler-related issues they encountered. They felt that they had been somehow cheated out of the adoption experience they had envisioned.

I have talked to parents who fully admitted that they "settled for" a toddler adoption when they would have preferred an infant adoption, but believed that children under age four were the next best thing. For many of these people, toddler adoption was really a *third best option*, with biological parenting being their first choice, healthy infant adoption their second, and anything beyond that a far-off third choice. Toddler adoption allows many of these individuals to rationalize that they are at least adopting the child closest in age to their preferred choice. Unfortunately, this kind of thinking may interfere with Mom and Dad's ability to accept the unique needs of their adopted toddler.

Parental age may also be a contributing factor in an impulsive decision to adopt a toddler. Older parents may accept a toddler referral, rationalizing that they aren't getting any younger so they'd better accept any referral that comes along. Desperate people sometimes make rash and inappropriate adoption plans. While in Peru, I met a woman who had just arrived at our hotel and was anxiously awaiting the delivery of her new daughter. Cheryl seemed anxious to talk, so I said I'd be happy to wait with her. She proceeded to tell me how she and her husband had been rejected for confidential infant adoption programs by numerous domestic adoption agencies because of their age and had ruled out open adoption because they didn't feel they could handle ongoing contacts with a birthmother. They had applied for adoptions from both Korea and India, but subsequently decided to accept a waiting child referral from Peru because it seemed a faster route and because they had been led to believe that many of the available children were of European descent.

While I listened in stunned silence, Cheryl went on to tell me that her in-laws had promised to pay all adoption costs if she and her husband could produce a Caucasian-looking grandchild. She showed me the small snapshot of the little girl she was waiting for, explaining that the attorney responsible for handling the adoption had assured her that Mara had "European" features. In a short time, the obviously Indian child arrived at the hotel, escorted by the attorney. Cheryl took one look at Mara, handed her back to the attorney, and was on a return flight to the United States that afternoon, fortunately for everyone involved!

Desperation may make people susceptible to the power of suggestion. Professionals who are strongly committed to finding permanent homes for all children may consciously or unconsciously take advantage of the vulnerability of some people to accept a referral that they would not normally have made. The social worker who completes a homestudy literally holds the future of a client's ability to parent in his or her hands. Therefore, it is hard not to feel pressured to accept a referral that is recommended by workers. Pat Johnston suggests that rarely is such pressure intended or consequential, but that many adopters feel their own sense of guilt in response to the reasonable suggestion from agency workers that couples give at least careful thought to all of the options open to them in building a family by adoption.

Adoptive parents who make rash or misguided decisions to adopt a toddler may continue to deny the differences, feel cheated, resent the intrusion of unanticipated adoption related challenges, and/or end up feeling further victimized.

In the worst case scenario, the adoption may disrupt. Fortunately, many parents who do not deliberately choose toddler adoption make the necessary adjustments during or after placement, usually with the help of friends and family, or with professional assistance.

The most satisfied parents to whom I've talked, however, were those who were motivated to adopt a toddler because they enjoyed that age child, anticipated their child's unique needs, and felt empowered to address those needs. Most also recognized that there are unique rewards associated with toddler adoption.

Unique Rewards and Challenges of Toddler Adoption.

Even though most of this book is about the unique challenges of toddler adoption, I would be terribly remiss if I did not also talk about the exquisite joys. Many parents and siblings are delighted by their toddler's immediate ability to laugh and play. The toddler's capacity to smile is one of his key advantages over a very young infant. Being smiled at is a landmark event for all parents. When parenting an infant, you watch and wait for that first smile, often mistaking other grimaces for the anxiously awaited event. In a number of his publications, Foster Cline has described reciprocal smiling as the bonding mechanism between human beings...the very essence of our humanness. Throughout life a smile evokes a smile and is therefore of primary importance in the development of any relationship. Parents often describe how thrilled they are to be rewarded with laughter and smiles from their new toddler. In fact, every adoptive parent of toddlers whom I've asked was able to cite the exact time and place when they were first rewarded with a smile from their new son or daughter. Gustavo's sister Natalie was the recipient of his first smile, about an hour after he joined us at the hotel in Cusco, Peru. She describes with pride how he looked her right in the eye and laughed when she surprised him with a new toy.

People who enjoy the toddler's emerging self identity, desire to learn, sense of humor, and communication skills are great candidates for adoption. A toddler is completely unpretentious and honest about his feelings. You always know where you stand. The whole world is before her and it is a joy to watch her explore and conquer her environment. Everything is fresh and new. He studies his world with the precision of a scientist. She delights in the ludicrous and the unexpected. His nonsensical words and nongrammatical but logical sentences are delightful. To see the world through a toddler's eyes is to find the child inside yourself once again.

A number of parents described how uncomfortable they were with "fragile infants" and how much they enjoyed the physical competence of their new toddlers. One mom reported, "I'm always afraid to pick up infants because I'm afraid they'll break, but I felt comfortable right from the start holding, hugging, and playing with Sara." A dad said, "With infants, you always worry about whether they're getting enough to eat and gaining weight, but A.J. loved to eat right from the start."

Many parents emphasized how rewarding it was to watch and feel at least partially responsible for their children's development, especially in the first year after placement. Most toddlers make tremendous developmental gains following their adoption. Parents use words like *awesome* and *miraculous* to describe their child's incredible rate of growth. For example, many parents shared delightful stories of how their children's vocabularies doubled or tripled in the months following their arrival home. Toddlers normally acquire skills at an amazing rate, but because so many adopted toddlers display developmental delays at placement, their development appears even more accelerated. For example, Gustavo didn't walk when he was first placed with us in Peru, but within days he was cruising around the furniture. By the time he came home he was walking.

Many families reported enjoying their toddlers ability to interact immediately with siblings and join in family activities. One mom described how thrilled her three children were when their new brother joined in the fun of building a fort under the dining room table on his very first night home. In contrast to the disappointment many siblings experience when a new baby comes home and can do nothing but sleep, cry, and eat...the toddler can immediately join in many activities. I recently talked to a mother whose newly arrived toddler, with the rest of the family, had just returned from a wonderful vacation at Disneyland. She pointed out that they would have had to cancel the long anticipated trip if a newborn had joined the family. Another family of avid outdoor sports people reported enjoying the fact that their newly adopted toddler could immediately be included in family camping activities. Gustavo had become an avid sledder by the time he'd been home a week. Older siblings may have mixed reactions to a new toddler in the family, but most enjoy having an "immediate playmate."

On a deeper level, many families described the tremendous personal growth and family bonding that grew out of their toddler adoption experience. Struggling together to build family created strength of character and capacity to weather other challenges. Parenting children who have been neglected or otherwise abused creates special opportunities. Nathan and Joey's mom described humbly coming to terms with her own "perfectionism" as she shared her sons' struggles. She wrote, "I have peace knowing that I love my children and that they are growing up in a safe, loving place. I realize that there are not perfect solutions in this world-gone-awry. Dealing with my perfectionism and background issues has freed me to love my sons, throw myself into doing everything I can for them and not worry about tomorrow."

Many adopted toddlers arrive home with behaviors and needs that do not fit our society's definition of "good" children. In our society, babies and children are often labeled as good when they are easy to care for, cheerful, and undemanding. However, these babies are not loved more than the so-called "difficult" children. In fact, I believe the bonding process may be delayed by a particularly undemanding child. Adversity strengthens the fabric of parental love. Just as surviving our daughter's infant crying jags strengthened our commitment and confidence, sharing our son's struggles to adapt and attach strengthened our family bond. The goodnight kiss of any child is ever so sweet, but the first goodnight kiss from a toddler who has struggled with attachment is exquisite. While none of us choose to create problems for our children or ourselves, we should appreciate the learning and growth opportunity inherent in meeting and conquering challenges. All of the families who provided information for this book felt that their family bonds became stronger through toddler adoption.

Parents of transracially adopted toddlers reported growing in many other ways. One dad described his expanded appreciation of human beauty after observing the tenacity and inner strength of the people from his new son's country of origin, a country in which the majority of people live in abject poverty. Other parents described how their enhanced appreciation of literature and art from their child's culture had broadened their horizons. A number of parents reported having acquired a much deeper understanding of the history of the world and its people through their international adoption experience than they had been exposed to in American high schools and colleges. Some parents described their heightened appreciation of multiculturalism through incorporating holidays and celebrations from their child's culture into their family traditions. Still others reported an expanded political perspective as they studied the history and current events of their child's country of origin.

All of us who are privileged to be parenting adopted toddlers have grown in ways we never dreamed. Our children are exquisite and precious individuals who have enriched our lives beyond description. Our lives have even been enhanced by the difficulties we've encountered. Now let's talk candidly about those difficulties.

When people make the decision to pursue toddler adoption, they are making a decision that will affect their lives and the lives of their descendants forever. It is not a decision that should be made quickly or easily. Prospective parents are advised to assess candidly their readiness to deal with the special challenges often related to toddler adoption and their resources for meeting those challenges. Careful preparation now will help people avoid unnecessary time and expense later. Prospective parents are advised to try to picture themselves dealing with the types of issues described in the following section.

Toddlers with Specific Developmental and Adoption Related Problems.

Before committing to adopting a toddler, people will want to learn everything they can about toddler development to help them separate behavioral challenges that are characteristic of *all* toddlers from those behaviors indicative of developmental delays, grieving, or attachment challenges. If Dad did not know that most toddlers are given to occasional temper tantrums, he might think his adoption is a total failure the first time his child pitches a fit or drops to the floor in the grocery store when Dad won't buy the enticingly displayed candy at the check-out counter. However, convulsive raging that is frequent and prolonged and abject despair which does not respond to comforting are not normal toddler behaviors. Finding out that toddlers typically develop "food fetishes" that make macaroni and cheese the only acceptable food of choice for weeks on end will provide parents with a more balanced perspective on the normalcy of their new child's eating habits, but it isn't normal for a toddler to show absolutely no interest in food, or to hoard or gorge food for days on end.

Familiarity with normal development will help people correctly interpret referral information, especially any assessments that have been done with the child. Because cognitive, language, physical and psychological milestones normally occur in a rather predictable pattern and sequence, serious deviations from those normal patterns are fairly predictive of developmental problems. Significant delays in the acquisition of developmental milestones and/or certain milestones developing ahead of their predicted occurrence often indicate serious cognitive, psychological, or physical problems. It's important to understand that children's reactions to devastating events such as abuse or the loss of their primary caregiver are greatly affected by their developmental level. The transition to a new family is particularly difficult for toddlers because of their stranger anxiety, lack of language skills, and the developmental tasks that they are dealing with. Older children can participate verbally in the selection, preparation, and transition to a new home, while toddlers have to be prepared and transitioned in very concrete ways. Knowing a toddler's developmental level provides a necessary context for understanding their reaction to the adoption process. It is extremely important that people are willing to parent their toddler at his or her developmental level.

A father whose Korean-American daughter is now five years old said, "I knew we had reached an important stage of adjustment when our daughter's neglect during infancy stopped being the overwhelming influence on her behavior, and we finally were able to stop attributing every problem to our daughter's being adopted...then we stopped thinking in terms of our adopted daughter, and just thought of her as our daughter." As children age, adoption will be one of many variables affecting their development, however many adopted toddlers carry baggage that has an overwhelming influence on their behavior and development, especially during the first months following placement. It is essential to learn as much as possible about the many factors affecting a child's well being.

Toddlers Have a Past

Child development specialists have long agreed that personality, interests, and abilities are affected by what happens to the child even before he is born, and are a result of both nature and nurture. In spite of this, some people naively cling to the belief that the child who cannot consciously recall events prior to age three will have no memory of his life prior to adoption. Furthermore, these same people may erroneously conclude that if you can't consciously recall something that happened to you, it won't have any effect on you. Unfortunately, these attitudes are sometimes reinforced by the very professionals who are supposed to help prospective adoptive parents make informed decisions. If I had nickel for everyone who has ever said to me, "Aren't you glad you got Gustavo early enough," and "You're so lucky he wasn't talking yet so he won't remember anything that happened to him," I'd be a rich person. If the toddler's ability to recall and be affected by his early life experiences is not acknowledged, professionals and parents may be inclined to ignore his preparation and transition needs.

Parents should be able to accept the fact that their child will arrive with an intact temperament and personality. While even the newborn arrives with certain inborn characteristics, parents of infants have the luxury of coming to terms more gradually and gently with their child's inherent temperament than do adoptive parents of toddlers. One of the delightful rewards of toddler adoption is discovering who children are and being able to influence their values and interests, but if parents set out to make a major overhaul of their child's personality, they will be disappointed. The parent who can delight in discovering the child's personality and temperament rather than creating or conforming the child is a good candidate for toddler adoption. The successful adoptive parent strives to learn as much as possible about her child in order to accommodate that child's needs within the parameters of behavior necessary to live safely and compatibly with others.

Many toddlers become available for adoption because their birth parents were unable to parent for a variety of reasons, including poverty, societal discrimination, chemical dependency, mental illness, and multigenerational patterns of incapable parenting. Many of our adopted children have not enjoyed the type of early nurturing which we would have provided if we had had the opportunity. Our influence will always be inextricably mingled with all of their other life experiences and with their genetic composition. A popular saying among successful adoptive parents of children past infancy is that we can replace, but never erase our children's early life experiences. Yet, if parents pessimistically believed that children are doomed to repeat the patterns of their birth parents or that children who experienced early neglect and abuse are destined to life-long mental illness, they would be very poor adoption candidates indeed. It is appropriate to use any information available about potentially damaging genetic issues or early life experiences as red flags that can help parents make better informed decisions affecting their child when questionable or troubling issues come up. For example, knowing that some mental illness has a genetic link should alert parents to know and *watch for,* not *wait for*, symptoms of the illness.

People who believe that children who have experienced poor parenting during infancy will never form healthy attachments to new parents are also poor candidates for toddler adoption. It is important to know as much as possible about children's pasts, but then parents need to proceed with optimism and determination. I have found no compelling evidence to support the widely held misbelief that there is a sensitive period immediately after birth when bonding *must* occur or the opportunity will be lost forever.

As adoptive parents, we are challenged to balance our anticipation that our children will grow to be healthy, happy adults, with awareness of any special difficulties they may have related to their adoption or early life experiences. People who are committed to incorporating a child's past while building a foundation of security and trust for the future should consider toddler adoption.

Toddlers Need to Be Dependent and Independent.

A major developmental task of a toddler growing up in a healthy functional family is to form an identity separate from the parents. The ability to develop autonomy is predicated on a foundation of healthy attachment and a positive self-concept. Fortunately for most children, this foundation is built in infancy and sustained throughout life. Toddlerhood is normally preceded by a year of healthy dependency and a consistently loving relationship with the primary caregivers. This sets the stage for the long journey toward independence. Under the best of circumstances, the simultaneous push-pull of these two forces is challenging both for toddlers and their parents, but it can be overwhelming for insecure or unattached toddlers and their families.

It is a sad irony that the very children who *most* need to experience appropriate dependence often keep their adoptive parents at bay through their anger, grief, and biological urge to begin the long journey toward independence. The child who has experienced neglect or other abuse, or who has experienced multiple disruptions from a caregiver has not internalized the attachment cycle of need-rage-relief-trust essential to internalize trust and security (see Chapter 7). At the same time that this child's developmental time clock is saying, "It's time to differentiate yourself from your primary caregiver—your foundation," his heart and brain knows that he has no foundation. How can you separate yourself from what you've never had? The very children who have the greatest need for consistent, focused, responsive care are likely to be the most rejecting when it is offered. It takes very determined parents to intrusively and persistently impose attachment strategies upon a resistant child. The challenge of parenting the adopted toddler who has missed out on the attachment process is to regress the child back through the stages of trust and healthy dependence while simultaneously fostering acquisition of the toddler's normal developmental tasks.

Prospective parents should ask themselves whether they can accept the potential challenge of parenting a child who is experiencing this type of ambivalence about dependence and autonomy. People who have a very strong need to parent a child who seeks and responds to nurturing, love, affection, and care from the time of placement will probably have difficulty adjusting to the independent toddler who may initially disdain or simply ignore their overtures. Likewise, people who have a strong desire for a child who is physically helpless and psychologically dependent should probably pursue an infant adoption or adoption of an older child with severe developmental delays.

Clearly, people who are looking for a helpless, dependent infant are not going to have their needs met through toddler adoption. On the other hand, neither are toddler adopters who accept or even reinforce inappropriate independence in their children. Unfortunately, some parents welcome a toddler's prematurely inappropriate independence because it frees them from the time and effort required to recreate attachment. Such parents may be happy with a toddler who is self-reliant, aloof and undemanding, but eventually the lack of attachment will manifest itself and the problem will be much more serious and difficult to address than it might have been at the toddler age. For example, two parents at a workshop told me that they were very pleased with their recent toddler adoption because their daughter Emily was so self-sufficient and undemanding. They reported, "We were worried about having to totally change our lifestyle, and instead we've found that Emily actually requires very little care. In fact, she likes getting herself ready for and going to bed all by herself...she doesn't even want a book or tucking in...she just goes off to her room after dinner and we have the whole evening to ourselves." Sadly, not intruding upon this child's isolation was further driving a wedge between her and her parents—impeding their attachment to each other. Learning to trust and depend on new parents while trying to differentiate from parents is a confounding developmental challenge for toddlers who have attachment problems, and an equally confounding task for parents, but a task that must be faced squarely.

Can You Deal with the Toddler Who Resists Attachment?

Most people who are contemplating an adoption fantasize about the moment of their meeting face to face. They probably envision gazing into each other's eyes, theirs filled with tears of joy. Their son reaches out as they enfold him in their arms. Time stands still while parents and child instantly bond. Whatever a person's particular variation is on this happy scene, it probably does not involve a child who totally ignores adults, violently rejects them, or screams in terror at the sight of them. Yet, according to the parents whom I've interviewed, that is a typical reaction of a toddler without any understanding of what's going on, to her new adoptive parents—a reaction that is typical from a child who has been wrenched away from a familiar caregiver, or a child who has serious attachment challenges. In only four cases of toddler adoption which parents have described to me did their new child display positive and accepting behaviors at their first meeting. Three of these involved situations where the first meeting was during a preplacement visit with the former caregiver present, and the fourth involved an unusually resilient child.

Rage and rejection are very common behaviors in children who are grieving the loss of a loved one or are experiencing attachment problems for other reasons. Attachment problems, caused by a variety of circumstances typical to institutionalized children and those who have experienced neglectful and disrupted care, are *very* common in toddler adoptions. In fact, when asked what advice they would give others contemplating toddler adoption, most of the adoptive parents with whom I've talked advised, "Expect problems with attachment." At the very least, the adopted toddler is faced with the enormous task of transferring attachment from one caregiver to another. Even more challenging, however, is the daunting task of building attachment, literally from the ground up.

Toddlers frequently resist adoptive parents' attempts to get close to them as a way to protect themselves from getting hurt again or as a way to protect their attachment with the former caregiver. For the toddler who has enjoyed a previous healthy attachment with a former caregiver, using transition strategies such as those described in Chapter 4 will help him overcome seeing you as the object of his most intense stranger anxiety. On the other hand, when the toddler's needs have not been met in infancy, he responds to that rejection by becoming rejecting.

News stories which depict orphanage children reaching out through their crib slats, seemingly imploring someone to love them, are extremely misleading. Children who, early in life, reached out to have their needs met simply do not continue in a holding pattern until someone meets those needs. Children who have experienced inadequate stimulation, intermittent care, or a series of caregivers in institutions learn early not to continue their fruitless efforts to engage a caregiver. Children who have been severely neglected learn from an early age to count on no one but themselves. Toddlers who have been abused have long since learned that adults are unpredictable and can hurt you very badly, so you have to protect yourself in whatever way you can.

Children acquire amazingly adaptive skills very early in life to protect themselves against what they perceive as any threat to their defense systems. For toddlers this may involve autistic-like passive behaviors, appearing unresponsive to any stimuli, or it may involve violently aggressive behaviors. One little boy who could not yet walk had developed the ability to totally disarm adults when they attempted to hold him. He would suddenly throw his arms back and arch his back. Fearing that he would fall, the adult naturally grabbed him around his back and legs. Having thus occupied the adult, the toddler quickly leaned forward again and dug his fingernails into the adult's eyes.

Never underestimate the potentially strong attachment that a child has for a former caregiver, even to one who provided inadequate care. Children who are strongly attached to their former caregiver will reject all attempts to separate them from the object of their attachment. If a child is not adequately prepared and gradually transitioned to his new caregiver, the new caregiver is more likely to be viewed as the enemy than as a potential love object. During acute grieving over a lost attachment, toddlers are likely to remain detached and potentially aggressive rather than seeking a parent's support.

The good news is that at least parents know where they stand right from the start. The bad news is that rejection is very hard for any new parent, but especially for one who is feeling tentative about the decision to begin with. Parents of adopted toddlers must be resilient enough themselves to understand rejection while simultaneously focusing on attaching with their child even when it appears the attachment is not reciprocated. Prospective parents need to consider whether their egos can handle unreciprocated love. As one mom lamented, "It was so hard for so long—I was so in love with her, and she was so not in love with me." Friends and family members say naive things such as, "I bet Johnny is *thrilled* to be with you after living in an orphanage," when, in fact, Johnny is violently rejecting Mom. This issue is discussed in Holly Van Gulden's and Lisa Bartels-Rabb's book, *Real Parents, Real Children*. They point out that the benefits of adoption for the child—having a family of his own, being rescued from an abusive home, or joining a family that can economically provide necessities, even luxuries the birth family never could—are so wonderful that we have difficulty understanding how an adopted child could be anything but happy. But the reality is that many adopted toddlers are anything but happy, some for quite a long time.

Parents of adopted toddlers should be able to depersonalize rejection, understand its origin, appreciate the honesty of it, and remain steadfast in their determination to connect with the rejecting child. They need to maintain a long-range perspective, rather than require immediate responsiveness from their child. It may take weeks, months or even years before their love is reciprocated.

Because grief and attachment issues are so common in toddler adoptions, Chapter VI is devoted to the issue of parenting the grieving toddler, and Chapter VII is totally devoted to a discussion of attachment indicators and strategies to enhance the parent-child bond.

Losses Inherent in a Toddler Adoption

All adoption involves losses, but there are some losses associated specifically with toddler adoption which need to be honestly confronted by potential adoptive parents.

Toddler adoption is fraught with many emotions, but one I hadn't anticipated as a new adoptive mother was my grief over the loss of my son's infancy. I mourn all that I will never know and the fact that we weren't able to parent him for his first year and a half. How did he look and what was he like as an infant? Did he have a head full of hair at birth? Was he colicky? When did his first tooth appear? Who was the recipient of his first smile and who comforted him when he cried? Sometimes the pain catches me unaware, as when I see an infant who looks like I imagine Gustavo must have looked, or when he says, "Let's pretend just for today that I came out of your tummy," or when family photo albums seem to mock the absence of Gustavo's baby pictures. There is also an element of irrational but innate guilt that complicates parents' feelings. While parents know they are not responsible for the hurt their child experienced, they reason that if they had known about him sooner, maybe, just maybe, they could have prevented some of it. Now that Gustavo has reached the age where he is beginning to understand how much time elapsed before he joined our family, he is beginning to share this sense of loss. He has become poignantly aware of the fact that, unlike most of his friends, he has no baby pictures or stories about his infancy. Other adoptive parents may find that, like us, this sense of loss doesn't hit until after the child is permanently settled into his home, but it's an important issue to think about as people contemplate toddler adoption. As with many losses associated with adoption, parents will be dealing with their own feelings and simultaneously supporting their child's grieving process.

Reparenting is a strategy discussed in Chapter 7 to enhance attachment. It involves deliberately regressing the child back through certain aspects of infant development. Reparenting can be a very effective strategy for children having attachment difficulties, but it can also help parents resolve their own grief about the loss of their ability to parent their toddler in infancy.

Another loss experienced in toddler adoption is the loss of the type of reinforcement you get from other people when you are parenting an infant. Infants just naturally attract people. Everything about them engages adults, including their smell, sound, and appearance. When you are parenting an infant, people smile at you, coo at your baby, and are very indulgent of your needs. People get up and offer you their seat on the bus, they smile and cluck when you're attempting to soothe a fussy baby. However, these same people can be much less tolerant of a curious toddler. When the toddler is acting out, others may be disapproving or critical. A toddler's sticky touch is rewarded with a cringe and "Oh, ick!" Toddlers, unfortunately, have an unpopular reputation.

Prospective toddler adopters should think about whether they have a strong need for others to be solicitous of them, or whether they can grin and bear those moments of intolerance from people. Whenever Gustavo pitched a tantrum in public, I would quickly scan the crowd for a friendly face and make eye contact with an understanding kindred spirit for sympathetic support. Having found out how much this helped me in moments when I was feeling overwhelmed, I now always make it a point to look directly at parents of toddlers and smile. I make positive comments about toddlers, offer assistance to parents struggling to balance an arm full of groceries and a squirming toddler, and smile reassuringly at parents whose toddlers are raging out of control.

As obvious as it may seem for anyone contemplating *any* adoption, coming to terms with the fact that adoptive parents will not be their child's one-and-only parent is a loss to be reckoned with. Independent of the quality of the care, toddlers have been actively parented by others—sometimes several others—before coming home. It amazes me when prospective toddler adoptive parents tell me that they would prefer to adopt a child who had *never* had an attachment to another caregiver over one whose attachment was secure so that they could be the first ones the child really loved. How sad! This view represents a terribly misguided understanding of attachment. Transferring attachment is infinitely easier than establishing attachment with a toddler who has never known one. Parents who feel a strong need to be their child's first and only psychological parents need to reexamine the entire premise of adoption. Parents who can accept and reinforce the role other caregivers have played in their children's lives are wonderful candidates for toddler adoption.

Another loss which all adoptive parents of older children experience is the loss of personal time and space. Unlike infants who stay where they are placed, toddlers infiltrate every square inch of a home that is not under lock and key. Because parents want to enhance their child's sense of belongingness, they will not want to restrict her from many areas of their home, but that does mean they have to rethink their private space and possessions. If you don't want something broken, you have to move it. First time parents find this a more difficult adjustment than do experienced parents. Infants also spend more of their day sleeping than do toddlers, so personal time is also lost (some say nonexistent) when adopting a toddler. It is tiring to keep up with toddlers because they have the capacity to get into everything, without the judgment to go with their motor skills. Parents of toddlers who are struggling with attachment issues often find it difficult to leave their child with caregivers, thereby increasing their loss of personal time. Couples may find that they initially have little time and energy for their own relationship. While all of these issues improve with planning and experience, the loss of personal space and time is still an important consideration in adoption planning.

Do You Have the Resources Needed for a Toddler Adoption?

When developing an adoption plan, people will want to consider whether they have adequate resources for a toddler adoption. The adoption planning process recommended by Pat Johnston in *Adopting after Infertility* advises prospective parents to gather practical and concrete information about each of their resource needs, including time, finances, emotional energy, and physical capacity.

Toddler adoption should not be viewed as an instantaneous route to parenting. While the time between referral and placement is usually shorter than the wait for a healthy newborn, the time factor alone can hardly justify the decision to adopt a toddler. Careful planning for the transition of the toddler and incorporating the new child into the family is very time and energy consuming. Johnston advises people to examine the restrictions imposed by their jobs. Is flex time available? Can parents take a medical leave? Can they take a parental leave? Many new parents who contributed information for this book discovered, some to their surprise, that they needed much more time at home with their newly adopted toddler than they had anticipated, and some even decided to take a long-term (one to three year) leave from work to care for their child's special needs.

Age is another factor that needs to be taken into consideration in deciding what age child to adopt. While adults may feel perfectly capable of keeping up with a toddler at age fifty, they need to consider whether they will be able to keep up with a teenager in their sixties. People's health, family history, and support resources obviously need to be considered also.

As distasteful as it is, financial resources are another reality to consider. The total cost of an adoption is often more than the sum of the up-front costs of a homestudy and adoption agency fees, and those costs can vary considerably. Adopting a toddler domestically through public or private non-profit agencies is usually the least expensive route. Subsidies may be available to help with on-going costs and medical expenses in placing some waiting children. Private agencies and non-agency intermediaries are far less often involved in the placement of older children and often refer children with disabilities to the public sector agencies. I do know of one situation, however, where a privately arranged open infant adoption resulted in the birthmother's decision to place both her newborn and her toddler with the adopting parents. The cost of private adoptions varies considerably from state to state and even among attorneys and agencies within a state.

Many toddlers join their families through inter-country adoption, usually a more expensive route than domestic adoption. Adoptive parents are almost always responsible for travel costs. When parents travel to their child's country of origin, they have to be prepared for unexpected delays and unanticipated expenses. What will happen if people get detained while adopting their child? My husband was in Peru six weeks longer than anticipated, and the financial drain was soon evident. Are employers flexible enough to allow unexpected delays in returning to work? Is a leave affordable? For how long? One couple who adopted from Peru was detained for eleven months and ended up selling their home to cover their costs. In some countries, adoptive parents have to pay all fees in cash. One couple told how they had traveled to South America to adopt their two toddlers with $15,000 in cash literally taped to all different parts of their bodies, their reasoning was that if they were mugged it would take too long for the robbers to strip them of all of their money. In many countries, food and other products needed to care for children cost much more than they do in the United States. Diapers cost three times as much in Peru. With international adoption, there are follow-up costs associated with subsequently adopting the child in the United States, obtaining citizenship, and getting a U.S. birth certificate.

Whether a child comes from half a world away or right nearby, however, there are still often overlooked costs to consider for many essential items that a toddler will need. A place to sleep, car restraints, essential clothing, and toddler safety devices in the home are all necessary expenses. Many adopted toddlers require immediate health, and, possibly, therapeutic care. Prospective parents should determine what their health insurance coverage includes prior to accepting a referral. Health maintenance organizations typically require a referral from the primary care physician before insurance coverage will apply to specialists. If that is the case, talk to the family physician about a child's potential needs prior to placement. Toddlers who have special medical or physical needs may require adaptive aids for activities of daily living such as feeding, walking, communicating, or transportation. Children with diagnosed language or learning disabilities will need early intervention. As much as possible, anticipate these additional resource needs, recognizing, however, that toddlers' special needs are often not diagnosed prior to adoption. Services and treatment for children with special cognitive, physical, and emotional needs are discussed in detail in Chapter 5.

The emotional energy required to parent any toddler is great, but the emotional energy required to parent the *newly adopted* toddler is enormous. All life changes are stress producing, but expanding a family through the addition of a toddler can be especially stressful. While it's difficult for people to assess objectively their emotional energy, it will help to consider how other stressors are managed. Pat Johnston advises that parents who have adequate outside support often find that their emotional reserves are increased as a result.

An often overlooked resource needed in toddler adoption is physical stamina. Physical and emotional energy are interrelated. It's difficult to stay emotionally balanced if you are sleep deprived. Most newly adopted toddlers do not sleep through the night, and unlike an infant, toddlers may wander when they awaken. Therefore, at least one parent may be getting up frequently for a period of time. The developmentally delayed two-year-old who is not yet walking is one heavy load to carry! Parents who have raised their children from infancy gradually build up the strength to be able to carry a toddler occasionally, but the new toddler parent is often unprepared for the physical strength required to care for her new child. When an adopted toddler displays aggressive behaviors, restraining him simply to keep him safe can require considerable physical agility and stamina.

What if Mom or Dad Have a Disability?

My circle of friends and acquaintances who have been rejected by private and state agencies for domestic healthy infant adoption includes little people (formerly referred to as dwarfs), a woman who had had cancer six years before applying to an adoption agency, a traumatic brain-injured woman, and an individual with muscular dystrophy. Yet each of these individuals was determined eligible for selected special needs adoptions. A man and woman, both individuals of small stature, successfully adopted a toddler from Peru after repeated encounters with domestic agencies that would only approve them for adoption of an infant of small stature.

There is no proven correlation between the capacity to parent effectively and the absence or presence of a non-life-shortening disability. Society wouldn't think of removing children from parents because of an acquired disability, yet individuals with disabilities often face subtle or overt prejudice when attempting to adopt, especially when attempting to adopt a "healthy" infant. Attitudes are slowly changing, but most people with disabilities still encounter barriers.

People who have disabilities should not be summarily excluded from parenting just as they cannot be arbitrarily discriminated against on the basis of their disability in other situations. Each person needs to assess his or her own desire and needs and pursue appropriate goals. Because few social workers or other professionals associated with the adoption process have training in disability accommodation, the prospective parent needs to be as prepared to self-advocate and educate the system as to their abilities and accommodations as they often have had to be in other aspects of their daily lives. An individual's *ability*, not disability, should be considered in deciding whether parenting through toddler adoption is appropriate. While physical, cognitive and emotional capacities may be legitimate considerations in determining whether an individual is capable of caring for a toddler, one's disability should not automatically preclude a person from eligibility. Each individual's situation is unique. Children who are securely attached to their parents tend to learn to accommodate their parents' disability-related needs, but until attachment occurs, parents with disabilities may need special assistance. For example, the toddler of a friend who is severely visually impaired uses sound to keep Dad informed of her whereabouts. Beginning at the age of nine months, she has vocalized whenever her father is in her vicinity. However, a newly adopted toddler may initially need to be equipped with a sound device to accommodate a parent with a visual impairment.

People who have a disability and plan to travel to their adopted child's country-of-origin may encounter specific challenges. Developing countries are not as progressive as the United States in terms of disability accommodations and accessibility. Anyone who has accommodation needs should try to determine what barriers may be encountered in another country and plan accordingly. For example, wheelchairs are unusable in most of Peru due to road and sidewalk conditions. Most countries from which children may be adopted have nothing equivalent to the long-fought for U.S. federal Americans with Disabilities Act, which mandates accessibility and accommodations for individuals with disabilities. People with physical and sensory disabilities may experience challenges, but with planning and assistance, even the most insurmountable obstacles have been overcome.

Single Parenting and Toddler Adoption.

Four parents whose stories contributed to this book were single at the time they provided information about their toddler adoptions. Three of these individuals were single when they made the choice to adopt, and one parent divorced shortly after placement. One of the parents who began the process as a single parent actively sought a toddler because she felt a toddler would be easier to care for alone than would be an infant. The second initially pursued infant adoption, but after being turned down by numerous agencies because of her single status, accepted a toddler. The children of both of these parents were reported as having little transition difficulty, although one of the parents did leave work shortly after placement because her daughter demonstrated severe separation anxiety each day when left in day care. The third parent who adopted as a single actively sought a toddler because she felt an infant would be too much work. Sasha arrived at age two-and-a-half, and after the first week began demonstrating significantly challenging behavior, described by her mother as violent temper tantrums, physical aggression and inappropriate affection toward men. She reported, "No one prepared me for a two-year-old who would bite me, scratch me, hit me, keep me awake all night, take up all my time...as a single person my time had been my own...no one can prepare you for this!" The daughter of the parent who divorced shortly after placement also demonstrated numerous challenging behaviors associated with grief, and continued to display attachment problems as she got older. The custodial parent thought that losing a parent to adoption and then another parent shortly after placement contributed significantly to her attachment problems. By his own admission, in fact, this parent's own grieving process distracted him from parenting effectively.

Many of the parents who had partners emphasized the importance of sharing parenting challenges and joys. A number of parenting couples commented that they didn't know if they could have done it if they hadn't had each to lean on. In fact, two people are not even sufficient. Extended family, whether biologically related or not, are essential to raising healthy children.

Single parenting is challenging with a child of any age. Single parents should not presume that a toddler will be less demanding than an infant. In fact, many are *more* demanding, but in different ways. Single parents who select toddler adoption should consider their resources carefully before making their final decision, especially their support systems and contingency plans for their child's continued parenting should they become disabled or even die. To be perfectly honest, I would not even consider adopting a toddler as a single parent unless I had a support system of family or friends who were committed to intensive and sustained involvement with my child. I would also recommend adoption of a toddler who has had a secure attachment to his caregiver and no more than two disruptions.

What about Siblings and Adopting a Toddler?

People who have children will want to consider the effect of a new arrival/competitor into the existing family makeup as they develop an adoption plan. Depending on the age and number of siblings, parents will want to find ways to involve and prepare their children for the adoption of a toddler who may be a bundle of contradictions as he establishes himself in the family. Older siblings particularly need to be involved in the decision to adopt a toddler. If the older sibling has been included in the decision process, he will be more committed to making the adoption work.

Slightly more than two-thirds of the children described in this book arrived home to one or more older siblings. Interestingly, older siblings (six or more years older than the adopted toddler) demonstrated the greatest range of reactions. Older siblings were described from one end of the continuum or the other: from loving, maternal, solicitous, and happy, to resentful, jealous, hostile and depressed. Not surprisingly, the older siblings who were very involved in the adoption decision and process reacted the most positively, and those who were opposed to the plan from the start had the most negative reactions. The older siblings who were "onlies" displayed more resentment and jealously than children in families that already had two or more children. The bottom line: making room for another seat at the table requires more than just sliding over and readjusting the chairs!

Siblings who were closer in age to the adopted toddler seemed to develop a more typical sibling relationship more quickly than did older siblings: soon becoming best friends and worst enemies. Individual personalities and temperaments appeared to be the primary determinant of close-in-age sibling relationships. Children described as introverted, protective, possessive and having difficulty with interpersonal relations had difficulty adjusting to a sibling. One family who adopted two-year-old boys in two consecutive years described how they had mistakenly assumed that the second child would help the first child's adjustment. Instead, the older son displayed more intense attachment problems after the arrival of his two-year-old brother. Gender did not appear to be a major variable, although same-gender siblings were typically described as having more intense relationships, either positive or negative. Specific strategies for sibling preparation and transition are described in Chapter 4.

Feedback from Parents Who Have Adopted Toddlers

I have had the privilege of talking to many parents of adopted toddlers. Something that I always try to glean from those conversations is a sense of how Mom and Dad feel about the adoption process and the outcome. Do they feel that they made a good decision? Were they satisfied with the manner in which the homestudy was conducted and the adoption occurred? Were they adequately supported by family, friends, and professionals? Do they believe that they made an informed decision? And the most important question, if they knew *then* what they know *now*, would they do it again?"

The majority of parents expressed a strong degree of satisfaction with their toddler adoption. While there isn't an absolute profile of satisfied parents, there are characteristics of both the parents and their adoptions that are strongly related to parent satisfaction. Interestingly, parent satisfaction had little relationship to the difficulty of the adoption or to the status of the adopted toddler before, during, or after placement. Some of the happiest parents encountered and overcame the greatest bureaucratic barriers to their adoption and are parenting children with the most challenging medical and emotional needs.

Two factors did come up repeatedly in the families who were highly satisfied with their adoption. First was their *intuitive belief in the rightness of their adoption*, and second, that they had made an *informed decision* regarding adoption at the toddler age. Over and over again, satisfied parents indicated that the main criteria by which they decided to accept their particular child's referral was the degree to which they felt a sense of the "rightness" of the match of child to family. This was often expressed as a belief that there was some power beyond themselves—be it fate, the human spirit or a supernatural force that led them to their particular child. For some families this was expressed as a spiritual belief..."We know he is God's gift to us,"... "God meant for us to have this child." Other parents said that they intuitively knew that their child was meant to be their son or daughter..."I knew as soon as I heard about her that she was the right one." One dad who worked as a radiologist was reviewing medical information about children with physical disabilities who were residing in an orphanage in Central America. He intuitively sensed that one little girl whose case he was studying was meant to be his daughter. He and his wife subsequently read as much as they could about adoption of a two-year-old and made arrangements to meet her medical needs. Four months later they were on their way to meet their new daughter. Another father wisely advised, "You must believe in your heart that this (toddler adoption) will turn out to be the best decision you ever made!"

Parents who expressed the greatest satisfaction with their adoption said that they had made a deliberate decision to adopt a toddler-age child, or if their child had originally been referred at infancy but not placed for a year or more, that they had adjusted their expectations and were comfortable with the change. There was a strong relationship between how satisfied parents were with their adoption and how realistic their expectations were regarding the child's needs and behaviors. Satisfied parents were knowledgeable about child development and the challenges of adopting a toddler-age child. They recognized that there would be weeks, months, or even years of adjustment. In contrast, Molly's mom, who described her adoption as somewhat frustrating, reported feeling disappointed because she had envisioned playing with a happy baby...not with someone who was screaming all the time.

Satisfied parents were motivated to adopt a toddler because they wanted to nurture, not mold, their child. They recognized that adoption involves a two-way bonding, parents to child and child to parents. One mom succinctly described her reason for adopting her daughter. "A child needed us and we needed her." Another mom and dad who had adopted two toddlers declared, "Our children are so precious to us because we almost didn't have them. Every day we give thanks for their presence in our lives." Successful parents respect and celebrate the individuality of their child. Parents who give birth have a tendency to watch for certain characteristics and talents to emerge on the assumption that they will recognize certain aspects of themselves in their children. Knowingly or unknowingly, this may result in birth parents trying to influence those characteristics. In contrast, effective adoptive parents cherish every new talent and interest that evolves, even the ones that are not like theirs. Some adoptive parents even celebrate the fact that their children are not saddled with certain genetic characteristics and traits. One dad joked, "Thank goodness my son isn't genetically related to me so he didn't inherit my klutz genes." A key element in successful parenting of adopted children is being open and excited about the innate talents that children display. Successful and satisfied parents accommodated to their child's personality and temperament rather than trying to form the child to fit their expectations. Lisa's mom observed, "When she's good, she's a wonderful child, but when she's not, look out! She's very strong-willed and temperamental, but I wouldn't change her for the world."

Interestingly, over half of the families who provided information for this book stressed that their ability to maintain a sense of humor and pragmatism was related to feeling good about their adoption. As one dad suggested, "When you've got to laugh or cry, try to laugh!" Related to this, many parents emphasized the need for patience and not getting too "up tight" about how well and quickly everyone adjusts. In fact, one dad recommended, "Expect it to take longer than you anticipated, and then you'll be pleasantly surprised if it doesn't!"

A strong support system is an important factor in parent satisfaction. Spouses who are able to lean on each other and on extended family, and single parents who have a strong extended family or friendship support system feel less isolated and better able to weather the storms as a toddler adjusts to his new life circumstances. While very few parents reported being able to find adoptive parent support groups that focused specifically on the challenges they were facing, a couple of families indicated that it was extremely helpful to connect with one or more families who had adopted toddlers. Many parents expressed the hope for more toddler-specific adoption support networks as parents and professionals increasingly recognize the unique issues associated with toddler adoption. Clearly, the need exists.

There does not appear to be any difference in satisfaction between new and experienced parents of children who were described as relatively easy-to-parent. However, experienced parents seem to have an edge when it comes to parenting children with extremely challenging emotional and physical needs. For example, Nathan's adoption at age one-and-a-half was reported to be easier for his parents because they had already experienced toddler-related adjustment issues when they adopted Joey at age two. Mom and Dad indicated that they had really struggled with Joey's persistent tantrums, but were much better able to deal with Nathan's angry and grieving behaviors because of their similar experience with Joey.

A final notable characteristic of satisfied parents was their ability to take one day at a time and maintain a balanced perspective in the presence of chaos. Many toddlers seem to take one step backwards for every two steps forward in their adjustment and development, but it is important to think in the long range rather than in terms of today's setback. Rather than comparing the two-year-old adopted toddler's development to that of the two-year-old neighbor raised from birth in a secure, nurturing environment, compare the child's development today with where he was three months ago. A number of parents wisely recommended that parents of adopted toddlers take each day as it comes, celebrate every accomplishment no matter how small, and don't get overwhelmed worrying about the future!

I've only met a few people who have said that they would not have adopted a toddler if they had known how difficult it would be. These are the parents who also reported feeling coerced into toddler adoption in the first place or were very naive about attachment and grief issues. Whether these disappointed parents were deliberately misled about the challenges associated with toddler adoption in general and the potential for their specific child's needs, or whether they disregarded information from their social worker or others, is hard to say. Significantly, these were also the parents who reported that they felt isolated and lacked support or validation by professionals and extended family.

When asked, "If you knew then what you know now, would you do it again," the overwhelming majority of adoptive toddler parents have responded in the affirmative. "Absolutely yes," "In a heartbeat," and "Without a doubt," were typical responses. I am confident that I speak for the vast majority of adoptive toddler parents when I assure prospective parents that to adopt a toddler is to embark on the most exciting and fulfilling journey of your life.

Time-out for Some Personal Reflection.

At this point I need to invite the reader to step back and take a deep breath or take a break from this book. I know how overpowering it can be to hear about the many issues facing adopted toddlers and their parents. Sometimes when I listen to other adoptive families' stories, I feel overwhelmed...and my family has been through many of the same struggles! So if prospective adoptive parents are feeling pretty overwhelmed right now, that's OK. I don't know how my husband and I would have reacted to all of this information before we adopted Gustavo. I think we would have needed some time to digest it and contemplate the things that we could do to build a healthy family in spite of these challenges. One thing I am sure of though is this: as frightening as this may be, it sure would have been better to have had this information when we were making our adoption plan than it was to have to find it out when we were already parenting. By the time we figured this stuff out, we had no idea where to turn for help! We had to learn through the very slow process of trial-and-error, and by tracking down other adoptive families for information and support!

People who are prepared to accept the inherent joys, as well as the potential difficulties of toddler adoption can look forward to an incredible journey. I hope that readers will be reassured by the fact that the remaining chapters in this book are devoted to helping people develop parenting strategies which will help their toddler adoptions turn out to be as satisfying as toddler adoption has been for the vast majority of those whose successes are the stuff of which this book is made!

CHAPTER *Three*

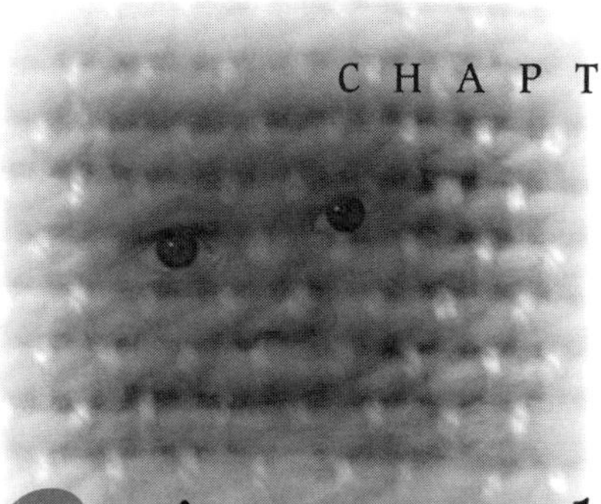

Getting Started on Adoption

Planning for parenthood through adoption involves more than an endless round of meetings and paperwork. It also means embracing the decision to adopt and confidently letting the world know with your words and actions that you have made an important decision to become parents. Adoption is a decision of entitlement, not one of justification.

Paul and Linda were excited about their choice to adopt an international toddler, but worried about their ability to connect and communicate with a child whose culture was so different from their own. When they joined an adoptive parents support group and heard how helpful it had been for some families to learn the basics of their child's language ahead of time, they immediately enrolled in a class at a nearby community college to help them prepare. In their new group, they also found support for their adoption decision, freedom from personal questions, criticism, and unwanted advice, an on-going dialogue on many issues involving adoptive parenting, and a sense of real understanding during the months of uncertain waiting and delays.

In a society where becoming a parent is often measured by the growing expanse of the expectant mother's waistline, expectant *adoptive* parents can feel overlooked and under-appreciated. One of the best ways to counter these feelings is to embrace your decision and your right to become a parent through adoption.

Preparing home, head, and heart for a new child is among the greatest joys of parenting. Because adoption can feel like an "invisible" pregnancy with no clear beginning and no due date, some adoptive parents have difficulty openly embracing this joyful time out of fear that it will all be whisked away in an instant. The secure and visible sign of progress—an expanding waistline—that signals to everyone an entitlement to some personal pampering as well as the pleasures of anticipating and preparing for a new addition to the family is absent, and this, alone, can make the entire adoption endeavor seem tentative. In fact, adequate attention to the preparation and transition phases of adoption are essential for both parents and child. Planned activities and involvement in the important stages of adoption planning, personal preparation, child preparation, and transition are as critical to the success of an adoption as any prenatal care for a pregnant mother-to-be!

First Steps.

Preparing for parenthood—whether through birth or adoption—inevitably involves attention to the "nitty gritty," the basic activities that will increase the probability of a positive outcome. Whether this means keeping medical appointments, attending Lamaze classes, and eating properly on the one hand, or meetings with a social worker or attorney, attending adoptive parenting classes, and completing endless piles of paperwork in a timely fashion on the other, the importance of these activities cannot be underestimated.

For adoptive parents, an essential step in the preparation process is completing a homestudy and related paperwork. All adoptions in the United States require an applicant evaluation and approval or endorsement from a qualified individual or agency in keeping with the regulations of the home state. This evaluation and approval process is often called a homestudy. While some states allow a licensed social worker to complete the homestudy and approve individuals for adoption, most states require an endorsement from a certified agency representative.

Many agencies have specific selection procedures or criteria that must be met in order to begin a homestudy. Meeting agency criteria is a challenging aspect of the adoption process. Having to qualify even to be considered for parenthood can feel demeaning, especially when the agency's criteria seem arbitrary and capricious. Agency qualifications are not necessarily the qualifications which are really essential to being an effective parent, however. In *Adopting After*

Infertility, Pat Johnston puts agency qualifications in perspective by reminding readers that for many agencies, strict qualifications serve one purpose only—they are effective gates which serve to slow the flow of applicants and make the work manageable.

In the final analysis, the purpose of the assessment and approval process is to protect the interests of children. While this gate-keeping function has traditionally been called the homestudy or investigation, recent changes occurring in many agencies make it appropriate to relabel the process parent preparation. Johnston advises that a good parent preparation process requires a supportive and positive relationship between client and professional, and assists clients in building on their strengths toward the goal of becoming effective parents. The process is thus gradually changing from a process of evaluating the applicants' capacities and qualifications to parent, to a process of facilitating self-analysis and exploration of adoption. Increasingly, the person conducting the homestudy is empowering parents to assume as much control as possible over the adoption process. This is compatible with the movement toward empowering birth parents also to assume as much control as possible over their adoption plan. The goal of the homestudy process is to reach a mutual decision regarding a family's interest in adoption, and to explore various types of adoption. While directed to some extent by the resources and programs offered by the agency a client chooses, the goal is normally achieved through some combination of a social worker's visit to the home, individual meetings, and group meetings. A social worker who is committed to providing emotional support and an education to clients as well as the completion of the homestudy itself can be a wonderful resource in helping applicants explore their readiness to adopt a toddler. Referring prospective adoptive parents to other toddler adoptive families is opening them up to an invaluable resource. "Buddy family" systems are an important source of pre-adoption and post-adoption support.

If done well, the homestudy process can be likened to an educational cram course to prepare for lifelong membership in a special organization—The Parent Club. Preparation for "membership" requires pre-adoptive parents to listen, ask questions, take risks, change directions, explore feelings, challenge old ways of thinking, read, reflect, follow directions, make mistakes, revise expectations, deal with bureaucracies, draw up working plans and agreements, practice patience, wait, make new friends, build support networks, fantasize and dream. Through it all, they often feel scrutinized and judged, no matter how much integrity is built into the process. The end result, however, is usually well worth the effort.

A poem by Christine Futia as she awaited the arrival of her first child, Leo, from India sums it all up:

Song of the Waiting Mother

I'm pregnant, but my tummy isn't growing,
And no one ever calls me "Little Mom."
The public simply isn't overflowing
With questions that I'd handle with aplomb.

There are no special clothes to mark my waiting.
Nobody stops and smiles as I pass by.
The absence of a due-date is frustrating
And looking at the nursery makes me cry.

When I'm overdue no one will worry.
The phone won't ring and ring as friends check in.
I can't induce my labor in a hurry,
My new life as a parent to begin.

Adoption is a worrisome endeavor,
And waiting all alone is not much fun.
To be "with child" a year seems like forever.
Dear God, we're ready! Please send us our son!

C.F. 1987

As they complete their homestudy and related paperwork, there are numerous other things parents can do to help themselves prepare for their pending role as the new parent of a toddler. One of the most helpful things is to join, or if necessary, form a "waiting-for-placement" support network. Some people feel uncomfortable widely broadcasting the fact that they are waiting for a referral or placement. Others hesitate to talk about an event that will happen at some unknown future time, and still others seem to feel as though it might be "bad luck" to talk about a pending adoption. It is very disconcerting to have to deal with people who, upon hearing of an excited adoptive parent's adoption plans, question their motives or launch into horror stories of other adoptions gone-awry.

A peer support network, both before and after adoption, is a safe place to share joys and frustrations with others who know the territory. Often the most compassionate support comes from relative strangers who are just a few steps ahead in the process.

Because they, too, have experienced the excitement, frustration, anticipation, and uncertainty that are adoption's bedfellows, they are sympathetic with the range and depth of feelings that flood newcomers to the process. The friendships that are forged out of the mutual need for support can be powerful lifelines, both for now and in the months and years ahead after a child becomes a family member. Experienced adoptive families often consider it a privilege and joy to be involved with other new families through the waiting, placement, and post-adoption process. In addition to moral support, these parents are tangible proof that placement does happen!

Another wise move in preparing for parenthood is to cultivate relationships with other families that are parenting toddlers, especially if one's circle of friends does not already include families with young children. The change from a child-less to child-centered lifestyle often impacts a family's social life dramatically, and it is important to develop a repertoire of toddler-appropriate family activities. Families with toddlers, even though they may not have joined their families through adoption, are wonderful resources. Finding out where these families congregate, and what parks, playgrounds, restaurants, museums are toddler friendly is helpful, as is developing friendships with families whose parenting styles are appealing.

Building a Sense of Entitlement.

Families formed through adoption come to believe that they belong together and are deserving of one another. They feel entitled to that relationship. The entitlement process starts with the decision to adopt and preparations for that adoption. In *You're Our Child: The Adoption Experience*, (Villard Books: 1987) Jerome Smith describes the process as beginning with recognizing and dealing with feelings about what brought about the decision to adopt. It continues with recognizing and accepting differences, and includes learning to deal with the societal view of adoption as a second best alternative. In *Adopting after*

Infertility, Pat Johnston emphasizes that for preferential adopters (fertile people who choose to expand their families through adoption), the process includes clearly identifying and acknowledging their motivations for adopting and how those motives may affect their parenting and their children's feelings about their adoptive status. Furthermore, parents of adopted toddlers need to deal with the societal view that adoption of any child other than a healthy infant is often seen as a third best alternative.

Entitlement involves rehearsing the parental role in several ways. Once having made the decision to adopt a toddler, families often comment that suddenly, toddlers and their families seem to be everywhere. They are often drawn, as if by some inner force, into observing the many parent-toddler interactions around them, placing themselves in the role of the parent, and thinking about how they would handle a similar situation. As they visualize themselves in a parental role, they often begin to talk about hypothetical situations and how they would deal with them. The heightened awareness of toddlers in their environment, along with finally getting a formal referral, the first photo of their child, and the many other activities in which they engage as they wait, all contribute to the sense of entitlement in adoption.

A family who feels entitled to parent their adopted child also is one that is comfortable talking about their plans to adopt. Despite their own personal comfort, however, families are often unprepared for the questions, comments, and sometimes insensitive remarks they receive that challenge their motives or their right to parent through adoption. As in other areas of life in general and adoption, in particular, well-prepared is well-armed! In *Real Parents, Real Children*, Holly Van Gulden and Lisa Bartels-Rabb advise parents to think about how they will respond to challenging questions such as, "Don't you want children of your own?" or "Are you being fair to the child by taking him away from his people?" Adoptive parents of toddlers may have their decision challenged by questions such as, "Aren't you afraid to adopt someone with that kind of family?" or "Why would anyone want to adopt a child at such a horrible age?"

Some people may actually ask very personal questions about a toddler's past, such as, "Was he abused?" or "Do you know anything about her real parents?". For some reason, otherwise polite adults often feel compelled and even entitled to ask highly personal questions that invade privacy, integrity, and confidence at a time that should be celebrated and anticipated with joy.

Practicing responses to these types of questions puts adoptive parents in charge of how much personal family information to share with others. Responses such as, "I'd prefer not to discuss personal family information" put the parent back in charge. Said with a smile and a quick change of the subject, especially if one is reluctant to offend the questioner despite the inappropriateness of the question, usually gets the message across. Maintaining a sense of humor is always a good idea, too. Responding to the inappropriate but oft-asked question about the whereabouts of my son's real mother with an off-hand comment such as, "His mom lives a mile east of Downsville on Route 4, is 5'4" tall , and has brown hair," allows me to enjoy the expression on the face of the curious questioner as the meaning of my answer—a description of me, the speaker—dawns on them and they quickly change the topic!

A family's growing sense of entitlement is also affected by the way in which others respond to the announcement of the proposed adoption. When close friends and relatives fail to embrace the decision and offer their emotional support, it can be a great blow at first. There can be any number of reasons that families have for withholding their full support, ranging from ignorance about adoption to feelings of discomfort about the implications of the choice, to worrying that the adoption plan will fall through and someone they love dearly will be hurt—again. Whatever the reason, however, the net result is the often the same—feelings of excitement, entitlement and anticipation are downplayed or called into question. As family and friends struggle with their own feelings, it is still important for expectant parents to keep the lines of communication open and to tell those who are important to them of their need for others to participate in the joy of their planned adoption just as they would a pregnancy.

For many women, the sense of entitlement is also influenced significantly by the way in which they are treated by other women. Women who are mothers share a unique relationship. When a woman announces her pregnancy or it becomes visibly obvious, her status changes. Even women who are perfect strangers often respond differently to each other when a pregnancy becomes obvious. A kind of special sorority is activated at a moment's notice, and "club" meetings form spontaneously—at social gatherings, fast food restaurants, parks and public pools, while standing in lines, and at work. The agenda is simple. Members share personal information and compare notes about child bearing and child rearing. One has only to be a mother or mother-to-be to participate in the "meeting". The bonding process that occurs among mothers is a time-honored way for women to validate their maternal role and achieve a sense of community. Women who are waiting and hoping for a child sometimes feel excluded from this informal but powerful Sisterhood, but by sharing their own excitement and what little information they may have, they can claim their right to membership—and increase their own sense of entitlement at the same time. Women who will probably not be invited into participation based on an expanding waistline of a pregnancy should take the initiative and join in the "meetings," by asking questions and displaying interest in other people's toddlers. Experienced mothers, whether through adoption or not, are an invaluable resource not to be overlooked by their pre-adoptive sisters. Membership in the Order of Motherhood contributes to a woman's sense of parental entitlement. Go for it!

Interestingly, even though men are increasingly comfortable discussing their parenting role with other men, they do not experience a similar status shift among their male friends. While men who are fathers enjoy a certain camaraderie associated with their shared parenting role, there does not appear to be nearly the distinction made between men who are or are not fathers as there is among women who are and are not mothers.

"Nesting" Activities that Build a Sense of Entitlement.

Along with the legal work, the paperwork requirements, and the emotional work or reframing that is part of the preparation process are a number of other activities that strengthen a pre-adoptive family's sense of entitlement. These can include exploring child care alternatives and social networks, gathering information about the new arrival's heritage and culture, identifying a pediatrician and developing a plan for health care, preparing the toddler's room and personal space, choosing clothes and key items that will be needed immediately such as a car seat or stroller, and toddler-proofing the household environment for safety and peace of mind. From the intensely personal act of choosing a name, to the public pleasure of a surprise baby shower—each step in the preparation plan makes the pending adoption more *real*, and the sense of entitlement to parent *that* child and become a *real* family grows and strengthens. This is a critical stage of preparation, because when the *real* child arrives with *real* behaviors that challenge even the best laid plans, the new parents are apt to be less overwhelmed and better able to change plans if necessary.

Child Care Plans

The issues of taking a leave from work after a child arrives and planning for appropriate child care are usually explored with the social worker during the homestudy process. Employers who offer their employees maternity leave benefits cannot discriminate against adoptive parents who request the same period of time with their newly adopted toddler. Therefore, it is important to discuss a pending adoption and request appropriate leave from work just as one would in the case of a pregnancy. In cases where both parents are employed outside the home, it is often possible to plan back-to-back child rearing leaves that can double the time during which one or the other parent can be with the newly-arrived toddler. While plans may change once a child is home with the new family, identifying alternatives ahead of time can prevent a situation in which arrangements must be made hastily without time to thoroughly explore all options. Most parents recommend against finalizing child care arrangements prior to placement, however, as it is difficult to decide on the best setting for a child about whom very little is known. Some parents, in fact, described how they changed their minds about returning to work, switched from full-time to part-time employment, or even changed jobs to accommodate the needs of their new toddler.

Clearly, there is no one right approach to child care that works for all families. Family needs should dictate the final decision. One mom and dad who have adopted two toddlers coordinated their schedules so one of them was always home. Another mom anticipated enrolling her two-year-old daughter in a center-based day care within a month following placement, but discovered that both she and her daughter needed more time together to strengthen their relationship first. After her daughter had been home for three months, she arranged for in-home care while she returned to work part time. Another single mom who returned to full-time work after her maternity leave arranged for an in-home sitter, explaining, "I felt that this way she would have a consistent place and a person to claim as her own, and it seems to have worked. Our social worker recently commented that she seemed so at home in our house. I love our house and I think she picks up on that."

Parents of toddlers who experienced severe and prolonged attachment problems often find it very difficult to return to work in the first years after placement. While this can be a problem on many levels, understanding its potential and planning options around that possibility helps to keep it in perspective and plan for the emotional health of the whole family. As Carl's mother explained, "I chose to stay home rather than return to work, and spent incredible amounts of time for many years doing things with my son to help him form a bond to us. We never had sitters and stopped seeing family friends whom he had indicated he'd rather have as his parents. Getting him to accept that we were his family was a constant challenge." Karina's mom and dad reported that they didn't leave her with anyone other than grandparents for the first several months because she was so insecure, but admitted in retrospect, "This wasn't a good strategy because it was hard on us never to have a break." Another mom returned to work after her maternity leave, but quit after a few weeks because her two-year-old daughter did not seem to be adjusting to their separation. In this case as in so many others, necessity dictated the change of plans.

I have talked to a few parents who adopted children from orphanage settings who made the decision to place their toddlers in a group day care facility from the start, reasoning that such a setting would feel familiar to their children. While appearing to be a sensible choice, there is a potential problem. A child who has experienced neglect in institutional settings may respond very passively in a group day care situation, and not receive the attention and stimulation necessary to begin to make up for early losses. The reverse can also be true. A child who was described as being the "pet" of his institution may become aggressive and out of control in a group setting where, by his own internal standards, the "rules" suddenly have changed. Parents who choose a group day care facility need to be very confident that their children will receive individualized, responsive, and compassionate care.

Penny decided to work out of her home and employ an in-home mother's helper because her newly arrived daughter was displaying the same type of indiscriminate affection toward adults that had served her so well in the orphanage where she had lived for two years. While the helper assisted Penny with basic housekeeping and child supervision, she was careful to reinforce, not substitute for, Penny's rightful role as the primary caregiver. In my own case, both my husband and I returned to work a few months after Gustavo's arrival, and thus made the decision to hire a woman to come into our home to care for Gustavo. We reasoned that our son needed the consistency of being in his own home and the one-on-one attention she could provide. We found an experienced, dependable, patient, and compassionate young woman who fit all of our needs to come into our home. We were further blessed by her ability to stay with him until he went to kindergarten. I am certain that much of Gustavo's development can be attributed to the warm, supportive and consistent care he received from Janie. She and her family will always be very important extended family to Gustavo and Natalie.

Whether employing a full-time caregiver or an occasional Saturday night sitter, it is essential that those who care for children adopted as toddlers understand something of their unique needs. While it certainly isn't appropriate to share all the details of a toddler's life before coming to his permanent family, it is important that caregivers understand something of the behaviors that he might display that are out of the ordinary for children who have been raised in an environment of consistency and support. For example, it is not unusual for children who have suffered from early abuse, neglect, or deprivation to display behaviors characteristic of that experience for some time after placement, and this can raise questions or concerns for a caregiver who does not understand its impact. It is important, therefore, to be honest with potential caregivers and thoroughly investigate their experience, competence, and attitudes. It is also important to try to find someone who is committed to the position offered in an effort to avoid burnout and frequent turnover in caregivers. The loss of a caregiver is traumatic for all children, but even more so for adopted toddlers who are trying to make sense of their new world and who may have already experienced multiple disruptions in their short lives.

Regardless of the type of child care plan that is finally developed, it is also important for a toddler to have the opportunity to participate in organized group activities. Many adopted toddlers arrive in their families with physical, cognitive, and emotional delays. Informal group activities in a nurturing, watchful setting can provide a non-threatening environment in which they can observe the actions of peers and safely try out their own newly developing skills. Such settings also allow parents and professionals to observe the interaction—or lack of it—of the new toddler in this new environment and plan how best to meet his developmental needs. Group play also helps to build important school readiness skills, including sharing, handling conflict, language development and enrichment, taking turns in play, following directions, listening in a group, picking up and putting away, and interacting with peers and other adults on many levels.

Developing a Plan for Health Care

Families who feel entitled to parent a child also feel empowered to make decisions about that child's on-going health care. Adoption is often referred to as a "leap of faith." This is especially evident when it comes to accurate referral information describing a toddler's health and medical background prior to placement. The medical records which prospective adoptive parents must have presented to them by law in most states are often scanty, containing little more than the obvious and observable. Whether or not a toddler's referral information contains much about a particular problem that may require specific medical, psychological, or educational services, it is wise to plan for the worst and hope for the best.

Given the possibility that a child's medical needs—both anticipated and unexpected—may be extensive and costly, it is critical that potential adoptive families be familiar with the scope and limitations of their health care coverage before accepting the referral of a toddler whose medical background is largely unknown. Even in cases where a great deal of information is provided, the very real limitations in medical care for abandoned or orphaned children in some countries should raise questions about the accuracy or depth of that information. Missed diagnoses can be costly. While recent federal legislation prohibits insurance providers from treating adopted children any differently than birth children, the limits of individual coverage may be a crucial factor in deciding to accept a referral of one child over another.

Once a family has made the definite decision to accept a referral, however, they can begin to plan to meet that child's medical needs in a general way. A good way to start, especially if this is the pre-adoptive family's first child, is by talking to other parents about the pediatricians and dentists they have chosen and their own satisfaction with the care their children receive. Internationally adopted toddlers often have medical and dental problems that are less common in the United States, so locating doctors who have some direct experience with such issues can save time and money in arriving at a complete and accurate diagnosis. Families who plan to use a family doctor or dentist who is not experienced in diagnosing or treating the type of conditions their toddler may display, are advised to talk to that person prior to placement, which will allow them time to do some research about the child's needs and locate helpful consulting resources. While we were satisfied with our family doctor's treatment of Gustavo's intestinal parasites and fungal infection, we transferred Gustavo's records to a pediatric dentist after a very unsuccessful visit to our family dentist. It is important for a newly adopted toddler to visit a dentist as soon as possible and to do so without frightening the child unnecessarily. Children who have experienced pre-or-post-natal malnutrition or other forms of neglect are at high risk for dental problems and may need immediate attention.

There are some outstanding resources for families seeking help in understanding some of the medical challenges that care for their toddler may pose. One excellent resource is the International Adoption Clinic located at the University of Minnesota (612) 626-2928. Headed by Dana Johnson, MD., this clinic has amassed a wealth of invaluable information to help professionals pinpoint even the most elusive diagnosis. Another is *Adoption Medical News*, a newsletter designed to help families and professionals understand the unique medical issues that are often part of domestic and international adoption. The main contributor is Jerri Ann Jenista, MD, an immunologist and prominent specialist in health issues of adopted children. The adoptive mother of four East-Indian girls, much of Dr. Jenista's interest in this area originally stemmed from her need to answer questions about the health of her own daughters. *AMN* is available through Adoption Advocates Press, 1921 Ohio St. NE, Palm Bay, Florida, 32907, (407) 724-0815.

If a family accepts the referral of a toddler with identified physical, cognitive, or language disabilities, it is a good idea to become familiar with the supportive services that are available in their area. While some adoption agencies are excellent sources of information about federal and state mandates regarding insurance coverage, subsidies, eligibility and application processes for obtaining services, and mandated early intervention programs, families most often assume the burden of responsibility for locating and arranging services. Other excellent sources of information about service providers include a family's employer benefits office, the family doctor, state and local social services offices, local parent support networks, legislative offices, and local or county school system's office of special educational services. It's a good idea to get as much information as possible about the special services a child may need, where the services are available, and who pays. People who are adopting domestically can work with their agency to determine if subsidies are available for their adopted child's needs, including medical, child care, and mental health services. Unfortunately, many of these same support programs are not available to families adopting internationally, although there is some legislative work currently underway to change discriminatory practice.

Toddlers whose needs may include extensive surgery or assistive devices such as braces or hearing aids pose special problems to a poorly-prepared family, especially when it comes to the high cost of continuing care. It is important to arrange for a thorough assessment soon after placement by medical and rehabilitation professionals and to obtain a suggested course of action for continuing care. Families can contact their regional Center for Independent Living, Center for Rehabilitation Technology, social service office, local educational agency, or privately funded agencies such as the Easter Seal Foundation or the Shriner's Organization for assistance in diagnosis, referral, and possible funding.

Many of the parents who contributed to this book recommended that new toddler families investigate family counseling and child therapy options available in their area just in case those services are needed. In fact, some respondents advised new parents to go ahead and plan for family therapy as a worthwhile preventative measure as soon as possible after arrival. If nothing else is obvious, it provides a baseline assessment and reassurance that the toddler and family are coping well.

Becoming a Multi-cultural Family

Adopting a child from another culture, ethnic group, or race changes the character and complexion of a family—forever. Families who are uncomfortable with this aspect of adoption are well-advised to choose a different adoption path. Children are quick to pick up on feelings that transracial or transcultural adoption was little more than a desperate choice or second best, and they deserve better.

Families who make the effort to learn all they can about their toddler's heritage and the culture into which he was born are building a foundation for their child's growing self-esteem and comfort with his origins. Every family, community, and society has unique cultural practices and expectations of its members. Children who move from institutional care to a family and those who are adopted internationally typically experience the greatest culture shock after arrival. However, any child whose life has been marginalized through neglect, abuse, or indifference—whether living in a third world country or right near home—will experience a similar sort of culture shock that is part of a major adjustment in life circumstances and expectations. Families who understand this are better able to empathize with their child's behavior and thus, to ease his transition once he is home. Knowing something about child care practices, sleeping arrangements, toileting and hygiene, discipline, and even how children were carried takes on special importance when everything a child is experiencing is new and unfamiliar.

Cultures also vary considerably in the amount of structure normally provided for toddlers. Children from institutional settings may have been subjected to rigid schedules and rules, while street children may only understand inconsistent schedules based on raw survival. Adoptive parent and author Lois Gilman cautions that some children, especially those from institutional settings, may have little or no experience making decisions, playing independently, or even playing with toys. Others may have known only female caregivers, and may be very resistant to a new, enlightened father's efforts at active parenting. Again, the more parents know in a general sense, the better able they are to problem-solve and trouble-shoot down the line.

In this age of easily-available information, it is not difficult for families to become familiar with a new culture. Museums, libraries, restaurants, ethnic communities within the larger community, cultural heritage festivals, and even the Internet are rich and abundant sources of information. Families can incorporate artifacts into their home and their new toddler's own space that reflect her culture. Experimenting ahead of time with foods which will be familiar to the child is another way to feel connected. Locating a good ethnic restaurant helps to develop the taste standard for families who are unfamiliar with the unique textures, smells, and tastes of the food of their new child's country. Families who find that they like what they are learning and experiencing ahead of time are usually able to share that appreciation in a genuine way with their child after she arrives home.

Pre-adoptive parents often have concerns about making themselves understood to their new child when both speak different languages. While language fluency certainly can help to ease a toddler's transition, even parents who have a working knowledge of their child's primary language often rely on interpreters during the formal adoption process in another country. Those who have no ability to use the language beyond a few basic words or phrases may have to make use of interpreters in the beginning, but clearly, there is more to communication than words alone.

Parents who shared their thoughts on their first experiences in trying to understand their toddler—and to be understood in return—recommend that new families work on acquiring some functional vocabulary while they await their child's arrival. Joining a language club, enrolling in a language class, or buying a set of conversational tapes, compact discs, or books can focus parents' energies and allay their fears about communicating with their toddler in the first few weeks. One mother stressed the importance of learning some minimal survival phrases and words such as: I'll be back; I am your mama/papa; no; yes; I love you; food/eat; stop; come here; show me where it hurts; toilet. Once home and part of their new families, it is astonishing to witness just how quickly toddlers adapt to a new language and begin to make it their own. Considering how long it takes most adults to acquire even minimum competence in their use of a few basic phrases, the ease with which most adopted toddlers achieve new vocabulary and language skills can make anxious parents wonder if their effort was all worthwhile. Rest assured that it is. If nothing else, children are momentarily engaged by their parents' struggle at making themselves understood. And some day they may want help with their language homework!

Naming the Adopted Toddler

What's in a name? In most cases, the name chosen for a child carries a history, a story, a reflection of the time in which he was born, a burden, a destiny. A very important decision families will make prior to adoption is whether to retain or change their new son or daughter's name, and comfort with that decision is just another step in the process of entitlement to parent the child a family is accepting into their hearts and home. Unlike a young infant, the toddler knows and recognizes his name. In fact, his identity is strongly associated with his name. Children recognize their own name before their first birthday, and most begin saying their own name shortly after that. Adoption experts such as Vera Fahlberg and Lois Gilman caution that once a child is old enough to recognize his name changing a child's first name may infer that his identity is not acceptable, and that while certainly not every child whose first name has been changed has developed serious difficulties, there may be some risk in changing a name. Unlike the older child who may have an active role in the decision to retain or change her name, a toddler is subject to his parent's decision.

Personally, I believe that toddler's names should not be changed unless there are compelling reasons to do so. Having said that, however, I must honestly report that the majority of parents of adopted toddlers whom I've interviewed opted to change their children's names. The new name was often a traditional family name, or a favorite name the parents had looked forward to using. Some parents said they believed that the extended family would be more welcoming of a child who was given a traditional family name or was named for a family member. However, adoption author Vera Fahlberg cautions that a child should never be named to represent a fantasy held by a parent about children of a certain name. If Mom and Dad or Grandma and Grandpa have a strong need for a child who matches the fantasies they've associated with a specific name, the chances of finding that child are remote. The mother of a Korean daughter adopted at age one and a half recently told me that now, at age eighteen, the former "Kim Lee," renamed "Lela," is challenging her parent's decision to change her name. Alleging that Mom and Dad changed her name because they were trying to deny her ethnic heritage, Lela has initiated steps to legally change her name back to Kim Lee.

The father of a child who had been seriously abused told me that he and his wife felt that it was important for the child to disassociate with her prior experiences, including her name. Other parents changed their internationally adopted children's names to common American names because they believed that a child would more easily integrate into the community with a name that was not dramatically different. Gilman suggests that parents may also consider renaming a child if there is already a child in the family with that name. Another reason to rename a child might be if the given name has negative connotations that can lead to ridicule by peers, especially when combined with the new last name.

Many parents who renamed their children tried to transition their children gradually to their new names. For example, "Becky" was renamed "Bridget Kay" and nicknamed "BK." "John," who was going to become "Bill," was called "John Bill" for a period of time, eventually being called only "Bill." Some families decide to change a child's name to one which they believe will reinforce her cultural heritage. For example, one family selected a new name that means "Eagle" in their child's native language because they felt the name was symbolic of their son and his brave flight to his new home.

Other parents modified their child's given names. This was done to retain some vestige of the child's given name as a way of showing respect for the culture and family of origin. For example, some children were renamed the English translation of their given names. Thus, "Roberto" became "Robert."

Some internationally adopted children's given names were retained, but the initials were used to provide a more "American" sounding name. "Juan Carlos" was nicknamed "JC." "Stanislas" is now called "Stan." The most common modification was to give the child a new first name, and use the given first name as the middle name, so "Maria Isabella" became "Chandra Maria."

Some parents felt a new name was symbolic of the child's new start. This reasoning can be explained to the older child. Parents who adopted a four and a five-year-old described how they retained their children's names for the first six months, during which time they discussed the symbolism of a renaming and together, with their children, selected new names. The family then conducted a formal renaming ceremony at which time the children symbolically let go of their former names and assumed their new names.

Few families with whom I've talked retained their children's given first names. We retained Gustavo's name but gave him the same middle name as his father. His whole name, Gustavo James Best, is an interesting mixture of Quecha, Spanish, and English culture, consistent with the blended cultures of our family. Gustavo came to us with literally no possessions other than his name: no clothes, blanket, lovey, or toy. We felt it was essential to retain the name his birthmother had chosen for him. In fact, we incorporated his naming by his birthmother into his life story. Gustavo means the *holder of the staff*, or *brave and strong ruler*. Therefore, we incorporate his naming into his life story by saying, "Your birthmother picked out the very special name of Gustavo for you, a name that means brave and strong, because we know that she wanted you to be brave and strong as you journeyed to your new family. She must have also picked out that name because you are of the true blood of the Inca, a very brave and strong people."

While we recognized that his name would set him apart from the masses of Jasons and Joshes that fill his generational peers, we knew that his obviously Hispanic appearance would distinguish him as being of a different cultural heritage than the majority of his peers anyway, so having a compatible name was a logical choice. We are proud of his Quecha heritage and welcome the opportunity to show that pride through his name. So far we have not experienced teasing from his peers. To the contrary, we have been pleased at how accepting his peers are of his unusual name. In fact, they seem to enjoy being able to pronounce it correctly. There are a number of Southeast Asian families who have moved into our area in the past several years, so children are becoming increasingly familiar with names that are different from those to which they are accustomed. In fact,

Gustavo's peers have been more accepting of his name than have adults, many of whom either make little effort to pronounce it correctly or try to Americanize it by calling him "Gus."

If, after careful deliberation, parents do decide to change their child's name, it is helpful to solicit the help of his current caregiver in transitioning him to his new name. For example, if "Juan's" caregiver will start calling him "John" before he leaves for America, it will be one less abrupt change in his life.

Practical Preparation: Clothing, Equipment, and Personal Space

An exciting activity associated with becoming a new parent is the ritual of accumulating and preparing the physical evidence of the long-awaited child's presence—clothing, equipment, and personal space. Immediate and extended family as well as friends and colleagues are often welcome participants in this process. Grandma and Grandpa ceremoniously give Dad the crib that he slept in as a baby. A sister knits a receiving blanket. Mom and Grandma shop for just the right coming home outfit. Mom and Dad browse garage sales to find an infant swing. Friends give up their Saturday afternoon to help paint the nursery. Aunt Sally hosts a shower, and everyone at the office chips in to purchase a high chair. A friend introduces Dad to the lingo and etiquette associated with twenty adults pawing through a table of sleepers at a garage sale.

Yet choosing clothing and preparing a toddler's room to reflect his needs, interests, culture, and even personality has a much deeper meaning than the mere accumulation of material possessions. It is a declaration of intent, an affirmation to yourself and the world that a child actually is joining your family. For a variety of reasons, families anticipating a toddler adoption may be short-changed in this area. There may be little time between referral and placement. Expectant adoptive parents may hesitate to ask extended family members or friends to help them prepare for their child's adoption because they aren't sure when or even if the adoption will really occur. And, saddest of all, family or friends may regard the adoption of a toddler as different than that of the birth of a child born into a family or even that of an adopted infant. Adoptive father and noted adoption author David Kirk shared how this played itself out in his own family when his wife's parents handed down a treasured heirloom cradle to their birth grandchildren but not to their adopted grandchildren.[1]

It is important that new families not deny themselves the opportunity to engage in and enjoy preparing for their child's physical needs. It is an exciting,

1 Kirk, David. (1995). *Looking Back, Looking Forward, An Adoptive Father's Sociological Testament.* Indianapolis, IN: Perspectives Press.

informative, and reassuring part of the anticipation and preparation phase of adoption, and an opportunity to welcome the involvement of close friends and family. If extended family members treat a pending adoption differently than they would a pregnancy, try to educate them gently, but don't be burdened by their own unresolved issues or lack of understanding about adoption. If they seem distant or unsupportive now, they most likely will fall into line after placement. On the other hand, if family members offer to share a piece of heirloom furniture or a special item of clothing that is clearly inappropriately sized for a toddler, try to incorporate these things in some symbolic way. The family cradle can be filled with special stuffed animals and placed next to the child's bed. Even an infant-sized christening gown can be gently taken apart and restitched to create something new while preserving the sentiment and uniqueness of the original.

Indulging in window shopping and browsing in stores that specialize in items for toddlers is both fun and educational. During the months when I was waiting for Gustavo, I loved to visit children's stores and fantasize about my son playing with the toys. I would hold up little boys' outfits and imagine how cute they would look on him. Doing these types of things made me feel more connected to him during the wait.

Just as it's exciting to imagine dressing up a child, doing things with him, and building rituals that will help bind him securely to his family, it is also fun to plan for the practical needs of a new toddler. Even if parents use a family bed, or siblings share a bed or room, each child should have some personal space where she can keep her own belongings. However, don't go overboard decorating before placement. Once parents get to know their child, his own space should reflect his special interests and preferences. Waiting will provide the opportunity for the toddler to have some input into his room arrangement and decorations. Gustavo's initial furnishings consisted of a crib, a Mickey Mouse table with chairs, a toy box, and a dresser. During the year following placement, his passion for trains evolved. We then had a wonderful time planning and decorating his bedroom with a train theme. He was very proud to be involved in selecting his bedroom furnishings and decor. His strong interest in trains was reflected in his selection of a Thomas the Tank Engine bed ensemble, pillow, lights, and rug. Two years later, he was still proudly telling visitors, "My mom painted those trains on my wall 'cause I like trains!"

There are a few pieces of equipment which are important to acquire prior to the toddler's arrival. A car restraint device is mandatory. Unless a child is familiar with and prefers riding in the booster type seat, a full-size carseat designed to fit children through the preschool years is preferable. Toddlers can escape too easily from the booster seat. They ride higher in a full-size seat and are therefore able to see out of the windows. Seats with a reclining function are nice for car naps. It is also a good idea to secure a portable stroller. Many adoptive parents are not prepared for the physical stamina required in caring for a toddler. It's nice to have a stroller handy when Mom can't carry a tired or non-mobile toddler. A child carrying backpack is not essential, but great for parents who can physically manage it. In fact, a backpack has advantages over a stroller. The child can be carried over any terrain in a backpack, and it keeps the child in physical contact with the person carrying the backpack.

Pictures and photographs are an essential element of a child's personal space and the family home. Pictures can provide tangible evidence of the child's past, the placement transition, and her membership in her new family. Colorful artwork from the child's country of origin, photographs of close friends from the orphanage, a group picture showing the adoptive parents and former caregiver together with the toddler, and a collage of photos taken during Mom and Dad's stay honor the memory of a child's transition to her new family. These types of pictures create an inviting environment, a sense of continuity, and a sense of permanence for children. Don't overlook the opportunity to display a child's artwork as soon as she joins the family. A refrigerator covered with a child's artwork proudly proclaims her to be a member of the family.

Toddler Proofing the Environment

Toddlers are naturally curious, and once they feel they have the "run of the house," anything is fair game for exploration. To encourage a toddler's creative exploration and feeling of belonging, I recommend toddler-proofing as much of the home as possible. Unlike parents of a new infant, toddler parents won't have a five to eight month reprieve before their child is an active explorer. One family described their traumatic first few weeks trying in vain to keep their two newly adopted toddlers out of dangerous situations. Their children's propensity for getting into every hazardous situation possible made sense when they found out that both youngsters had been confined to a restricted area of their orphanage which contained only cribs, tables and bare floors. The children were completely unaccustomed to stoves, cupboards, outlets, switches, electronic equipment, and bookshelves. Some children may not even be familiar with indoor plumbing.

Install latches on all cupboards or other containers that hold hazardous products. Toilets are particularly attractive to toddlers, so invest in a lid-locking mechanism. Cover sharp corners, remove slippery area rugs, and remove obstacles that complicate the lives of new-walkers. Install a gate if the toddler has not yet learned to safely negotiate stairs. Electronic equipment or anything else with dials is absolutely irresistible to most toddlers! One particularly enterprising family described how they fenced in a section of their living room for plants and electronic equipment rather than fencing their toddler into a confined space.

Remove poisonous substances to an inaccessible location and be particularly careful when using such substances. Poisonous substances often found around the house include after-shave lotion, ammonia, all medicines, ant poison, bleach, candle wax, dishwasher detergent and liquids, drain cleaner, glue, furniture polish, matches, moth repellent, mouthwash, nail polish, nail polish remover, nose drops, paints, perfume, plant food, shampoo, shoe polish, soap, spot remover, suntan lotion, toilet cleaner, and some plants such as mistletoe. Keep an emergency medical first aid kit handy that includes an emetic substance such as ipecac syrup to induce vomiting, and have the poison control center number listed by your telephone.

Preparing Friends and Family for Toddler Adoption.

If friends and extended family are involved throughout the adoption process, the announcement of toddler referral should not come as a surprise. However, close friends and family have their own preparation needs. They need to adjust their image of the new parents to incorporate their new family member. For example, if friends have been in the habit of calling at the last minute to go out on the town, they will have to adjust to the reality of needing to make child care arrangements or accommodate a different type of social activity which includes children. Most adoptive parents enlarge their social network through contacts made before and after adoption, but will want to maintain relationships with old friends as well. Friendships with people who have children will take on a new twist, especially for people who have been childless. In a manner similar to the renewed interest married people take in their single friends' pending nuptials, friends who are parents will probably be delighted to engage in extensive dialogues about the new child, especially if asked for advice. All experienced parents are valuable sources of information.

Family members are a potential source of both support or stress during the preparation and transition process. Families of people who have experienced infertility may still be grieving the loss of a biologically connected relative. Family members may also have to deal with their own lack of knowledge about adoption and their own prejudices. Sometimes they want the adopting parents to wait longer or to try harder to conceive.

Some parents report that extended family members are initially skeptical of their decision to adopt a toddler. Perhaps some family members secretly fear that a toddler will not be as easy to bond with as a cuddly infant. Others may be resentful that someone else got to parent the child during infancy, and still others may be concerned that a toddler who has experienced serious deprivation or abuse may never be able to fit into the family. Perhaps some members of the family worry that the adoptive parents are unrealistically optimistic about how easily and quickly the new toddler will overcome her attachment problems. Family members should be encouraged to express their concerns. Parents should share their concerns as well, and their plans to help their new toddler adjust. One of the best ways to involve the entire family in the adoption plan is to ask their advice and actively involve them in the preparation and transition activities. Ask questions—give assignments—seek help—stay connected. Sometimes prospective parents move into a world unto themselves or associate only with other waiting parents as they anticipate and worry about their pending adoption. Grandmothers can give advice on feeding the new toddler, grandfathers can be given the responsibility to pick up books on toddler development from the library.

Close friends and family members need to be prepared for the special needs of toddlers who are grieving and/or have attachment problems. Some people have more difficulty then others being actively involved with an adoptive family during the transition process. Be realistic and respect their needs while remaining open to the various forms of support they can provide. Some people can provide direct support and others can't. For example, a friend may have difficulty being around a toddler who is displaying frequent rages, but might drop off a casserole. Thank her and call her to chat while the child is sleeping. Try to be especially tolerant of childless friends who may feel very awkward and uncomfortable around a new toddler. I was visiting a friend a few days after he had arrived home with his newly adopted one-year-old and three-year-old children, when a mutual friend stopped in with a gift. This woman is childless, single, and the owner of a white convertible with white carpeting. She stood in the doorway of his cluttered, noisy home for five minutes before looking at her watch and saying, "I really have to get back to work." Before leaving she handed my friend a gift. We could hardly contain our mirth when the gift was revealed to be two dry-clean-only white snowsuits. However, it was the intent that mattered, and the snowsuits were used for church and other special outings.

Try to be tolerant of friends and family's misconceptions, stereotypes, or lack of knowledge. Sometimes adoptive parents forget that other people use insensitive adoption language out of habit, not to intentionally hurt. Perhaps we even used insensitive adoption language sometime in our past. When Grandpa says, "Why would Juan's real mom give him up?," gently respond, "I am going to be his real mom. His birthmother was unable to parent and, out of love, made an adoption plan that we have become part of." Lois Melina wisely reminds us that, adoptive parents forget that there was a time when they, too, may have had doubts about adoption, told racist jokes, or thought there was no choice but to conceive a child. Two excellent books for family and friends who are supporting an adoption are *When Friends Ask About Adoption: Question and Answer Guide for Non-Adoptive Parents* and *Other Caring Adults* by Linda Bothun, and *Supporting An Adoption* by Pat Holmes.

Siblings need to be specially prepared for the addition of a toddler to the family. While children should optimistically look forward to a new sibling, it is important that their expectations not be unrealistically idealistic. One of the best ways parents can help siblings prepare for a new family member is to talk about both the potentially positive and challenging aspects of the adoption. Don't build up unrealistically high expectations by saying such things as, "I know you're going to just love each other right away," or, "Won't it be grand to have an instant playmate?" Counter the instant playmate theme with a discussion of the realities of a sibling who will be interested in everything that belongs to an older sibling and the possibility of a sibling who is sad or even very angry.

Empower the older child by involving him in planning for his new brother or sister. For example, together go through the older child's outgrown toys and outfits to pick out things to be passed on to the new sibling. Natalie really enjoyed sorting through her discarded toddler toys and picking out the ones for

Gustavo. This was just one of the many things we did during Dick and Gustavo's extended stay in Peru. I think it helped her begin to feel connected to her new brother even before he came home. Talking with Natalie about her old toys also gave me the opportunity to prepare her for Gustavo's developmental level. For example, I told Natalie that Gustavo wouldn't be able to name the colors of the shape and color sorting blocks because he wasn't talking yet, but that if she helped him, I was sure he would soon be repeating her words. We talked about how her outgrown ride-on toys would help Gustavo learn to walk.

Help the older child identify which possessions and space will be off limits to her new sibling, and encourage her to devise a strategy for protecting her private space. Natalie was thrilled to have wall shelves built in her bedroom before Gustavo arrived. She spent hours arranging her "delicates" so they would be out of harm's way. Even though she had wanted wall shelves for years, we had previously told her that she was too young to safely climb the footstool necessary to reach wall shelves. Thus the wall shelves became another way to reinforce her self concept.

If children are going to share a room, help the older child clearly define and personalize his own space. Getting a new bedspread or even moving into a "big boy" bed can help an older sibling feel important and appreciated during the adoption process. If the older child's crib, carseat, or other equipment is to be used by the new addition, get the older child adjusted to different arrangements before the sibling arrives. Older children often feel displaced and resentful if their belongings are transferred directly to a new sibling.

It's extremely important for parents to keep the lines of communication open with their other children during the entire adoption process, but their developmental level has to be taken into consideration in deciding how much to tell them and when. While preparing to travel to Peru, we encouraged Natalie to talk to her friends about their toddler siblings and we made sure to visit some families with similarly-aged children. While we did not provide her with the details of Gustavo's first eighteen months, we did share with her that he had not had a home or a family and that it would take a while for him to get used to us. Parents can help their children anticipate and adjust to the changes which will occur in their lives during and after the adoption. Many families have commented that the greatest adjustment for most "onlies" is sharing the attention that used to be exclusively theirs. However, even in families with multiple children, siblings may feel resentful and jealous of how much time Mom and Dad are spending, first, arranging the adoption, and then, with the new sibling. Preschool-age children are beginning to enjoy their independence, but still expect and need a great deal of one-on-one contact with their caregivers.

School-age children are not immune from resenting a new member of the family. Older onlies are less dependent, but have spent more years enjoying unrestricted access to their parents. School-age multiple siblings have established relationships which will change with the addition of the new family member. Six-year-old Allison adored her ten-year-old brother Jeremy. She followed him everywhere. His wish was her command. All that changed when three-year-old Nadia joined the family. Allison and Nadia were soon inseparable and Jeremy felt like the outsider. Even though school-age children have had to learn to share the attention of a teacher with many other children, have numerous interests beyond the nuclear family, and are able to vocalize their concerns, they need special attention during the adoption process.

Time alone with Mom or Dad, extra attention from extended family, and special privileges such as getting to stay up later than the new sibling all help an older child to not feel displaced. Siblings who are actively involved in the adoption typically feel less resentful than do children who are surprised by an adoption. Children who are fortunate enough to have strong and healthy relationships with adults beyond their own nuclear family do not feel as disrupted by an adoption. On the other hand, children who count on getting all of their adult attention from their own parents are more likely to resent sharing that attention. Perhaps Grandma and Grandpa or a favorite neighbor can provide a "release valve," someone who will listen when children need a sympathetic ear or a place to escape to when they want to get away from their new sibling for awhile. Extended family members provide a sense of continuity for children. When the addition of a new child makes a sibling feel like her world is turned upside down, it's comforting to know that Uncle Jim and Aunt Barb will still come for dinner on Sunday just like they always have.

We found that bibliotherapy (using literature to expose and explore her feelings about her new sibling) was also very helpful for preparing and transitioning Natalie to the role of a sibling. Natalie was especially responsive to books that portrayed an older sibling and a highly spirited toddler, such as the Ramona series by Beverly Cleary (published by Morrow Publisher in New York) and the Fudgie stories by Judy Blume (published by Dutton in New York.) Ramona is a strong willed child whose older sister Beezus is sensitive, deliberate and restrained. Fudgie is an irrepressible little boy whose older brother sometimes feels misunderstood and overshadowed. Stories such as these provide wonderful stimuli for discussions about being an older sibling. Literature depicting families struggling with the same challenges faced by all families help siblings see the humorous side of familial relationships.

Just as parents constantly have to remind themselves that every challenge their children presents isn't related to adoption, they have to remember that every sibling encounter of the annoying kind can't be attributed to adoption. When Natalie stopped treating Gustavo like he was breakable, and instead started quibbling over who had more pudding and whose turn it was to sit on my lap, I knew they had become real siblings.

Many adoption specialists recommend planning some type of ceremony that in essence formally and publicly transfers to adopters the right to parent their child. An adoption ritual may be incorporated into some type of baptism for the child if parents prefer to have a religious ceremony. With toddlers who already received some type of religious ceremony, parents may instead incorporate an adoption ritual into a welcoming home ceremony. Parents may choose to develop some type of public statement of parenting or may ask someone else to install them as parents. A shower may serve this purpose as well, and may occur before or after arrival. Be careful, however, of not planning an overstimulating activity for the new toddler within the first months at home.

Embrace the preparation stage of toddler adoption. From the homestudy to the paperwork, from preparing the home to selecting a name, adequate preparation for parenthood provides people with the sense that they *are entitled to become parents*.

CHAPTER *Four*

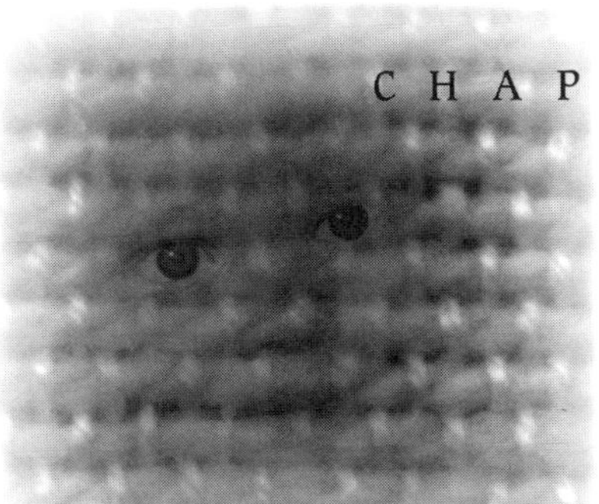

The Adoption Transition

Laura's life changed in the length of time that it took to say hello and good-bye. In the wake of her departure to a new family with new parents, she left a grieving foster mother. In the months that followed, Laura's own confusion and grief made her difficult to console. And her new adoptive parents, who had only tried to make the move as quick and painless as possible for all parties, felt helpless and at a loss for what to do to help their daughter.

Change came quickly for Ben, also. At two-and-a-half, he was brought to the airport by his birthmother, grandmother, and two young uncles, and handed over to a waiting American caseworker. He was swept away with the other passengers down the boarding tunnel and into the body of a jumbo jet. Nothing was familiar–not the faces, the sounds, the smells, the words. After a sixteen hour flight in which he was jostled, fed strange food, taken through customs by yet another stranger, and then reboarded for his final destination, Ben finally landed half a world away from home and was thrust into the arms of his excited new mother. For almost eighteen months, he watched...he waited...and said nothing.

The most frightening thing that can happen to a toddler is to be relinquished to complete strangers, yet that frequently happens in toddler adoptions. But it doesn't have to be this way.

A toddler's past needs to be connected to her future. Toddlers and their parents benefit tremendously when adoptions involve preparing and gradually transitioning the child to his new home and family. Advocating for a planned and thoughtful transition provides new parents with their first opportunity to assert their rightful guardianship role and claim their new toddlers as their responsibility.

Adoption specialists agree that abrupt moves are frightening for toddler-aged children. Toddlers may conclude that strangers may come and take them away anytime, thus long-term chronic fears are likely. Deliberate, thoughtful good-byes leave less "unfinished business" that is likely to surface at a later time in a child's development. A gradual and planned transition facilitates resolution of grief, allows for transference of attachment, and assists development of healthy attachment toward the permanent parent(s). Laura's arrival at age two illustrates this clearly. In retrospect, Laura's parents realized that it was a big mistake to comply with the foster mother's request to get the transfer over as quickly as possible. Laura's new family arrived at the foster home, said quick "hellos" and "good-byes" and took her away. The adults had erroneously assumed that a quick "good-by" would be easier for everyone. Not so! Both Laura and her foster mom experienced extensive prolonged grief. Laura had difficulty sleeping, cried inconsolably, and resisted attaching to her new parents. In a letter to Laura's adoptive parents, her foster mom expressed her feelings of anger, jealousy, and depression.

Critical components of the adoption transition include preplacement preparation, the actual placement, and postplacement strategies. While each adoption is unique, every toddler deserves to be prepared for and transitioned to his new family and home.

Preplacement Preparation.

Toddlers need to be as carefully prepared for their pending adoption as do their parents, who at least have the advantage of having initiated the whole process. Unfortunately this has typically not been the case. Many toddlers are moved abruptly from one home and family to another with little or no preparation. The mother of a daughter adopted at nineteen months from Korea lamented, "Toddlers have a really rough time. They're too young to understand why they're leaving their home, but old enough to know something's different."

Jordan's dad echoed these sentiments, "Kids who suddenly find themselves with strangers in a strange place are the 'bravest of the brave.' They understand so much and can express so little." Another parent likened his child's abrupt removal from an institutional setting to his waiting adoptive family to diving into an unknown body of water in the dark, without having time even to change into a swimming suit.

Many things contribute to this practice of quick transitions with little, if any, real thought to planning for a child's emotional well-being in the process. While time, travel, language barriers and a whole host of bureaucratic events play a significant role in this practice, the long-held belief that preverbal children are unable to participate in or benefit from preplacement strategies should be reexamined because it can be addressed advantageously. Adoption professionals owe it both to the children they serve and the integrity of the entire adoption process. In spite of the toddler's limited language and reasoning skills, there are a number of preplacement strategies that can be used to effectively prepare toddlers for their adoptions.

Introducing...Mom and Dad

The most frightening thing that can happen to a toddler is to be unceremoniously deposited with complete strangers. In many international adoptions new Mom and Dad's strangeness is further intensified by their physical appearance, dress, and even their smell. Toddlers deserve to have the opportunity to get to know their parents prior to placement.

In the ideal situation, this happens via pictures, letters, conversations, and actual face-to-face visits. Regardless of the method, however, the former caregiver plays an especially critical role in preparing the toddler to meet his parents.

A valuable basic transition strategy involves preparing a small photo album containing pictures of parents, siblings, extended family, pets, and the child's new home ahead of Mom and Dad's arrival or the toddler's trip home. Information for the caregiver or social worker to use when showing the pictures to the child should be included. Photos should be labeled so the caregiver can point out the child's bed, the family dog, and other places and items that will look familiar on arrival home. In the case of an international adoption, in the interest of accuracy it is helpful to have the information translated before it is sent. Laminating the pictures so they can be handled safely by the active toddler is also a good idea.

Sometimes before they meet their child parents have the opportunity to meet the interim caregiver, social worker, or others who work with the child and can then provide first-hand information for the curious toddler. Including a photo of the parents with the interim workers sets up a positive association in the toddler's mind as information is shared with him later. Depending on the technology available, video or audio tapes can be a wonderful way to introduce the toddler to his new family. One particularly creative and unreserved mother sent a tape of herself singing lullabies to her new daughter. The foster mother collaborated by playing the tape each night at bedtime. After the daughter's exhausting and stressful airplane trip to America escorted only by a stranger, Mom reported how excited her daughter was upon hearing her sing the now-familiar lullabies that first night they were together. If possible, parents should telephone their child to familiarize her with their voices. If they can obtain the current caregiver's cooperation, she can hold their picture up during the phone conversation.

Preplacement Visits

Whenever possible, parents should make preplacement visits specifically planned to transfer care of the child gradually from the former caregiver(s) to the adoptive parent(s). Ideally, preplacement visits should begin anywhere from one to four weeks prior to placement and continue until the toddler is placed in his new home. While this may sound unreasonable or impractical at first, some Central and South American countries have already revised their adoption laws to require one or two visits from parents-to-be totaling three to eight weeks, during which time social workers and caregivers meet regularly with the adoptive family as they get to know their new child, care for him, and work through transition issues that will help insure a successful final move home.

Preplacement visits benefit both the child and parent by minimizing the trauma of separation and loss. They can also help parents get ready to assume their caregiver role, and, most importantly, the attachment process can be initiated during preplacement visits. The former caregiver plays a critical role during preplacement visits, especially in cases in which a child is firmly attached to that caregiver. It is extremely helpful to toddlers to witness direct contact between past and the new parents. Young children benefit tremendously by tangible evidence that all caregivers are involved in and support the transfer of his care.

During the first preplacement visit, parents should be treated as important and welcome guests whose primary job is to observe the child and caregiver. Many toddlers are curious, yet resist being talked to or touched by a stranger. They should never be forced to interact with an adult, even adults who are their new moms and dads. Parents should assume an interested, friendly, but nonintrusive attitude. They might want to bring a small gift, but the toddler should not be forced to accept it. They can certainly be introduced as Mom and Dad, but it is unlikely that the toddler will internalize the meaning of those words in the first meeting.

Parents can gradually assume caregiver responsibilities during subsequent visits. It will be easier to integrate the new parent's roles with the former caregiver's style when they parent in a similar manner. In situations where parenting styles and routines differ, introduce changes gradually. Jenny's adoptive parents stayed in a nearby hotel for two weeks prior to placement so they could gradually assume responsibility for her care. Jenny had been responsible for much of her own personal care, including brushing her teeth. Jenny's parents realized that toddlers do not have the requisite coordination to brush independently, so they decided to gradually assume that responsibility. At first, her parents sat close to her while she was brushing, then prepared her toothbrush, then checked her teeth after brushing, and finally brushed her teeth after she had a turn.

Once the toddler is comfortable with his new parents on his home turf, he can go on outings with them. At first he may be more comfortable if he is accompanied by his current caregiver. On their first outing alone, Jenny's mom and dad took her to a favorite ice cream stand. Thus, even though her new parents were still relative strangers, she felt comfortable in a familiar environment.

If time and distance allow, the toddler can visit her new home prior to placement. If at all possible, the current caregiver should accompany the child during the first visits because she will take her cue about how to react to her new home from her former caregiver. Subsequent visits can be for extended periods of time, perhaps culminating in a sleep-over prior to final placement.

Getting Ready

There are a number of concrete strategies which can be used to help a toddler prepare for the move to her new home, including marking time, introducing new routines, reading books about adoption, and using language to reinforce the pending adoption. Toddlers have extremely limited time concepts, but they can be assisted in anticipating an event by being provided with tangible evidence of the passage of time. A common strategy is to mark off days on a large calendar. Beginning one or two weeks before placement, the toddler can cross off or put a sticker on each day leading up to placement. The caregiver helps him count the remaining days, reminding him that in five days, four days, etc. he will be moving to his new home.

Toddlers are creatures of habit, and most are upset by changes in their routines. The transition is enhanced by a caregiver who is willing to introduce new routines gradually and parents who are willing to eliminate old routines gradually. For example, Jenny's grandma and grandpa always let her sleep as late as she wanted in the morning. Having taken care of Jenny since early infancy, they enjoyed the luxury of sleeping late themselves. However, Jenny's adoptive mom and dad planned to have her get up at 7:00 a.m. with the rest of the family. Because Jenny's adoptive parents and grandparents cooperated in her transition, Grandma and Grandpa agreed to gradually begin moving Jenny toward a 7:00 a.m. wake-up beginning two weeks before placement.

Age-appropriate books about adoption can be used to help toddlers prepare for their adoption. Some books which are appropriate for toddlers include *Where the Sun Kisses the Sea* by Susan L. Gabel, *Through Moon and Stars and Night Skies* by Ann Turner, and *A Mother for Choco* by Keiko Kasza. In the first two books, toddler age children who live in "far-off" countries travel home to America to join their adoptive families. Some transition strategies are employed in both stories. In *A Mother for Choco*, Choco looks for a mother that looks just like him—yellow feathers, wings, and striped feet. Mrs. Bear looks different, but together they realize that she is a perfect for Choco because she hugs, kisses, sings, and loves him dearly. This book is especially nice for adopted toddlers who do not look like their adoptive parents.

Former caregivers can prepare toddlers for their adoption by including words that reflect their pending move and new status. Juan's foster parents began calling him John, the name selected by his new parents, a month before he came home to the USA. Jackie's and John's orphanage caregivers began referring to them as brother and sister as soon as they knew that they were being adopted together and made changes to their different daily schedules so they would eat, play, and sleep close to each other.

Important Preplacement Information

The more details parents can gather about their toddler prior to placement, the better prepared they will be to meet their child's needs. It is helpful if parents are able to obtain as much of the following information as possible, whether through preplacement visits, videos, letters, e-mail, or telephone conversations.

* The toddler's temperament and personality. Is she a night person or morning person? Does his activity level increase instead of decrease as he gets tired? How can you tell when she is on the verge of disintegrating into a tantrum? How does he respond to different types of stimulation? Does he enjoy gentle touching, boisterous interactions, or is he touch resistant? Is she an introverted person who needs quiet private time to regroup after loud and intense interaction with others, or is she an extrovert who thrives on lots of people and noise in her environment? Does he like to go to sleep in a dark, quiet room, or does he feel more secure going to sleep in a lighted room where music or voices can be heard? How does the toddler usually react to stressful situations such as frustration, hunger, tiredness, aggression by other children, strangers, and new situations? What coping mechanisms does she use to cope with stress?
* Sleeping style and practices. Find out everything possible about a child's sleeping habits. What is her usual wake-up time and wake-up style (fast and raring to go or slow and reticent)? Is she used to sleeping alone or with another person, and was that on a mat on the floor or in a bed? For example, knowing that a child is used to sleeping in a family bed may explain her fear later of sleeping alone. Find out if there is a pattern of sleep disturbances such as night terrors, and how the caregiver responded.
* Eating patterns, food preferences and dislikes. Understanding something about the food with which a child is familiar and the rituals that surround it can facilitate a toddler's transition to a new family. Parents of internationally adopted toddlers can use the preplacement time to learn to prepare a few simple foods and beverages that will be familiar to their child during transition. Even children adopted domestically may experience a significant change in their diet as families vary considerably in what they eat

and how they prepare it. Toddlers are notoriously picky eaters, so it's helpful to find out what particular food likes and dislikes the new toddler may display.

* Language. Every child and family has unique words, phrases, and pronunciations, often understood only by other group members. To communicate effectively with the newly adopted toddler, it is helpful to understand her unique terms for common words, especially in regard to favorite objects, eating, drinking, sleeping, and toileting.
* Behavior management style. In order to understand the adopted toddler's behavior and reaction to authority, it is important to know the behavioral expectations and discipline strategies used in his former setting. Behavioral expectations for toddlers vary considerably by culture and family. Rigidity and rules are the norm in many institutional settings, while child centered discipline is common in some cultures.
* Toileting routines and status. Is the toddler toileting independently? Under what circumstances? If not, what type of diaper is used? Does he wear diapers all the time, or only at nap and night time? What words have been used to refer to elimination and toileting? What incentives and rewards has his caregiver used?

Placement.

The Physical Transference of Care and Saying Good-by

A toddler cannot participate in a discussion of the transition process. He needs to experience the physical transference of care, and to witness the former caregiver's permission and support for his parents to assume their new role. The toddler pays careful attention to the former caregiver's face and voice, listening and watching as she talks to his new parent and invites the parent's assumption of the caregiver's role. The attached toddler is very perceptive of his caregiver's emotions and will pick up on nonverbal cues from that person as to how he should respond to his new family. Claudia Jewett Jarratt cautions that children who do not have the chance to exchange good-byes or to receive permission to move on are more likely to sustain additional damage to their basic sense of trust and security, to their self-esteem, and to their ability to initiate and sustain strong relationships as they grow up. The younger the child, the more important it is that there be direct contact between parents and past caregivers. A toddler is going to feel conflicting loyalties if she is made to feel on some level that she must choose between her former caregiver and her new parent(s), or if she is made to feel that she is expected to turn her back on her former caregiver as evidence of loyalty and love to her new parent(s).

It is important for the former caregiver to display honest emotions about the pending separation. If an attachment has formed, it is natural for both the child and caregiver to grieve their separation. This is no time for adults to try to be strong for the child's sake. A child's self-esteem is enhanced by tangible evidence that she was cared for and that her former caregiver will miss her but wishes her well. When adults express their feelings appropriately, it gives children permission to do so as well. Hopefully, carefully planned and executed preplacement transition strategies will have assisted former caregivers in adjusting their role and placing their confidence in the ability of the new parents to provide a safe, secure and nurturing environment for the toddler they have loved and cared for.

Caregivers who anticipate ongoing contact after placement may be better able to relinquish their role than caregivers who anticipate that "good-by" will be forever. Joelle's story illustrates this clearly. Joelle had lived with her grandparents since early infancy, but they had voluntarily relinquished their guardianship due to failing health and the heartfelt belief that Joelle would benefit by growing up in a family with younger parents and siblings. However, even though they had selected Joelle's adoptive parents, they initially spurned their request for preplacement visits. Through careful questioning, the adoptive parents discovered that the grandparents had incorrectly assumed that those would be their last days together as a family, and that their granddaughter would then be out of their lives forever. It was no wonder that they were not willing to share their last days together with her new family. However, the grandparents' attitude completely changed when the new adoptive parents assured them of their continuing role as Joelle's grandparents. In fact, the extended family had made plans to spend the upcoming holiday together before Joelle even moved from her grandparents' home to that of her new adoptive family.

Former caregivers may experience grief and guilt because they are incapable of providing permanent adequate care, or they may feel anger and resentment if they had wanted but were not allowed to continue parenting the child. Even the birth parent who voluntarily terminates guardianship may experience considerable ambivalence by the time of placement. Birth or foster parents who are struggling with their own needs may have difficulty meeting their children's needs during the transition period and at the time of placement. In cases such as these, it is important to have sensitive professionals available to help the former caregivers identify and express their feelings about the separation and support the toddler's transition.

The adoption of one family who contributed to this book was terminated shortly after placement because the foster parent actually wanted to adopt the child and could not bring herself to support the adoption. Her own distress when the adoptive parents were present and the lack of appropriate preparation of the child for his adoption contributed significantly to his growing sense of terror of his adoptive parents. After a month of unsuccessful attempts to "connect" with the child, the adoptive parents returned the child to the foster mother.

Saying Good-by to Friends

Professionals and caregivers often underestimate how powerful relationships can be between toddlers and their peers. Toddlers who, together with their peers, have experienced severe neglect, toddlers who have been together in understaffed institutional settings, or toddlers who have been in the care of older children often develop especially strong bonds. An older child may even have functioned as a toddler's most significant caregiver in situations where adults were not able to provide quality care.

Adult caregivers may not even be aware of peer relationships. Since toddlers cannot verbalize friendships, peer bonds are identified by carefully observing a toddler's behaviors. Watchfulness, a whole body reaction (wiggles, squirms, jumping) when a certain child pays attention to her, facial expressions, displays of empathy (distress when the other child is distressed), and seeking behavior when in distress, are all indicators of a strong peer bond.

In addition to experiencing a strong loss at placement, issues regarding the loss of a peer relationship may surface later. For example, as a toddler gets older, she may experience the loss of a peer as guilt that she was adopted while her friend was left in the institution. It is a mistake to underestimate the grief of toddlers who lose a significant friend. Toddlers need the opportunity to say good-bye to their friends. Some may wish to present their friend with a special farewell gift, or they may want to take something with them as a remembrance of their friend. Photos can be used to remember a friend in a Lifebook, and postplacement visits and letters can assist a child who is grieving the loss of a special peer relationship.

Transition Objects

Transition objects are those items that children take with them from one setting to another, providing comfort and a sense of continuity. Many children have a special blanket, plush toy, or other soft object that can be used as a transition object, while others cling to objects as diverse as a cup or toothbrush. For many children, the object's smell is as important as the way it looks and feels, so take care that these objects are not washed prior to placement. Even familiar sheets, blankets, bibs, and towels are reassuring to the toddler in transition. Transitional objects provide a way to bridge the gap between the child's current environment and his new home. Some toddlers may not be allowed to take things with them to their new home. Gustavo's caregiver was so poor that she did not allow removal of any blankets, toys, or clothing which the children had used. If this is the case, parents should try to send or deliver something to their child which he will be able to bring with him to his new home. Better yet, parents can offer to replace the toys or bedding sent home with the toddler. Many caregivers will be more than willing to exchange a used for a new item. John Bowlby reported on a landmark study of the adoption of securely attached toddlers which demonstrated that transitional objects had a major impact on reducing placement trauma. In this study, many of the toddlers' belongings, including beds, blankets, and toys, accompanied them to their new homes.[2]

Postplacement.

Honoring the Role of the Former Caregiver(s)

Some toddlers transition directly from a birth family to their adoptive family, while others transition from interim care to their permanent home. If a relationship has formed between a child's caregiver and the child, regardless of whether that person is a birth relative or not, it is essential to continue to acknowledge the importance of that person in the child's life.

While some new adoptive parents may find it difficult, even threatening, to accept the strong attachment their child has to previous caregivers, it is important to acknowledge and respect that relationship nonetheless. Parents should not try to change their child's positive feelings toward a previous caregiver. This may, of course, be easier said than done. One mother described how heartbroken she felt when her newly adopted daughter burst into tears whenever she saw a picture of her foster mom on the refrigerator. Adoptive parents who reference past

2 Bowly, John. (1973). *Attachment and Loss, Volume II.* New York: Basic Books.

caregivers and situations in a negative context, however, are setting themselves up for potential problems. Some adoptive parents want their children see them as the all-good parents and past caregivers or birth parents as the all-bad parents. This is as harmful as completely disregarding a child's past life. It is particularly damaging to developing self-esteem and will eventually create conflicting loyalties. Just as new parents hope former caregivers will support them, they have to continue to acknowledge and incorporate former caregivers into a child's life story.

In ignoring the important role played by early caregivers, parents can convey the impression that there is something wrong with their child's feelings. Ignoring feelings of anger or grief is confusing to a toddler at a time in her cognitive development when "magical thinking" is common. When parents pretend that their toddler's former caregivers don't exist, her magical thinking might lead her to a number of erroneous conclusions. She might decide that they didn't really exist, that a former caregiver has simply disappeared, or that she lived in some fantasy place to which she might return as quickly as she left. Fortunately, attachment to new parents is not dependent totally on a child either not having or losing strong feelings toward her early caregivers or birthfamily. On the contrary, a strong attachment to her former caregiver will help her attach to her adoptive parents.

What happens to the transition process when the former caregivers are not involved in the adoption? Our situation is a case in point. We did not have the opportunity to meet Gustavo's birthmother, and we had only a few minutes to talk to the woman who had cared for him in the two weeks prior to our arrival in Peru. She would not allow us to take a photograph, nor would she agree to our visiting her before we returned to the USA. In situations such as this, parents can develop a ritual that will symbolically remember birthparents and other caregivers as a way of validating the presence of the person and significance of the relationship. Some adoptive families conduct a simple ceremony for an unknown birthmother on their child's birthday. A candle may be lit, and the parent says something like, "We give thanks to Sara's birthmom for giving her life and for loving her so much that she brought her to the Safehouse so she could find her way home to us. We are thinking of her today and want her to know that Sara is happy, healthy, and very loved." Depending on a family's religious beliefs, a special message may also be incorporated into a prayer, such as, "Lord, we give thanks this day for Your divine intervention in leading Sara to us. We want to give thanks to Sara's birthmother for choosing to give her life. We believe that You are watching over her just as You watch over us and will help her know that Sara is healthy and happy."

Lifebook

A Lifebook documents a child's life-to-date. More than the traditional "baby book" often started for a family's birth child, a Lifebook is used after placement and for years to come as a way to help the adopted child connect his past and present life. According to noted adoption authors Vera Fahlberg and Claudia Jewett Jarratt, a Lifebook affirms the fact that everyone is entitled to his own history, confirms who he is, and provides a sense of full identity. A Lifebook provides tangible evidence to an adopted child of his continued existence. In most birth families, an individual family member's history is naturally preserved in both the oral and visual tradition. Stories of family members are told and retold, passed down from generation to generation. Physical evidence of each family member's history is present in pictures, audio tapes, videos, and artifacts that the person made, bought, or collected. A Lifebook provides knowledge about personal history for children who do not grow up in their family of origin.

Lifebooks typically contain pictures of the child from as young an age as are available, pictures of important people such as birth parents and other caregivers, copies of important letters and documents that marked different phases of the adoption process, and memorabilia associated with his life transitions. Photos of an internationally adopted child's country of origin are also important components of his Lifebook. Photos of the first meeting, former caregivers, first outings together, and placement day, are essential tools for communicating a parent's joy and love. Letters, cards, and other mementos celebrating the adoption are appropriate. One of the most prized artifacts in Gustavo's Lifebook is a hand-lettered sign that sister Natalie prepared for his arrival. It reads: "Welcome Gustavo I hop you lik it in our famly."

Parents often have to be creative in collecting material for the Lifebook. While we don't have a picture of Gustavo with his birthmother, we were able to obtain a photocopy of her government ID photo for his Lifebook. Magazine photos of real people who are not the actual birthparents or other caregivers should never be used as substitutes for real pictures, as a toddler's magical thinking tends to turn those people into the real birthparents. Artifacts which are three dimensional can accompany the Lifebook. While in Peru, we purchased a sculpture of a Quecha woman holding a small male baby and gazing pensively into the distance. We hold the sculpture as we discuss how Mathilde must have felt when she made the decision that she was unable to take care of Gustavo. Other artifacts which accompany Gustavo's Lifebook include his arrival outfit, his first teddy bear which Natalie brought to him in Peru, and the backpack his father used to carry him. Gustavo's Life "book" is a Life "bundle!"

Toddlers have limited capacity to understand the Lifebook as more than a story. However, the seed is planted for later understanding of and receptivity to information about his earliest days before becoming part of his adoptive family. The tone of voice and emotional demeanor of the adult telling the adoption story while showing the Lifebook is extremely important at this age. Respect, empathy, and support for everyone who has been part of the child's life history is important.

As a child grows, the Lifebook is used for a multitude of purposes, including helping a child deal with unresolved feelings as they surface. A child's Lifebook should be added to as he journeys through life. It also should be accessible to children any time they feel a need to thumb through it. The Lifebook, after all, belongs to the child.

The Lifestory

What child doesn't love to hear a story? When the story is her own, it usually becomes a favorite, and one that is told over and over again. Toddlers need to hear their adoption story told lovingly by those who care about them. Regardless of the amount of information available or even the accuracy of what is available, parents need to develop a Lifestory to share with their children. In the absence of specific information, it is acceptable to speculate based on what you know about the cultural habits or the situations of other children adopted from similar circumstances. "The word *maybe* is a gift from the English language for those of us who don't know the answers."[3]

The circumstances that brought Gustavo into the adoption loop are not unusual in cases of international adoption. There are no pictures of him prior to his placement with the private attorney who arranged his adoption at fifteen months. In the absence of a photo, we use our native Quecha sculpture of a woman and baby to serve as our symbolic representation of baby Gustavo with his birthmother. Having never had the opportunity to meet, talk, or obtain any letter from her, we have to create a representational message from her to Gustavo based on the actions we know she did take. For this part of his

3 Gulden, Lisa van and Bartels-Rabb, Lisa. (1994) *Real Parents, Real Children*. New York: The Crossroads Publishing Company. p. 37.

Lifestory, we rely on the fact that we do know his birthmother brought him to the attorney at fifteen months of age. We interpreted that piece of information in a part of Gustavo's oral life story as, "Mathilde brought you to Dr. Nelson and asked him to make sure to place you with a mommy and daddy who could take care of you. She must have felt good knowing that you would be with someone who would find a mommy and daddy to love you, and that you would be living in a house and be taken care of until you went home with Mommy and Daddy. She must have felt very sad that she was not able to take care of a baby, but she must have felt happy knowing you would have a mommy and daddy who would be able to take care of you. I think that's what she told you when she brought you to Dr. Nelson. I think she also told you how much she loves you, and told you to be happy, brave, and strong, because you are of the true blood of the Inca."

Discussions about early life experiences and adoption circumstances are setting the stage for later comprehension. Toddlers will not really understand such concepts as *adoption decision*, *termination*, *birthparents*, or *forever parents*. At this age, adoption discussions serve a variety of purposes. They create a climate of respect for all parties associated with adoption, build open communication, establish the habit of using appropriate, positive adoption-related terminology, and arm a child with answers to personal questions others may ask her. Toddlers assume the attitude that adoption is perfectly normal and wonderful when parents model that attitude themselves.

In an article titled "The Passing of Innocence," published in *Adoptive Families* (18/4, 1995, pp. 26-28), DiAnne Borders reports how her two-year-old delightedly mimics her enthusiasm for his racial characteristics and all things related to his birth country. However, she is also poignantly aware that in another year or so he will see and hear insensitive questions and comments from others, and knows she won't always be there to protect him from the racism he is sure to experience. Building the foundation now is the support a child needs later.

Adoption Related Books

While adoption-related books such as those recommended in the Preplacement section continue to serve an important role in adopted children's understanding and self-concept relative to adoption, they should not dominate their libraries. Children, whether adopted or not, should take the lead in book selection. Examples of excellent books which are not specifically related to adoption but reinforce important concepts such as unconditional parental love and the meaning of real love include the classic, *The Velveteen Rabbit* by Margery Williams, *On Mother's Lap* by Ann Herbert Scott, *Mama, Do you Love Me?* by Barbara Joose, and *Love you Forever* by Robert Munsch.

Postplacement Visits

While the conventional wisdom "out of sight, out of mind" may be true for some things, adoptive parents are wise to rethink this saying as they help their toddler make the transition to their new family. Without contacts to assure them that their former caregiver still exists, toddlers may expend unnecessary energy worrying, wondering, and fantasizing about former caregivers rather than directing their energy toward attaching to new parents. Worse yet, some may resist attachment because they may assume these new caregivers will simply disappear one day, too. One mother described how her budding relationship with her newly adopted toddler fell apart when she was hospitalized. Even though her daughter Sara was able to visit her during her hospital stay, she was extremely stand-offish, and refused to have any contact with her. Mom could not understand this reaction until she found out that Sara had experienced an abrupt disruption of a long-term foster placement when her foster mother became ill and was hospitalized. Sara never saw her foster mother again. Apparently, in Sara's mind, Mom's illness signaled another pending loss.

When a child has enjoyed a healthy relationship with a former caregiver, postplacement visits, when possible, can serve a variety of purposes. Postplacement visits not only provide tangible evidence of the continuing existence of previous caregivers, they also provide another way to transfer attachment gradually. In cases where personal visits are not possible, phone calls and pictures reassure a child of a former caregiver's continuing presence and love. In international adoptions, it is important to obtain as much information as possible to facilitate a potential meeting sometime in the future between the child and his former caregivers. Names and addresses of interim caregivers, birth relatives and attorneys may be useful someday when attempting to arrange a meeting between a child and his former caregivers. What is not gathered today may result in a cold trail in the future.

First Impressions of Parents and Their Children.

An airline commercial portrays a couple in an airport terminal pacing the floor anxiously, peering out the window, frequently checking their watches. Finally, a woman carrying a smiling baby walks toward the anxious couple, who we realize are the baby's waiting adoptive parents. This commercial portrays adoption in a refreshing and positive fashion. However, arrival scenes such as this are not usually as idyllic as the one portrayed in this commercial. In reality, newly adopted toddlers and their parents often do not fall in love at first sight.

Van Gulden and Bartels-Rabb report that according to A.B. Eagen, author of *The Newborn Mother: Stages of Her Growth* (Henry Holt and Co.), it is a rare woman who admits that she did not love her baby at first sight, even though research supports this fact.[4] During the first month after a child arrives in its new family, a woman's adjustment to her new role as a parent is greater than feelings of deep love for their babies. Love grows as the new mother cares for her children.

There is a real danger in anticipating an "instant bond" with a child, whether through birth or adoption. Many adoptive parents have shared that their emotions ran the gamut from fear, to awe, to exhilaration when they met their new toddler. The first thought of one father of a three-year-old with multiple medical needs when he saw his daughter carried off the plane was, "Oh my God! What have we done?" Two other parents described being absolutely nuts about their children as soon as they saw them, while another reported, "I was so excited and nervous I barely kept from crying. I felt awkward and was afraid to hold her because I thought she'd cry." Carl's dad was struck with how beautiful and tiny his twenty-eight-month-old new son was, but he wondered why he was screaming, kicking and punching. Another mom said she felt both fear and relief that her son was finally home. Mara's mom felt alarm and concern because she looked so awful and was so obviously terrified! Karina's and Lonny's mothers admitted that with all the negative behaviors and anxieties they exhibited at first, it was definitely not "love at first sight!"

Among the parents whose stories contributed to this book, however, there did not appear to be any relationship between first reactions and long-term attachment. Regardless of first impressions, the vast majority of the children and their parents developed a strong bond with time and integration into the family.

The adopted toddlers' first reactions to their parents also ranged from very positive to very negative. Not surprisingly, most of the children who arrived home via long flights were exhausted and disoriented and reacted to everything with extreme negativity. The toddlers who then had to face a lot of people and

4 Gulden, Lisa van and Bartels-Rabb, Lisa. (1994) *Real Parents, Real Children*. New York: The Crossroads Publishing Company. p. 114.

activity at the airport were particularly unappreciative. A low key welcome was unanimously endorsed by parents. Save the shower and welcoming party until the child has had a chance to settle in.

There were a few children whose reaction was very positive to at least one of their new parents the first time they met. Scott reached out to hold both his parents' hands. Sabrina crawled into her mother's lap and promptly fell asleep. These children are the exception however. Most of the toddlers' first reactions ranged from very stand-offish to downright hostile. Many refused to make eye contact and rebuffed all attempts at physical contact.

What Toddlers Made the Easiest Transition?

Some families who provided information for this book reported that their toddlers adjusted quickly to the family and displayed few recognized grief or attachment problems. Three striking similarities could be identified in this group of families. First, those toddlers who had experienced the fewest disrupted placements and changes in caregivers during their first year(s) of life tended to adjust to their new families with the least amount of difficulty. The exception to this were those institutionalized children who, although they had never experienced multiple placements, had experienced extreme neglect and initially resisted attachment to their new parents.

A secure attachment to a former caregiver was another similarity found among children who had little difficulty adjusting and attaching to their new adoptive families. Even those children who had been in orphanages made a better adjustment if they had experienced consistency in a caregiver relationship. For example, Lila's parents attributed her relatively easy transition to the special relationship she had enjoyed with one caregiver at her orphanage. Mara, on the other hand, was known to have had a series of caregivers prior to placement at age two and a half. At age eight she is progressing, but is still struggling with issues of attachment and self-esteem.

Toddlers who were prepared and gradually transitioned to their adoptive families adjusted much more quickly than those without preparation or transition. One mother and father of a domestically adopted eighteen-month-old described their son's successful transition. After first meeting their son at the agency and then being invited for dinner at his foster home, they were allowed to take him on short outings. Frequent visits at the foster home were also made prior to placement. When the final transfer was made, there was very little distress and their son is displaying strong attachment to his new parents at age three. Sharon, also adopted domestically at eighteen months, first met her new mom and dad at her foster home. Her new parents stayed at a nearby hotel for two weeks, visiting her frequently and gradually taking her on longer outings. Even after moving to her new home, Sharon frequently talked to her foster mom on the telephone. In both of these cases the parents took care to try to follow routines that were familiar to their children, and to talk with them daily about their former caregivers.

Not surprisingly, the toddlers who made the transition to their adoptive homes with the least amount of trauma also formed the strongest and quickest attachments to their adoptive parents. They also displayed the fewest long-term problems. Sabrina's case is a good example. Sabrina had lived with her foster mother, Carol, since early infancy. To help Sabrina prepare for her pending adoption, Carol showed her pictures and talked frequently about the family she would soon be joining. Letters, telephone calls, and visits preceded Sabrina's transfer to her adoptive home. Sabrina observed Carol and her adoptive parents talking and laughing together as they jointly cared for her for a week prior to her transfer. She left Carol's home with an album full of pictures of herself surrounded by her foster and adoptive families—tangible evidence of the continuity and "connectedness" of her life experiences. Sabrina also brought her favorite toys, blanket, and eating utensils with her when she moved home. During her first weeks at home, she frequently talked to her foster mom on the telephone. Carol continues to be an important extended family member. At age five Sabrina's cognitive, language, physical, and emotional developmental milestones are all right on target.

Stories from families who have adopted multiple toddlers provide especially convincing evidence of the significance of the role that stable, loving caregivers and a planned and gradual transition has in the success of a placement. Two families, each of whom had adopted two toddlers over a period of time, shared the stark differences in the adjustments of their children which, they believed, were directly related to their early care and the planning—or lack of it—in their transitions to their new families. In both families, one toddler had experienced chaotic and inconsistent caregiving with frequent disruptions while the other had the benefit of a stable foster placement and planned preparation for adoption. Joey and Roberto are brothers. Joey, who at six years of age still resists attachment, and has been diagnosed as having attention disorder and conduct problems, moved from a hospital to an abusive foster home and then to an orphanage prior to his placement at age two. Roberto, on the other hand, experienced few post-placement difficulties. But, unlike his brother, he had lived with a loving foster family from three days of age until placement at eighteen months. Roberto's parents related that they "were fortunate to spend time with his foster parents who obviously loved him very much. Roberto was their first foster child and since they had him for an extended period they had come to look upon him as their sixth child. "We will always be indebted to Roberto's foster parents, for without their care and concern I am sure we all would have had a much more difficult transition period," reported Mom. In both families the children who had been securely attached to their caregiver and had been prepared for their adoption grieved their losses and attached more quickly to their adoptive families. In contrast, the toddlers who had experienced multiple disruptions and neglect had long term attachment problems. Of course, in both of these cases there may have been other factors that affected the child's adjustment.

Other Factors Affecting the Toddler's Transition.

Clearly there is more to a toddler's successful adjustment to a new family than early caregiving and evidence of attention to transitional planning. What are some of these other factors? Interestingly, prior parenting experience seemed to be a mixed blessing, with no sure guarantee of having a head start on other parents new to the Parent Club. While experienced parents were better prepared for their toddler's instant mobility, many of the parents who had raised their other children from infancy felt unprepared for how different it was to begin parenting at the toddler stage. They reported believing that they could parent their new toddler as they had parented their other children as toddlers, and quickly discovered the error in their thinking.

Parental expectations also significantly influenced parental adjustment. Most parents who expected immediate bonding, tranquil nights, and happy children reported that both they and their children experienced confusion, shock, and stress following the adoption. On the other hand, the parents who anticipated and planned for a challenging transition were either pleasantly surprised when things went more smoothly than expected or were at least accepting of a difficult situation.

In some families, siblings appeared to play a positive role in the child's initial adjustment, while in other families siblings appeared to be extremely unsettling to the new child. Robert snuggled in with his new brothers on the very first night home, while Mara immediately rejected her older sister. Sibling relationships go both ways. In some families, existing children were crazy about their new toddler sibling from day one, and in other families the new addition was very unwelcome. Single siblings tended to be more resistant to the arrival of their new toddler sibling than children from larger families. Several families reported that their adopted toddlers and close-in-age siblings had difficulty sharing their parent's attention. This was especially true in situations where the adopted toddler was experiencing problems with grief or attachment, as well as in situations where the existing close-age sibling also had special needs. In most, but not all, families adopted toddlers bonded sooner with siblings who were at least four years older than themselves than they did with close-age siblings. It was no surprise that families who took time to include their children in the adoption process, planning, and transition of the new toddler sibling reported a much more satisfactory adjustment.

In some families, pets appeared to play a small, yet significant role in a child's adjustment to his new family. Three families reported that family pets provided a wonderful opportunity for their newly adopted toddlers to play and be affectionate. In fact, some parents said that their children were more affectionate with the family pets than they were with family members for some time. One of my favorite family photographs captured a heartwarming kiss Gustavo planted on the lips of our 125 pound Malamute a few months after arriving home. That kiss was one of Gustavo's first spontaneous displays of affection. I can understand why so many different therapy programs have recognized the benefit of the role animals can play in reaching people who are depressed, stressed, withdrawn, and angry. Some children seem to feel safer expressing affection toward an animal than they do toward an adult.

Finally, and not surprisingly, the number and type of other stressors occurring in a family at the time of a toddler's adoption seemed to play a significant role in adjustment. Toddler adoption requires a good deal of energy and resources before, during, and after placement. Marital difficulties, illness, financial concerns, moves, job changes, and a host of other changes both positive and negative will affect any family's sense of equilibrium and compound the challenges associated with integrating a new toddler into the family unit. One mom described a significant set-back in the attachment between herself and her daughter when she had to have surgery shortly after placement. Divorces significantly affected their children's adjustment in two other families. Having to return to work before feeling ready was very stressful for some parents and their children. Another family was faced with trying to recover financially from unbudgeted, unexpected adoption costs.

The Resilient Toddler.

Of course, there are exceptions to everything written thus far about the relationship between a toddler's early care, his preplacement preparation, the way his transition is handled, and his overall developing sense of well-being. Nothing is absolute. Some toddlers arrive home apparently unscathed by abandonment, neglect, lack of preparation, and even by multiple disruptions in their short lives. Some toddlers survive and even thrive in circumstances that would destroy most of us.

Child psychologists have long recognized the existence of such children, children known as "resilient." Not surprisingly, parents who described their adopted toddlers in terms of the characteristics associated with a resilient child also reported experiencing fewer challenges than the vast majority of other families. Scott is a perfect example of a resilient child. Abandoned at approximately age one-and-a-half in Korea, he was literally left on an orphanage doorstep. The orphanage where Scott subsequently lived for two years provided adequate physical care, but children there received very little emotional nurturing from the overworked staff. At three he was escorted to Washington, D.C., to be adopted by a European-American couple in their mid-thirties who had been well-prepared for any serious attachment and grief issues their toddler might have, and thus very surprised at how smoothly Scott adjusted to his new family and community. Two years later he experienced another major transition when his family relocated to a tiny Midwestern community in which there were few interracial families. When Scott was eight years old, his house burned to the ground and he had to move again. Through all of these disruptions and transitions, he has maintained an optimistic, empathetic, cheerful, and accepting attitude. His parents claim no credit for this. His mother provided the following description of her son's arrival: "Our first glimpse of Scott was as he walked down the jetway with his head erect, eyes alert and curious, and a firm grip on his escort's hand. When his father and I knelt in front of him, he looked his escort in the eyes, said good-by, smiled at us, reached out for our hands, and never looked back." At age nine, Scott is described by his teacher and mother as well-adjusted, happy, loving, secure, outgoing, and friendly. He is well liked by peers and teachers, and is an above-average student. His natural buoyancy and optimism are reflected by his response to his teacher when she expressed sympathy the day after his house burned down. Scott replied, "Thank-you, I feel bad about our things getting burned up, but the good part is that nobody got hurt and now we get to eat at the restaurant every night!"

The picture on the following page was drawn by this young man at age eight. He had been given an assignment to draw a picture of someone who has been very important to him in his life. Scott described his picture as being his birthmother as he imagines her–a woman who bravely but painfully delivered him to a place where she knew he would be taken care of and placed for adoption. His drawing reveals an unusually mature understanding of the loss involved in adoption: his and his birthmother's pain at the moment of separation, revealed in the tears being shed by both mother and baby. Their tears literally fill the picture. What are the resiliency characteristics that seem

(Scott Carlson, age 8. Permission to reprint drawing provided by Susanne Carlson).

to serve as protective factors against adverse experiences, and are they identifiable in toddlerhood? How is Scott different from the majority of adopted toddlers? Steve and Sybil Wolin describe these characteristics in their 1993 book, *The Resilient Self: How Survivors of Troubled Families Rise Above Adversity*. The capacity to be independent through separating, disengaging, and straying is a resiliency trait. The independent toddler finds physical and or intellectual safe harbors to which he can retreat in times of turmoil or fear. Some adoptive parents described their newly arrived toddlers as precociously independent. However, in toddlers it may be difficult to differentiate independence used as a healthy survival skill—independent behaviors that simply reflect the toddler's emerging drive for autonomy—from resistive behaviors that indicate attachment problems. It may be particularly difficult for toddlers who have had to acquire self-help skills for their own survival or who have assumed responsibility for caring for younger children to relinquish any control to their parents.

Mentally withdrawing or retreating is another resiliency characteristic some adopted toddlers may display. Joey had this technique perfected to the point that he was diagnosed as severely deaf. Another girl curled into the fetal position for a week after placement, unresponsive to touch, sound, or visual stimuli. Retreating to a safe place within oneself is actually a high level coping strategy for an infant or toddler who is unable to escape physically from an abusive, frightening, or overwhelming situation. It may serve a child well before and during placement, but it is critical to help him learn to trust that his new home is a safe place where he will not have to retreat inside himself.

Some children display the resilient behavior of initiative. Initiative involves the ability to assert oneself to assume whatever control one can over a situation. According to Wolin and Wolin, this characteristic is displayed by very young children who actively explore their environment, finding pleasure in poking around and conducting trial-and-error experiments. Children with initiative display an intrinsic motivation to master their environment. They have natural leadership skills and delight in problem solving. As toddlers, initiative may be displayed by a strong drive to master developmental tasks in spite of the lack of encouragement and resources normally provided by loving adults.

Insight, sensing, and intuition are also resiliencies that seem to protect children from succumbing to the disadvantages many adopted toddlers have experienced. Children with insight become very skilled at sensing danger early in life. In toddlers, insight may be manifested by watchfulness and an unusually good memory for people and events. Even when it isn't obvious, they are watching the environment, alert to signs of danger.

Some children display the resiliency skill of building intimate and fulfilling relationships with others. These resilient children learn to search out love by connecting with or attracting the attention of available adults at a very young age. This may be done by eye contact, touch, rudimentary language, and other engaging behavior. This is very different behavior from the superficial and insincere affection children with attachment disorders sometimes use to manipulate others. The toddler with this resiliency skill is often a favorite of caregivers at the orphanage or foster home, and typically receives more attention and personalized care than other children.

Another resiliency described by Wolin and Wolin that may be evident as early as the toddler age is humor and creativity, evident in the ability to turn reality inside out and direct energy into play. Resilient humor is not to be confused with the morbid and sometimes bizarre sense of humor displayed by children with attachment disorders. Toddlers display healthy, resilient humor and creativity by a happy disposition, spontaneous laughter, creative play, or an ability to play under the most deprived of situations. A stick and a rock serves nicely as a toy truck. Humor and play serve a restorative function for everyone, but are used especially well by the resilient toddler.

A final resiliency described by Wolin and Wolin is morality. The seeds of morality are sewn early in life when children begin judging the rights and wrongs of their daily life. The earliest signs of morality can be seen in a toddler's compassion for peers, distress when other children are hurt or frightened and attempts to assist them. Retrieving a bottle for a crying baby is a very early indication of budding morality.

Looking Ahead at Continuing Transition Needs.

The lives of adoptive parents and children are always in transition. Helping adopted children connect their beginnings to their present lives with us doesn't end with the transition at placement. Parents need to deal with adoption related issues over and over again as their children reach new levels of cognitive and language development. Sometime between the ages of twenty-four and thirty-six months, many children will begin correcting Mom or Dad if they make a mistake or forget part of their Lifestory. Shortly thereafter children begin to fill in factual names, places, and events when invited to share in the story telling. Preschoolers' reasoning is very limited and most do not sense anything unusual about being adopted. My three-and-a-half-year-old adopted nephew announced proudly, "I'm adopted." He then added, "And there's a kitty growing in my tummy." Children spontaneously announce to the store clerk such things as, "My mommy came to get me in a big airplane," or "I'm from Peru!" At this age parents should continue to build the factual foundation that will help full comprehension later on and instill a sense of pride and positive feelings about adoption.

Preschoolers often obsess on the question, "Why?" It's important to remember that even though the question may be applied to any aspect of the adoption story, preschoolers aren't ready to really comprehend the intricacies of why their birthmother wasn't able to take care of them or why they don't live with their birthmother anymore. Simple answers that show respect for everyone involved and stress the positive outcome of adoption are best. Feelings associated with the adoption process are more important than details at this age.

Around the age of four, children usually start thinking about their story at a deeper level. This is the age at which children typically notice pregnant women and become very curious about the birth process. Children at this age are concrete thinkers who work hard at trying to understand their world. A good example of this is provided by the four-year-old birth child who participated in the adoption of his new sister. Coincidentally, he knew another family who had an adopted daughter and a birth son. One day he confidently announced that he knew where babies come from: "Boys are born out of mommies' tummies and girls are adopted!" Shortly after his fourth birthday, Gustavo announced that he planned to find Mathilde (his birthmother) when we went back to Peru. When asked why, he declared that he wanted to see the other Gustavos that came out of Mathilde's tummy. After considerable discussion, we realized that he thought Mathilde was the "grand birthmother" who birthed all the children adopted from Peru. The preschool child's desire to categorize information into digestible and understandable facts is also revealed by their reaction to birth siblings. At four, Gustavo alternated between insisting that he "was born out of Mommy's tummy just like Natalie," and proposing that Natalie must have also been adopted. One day he advanced the following theory. "I know what! Let's say that I was adopted from South of America and Natalie was adopted from the Mall of America!" He had no idea how fitting this idea really is, as Natalie is the consummate shopper!

Books about adoption and a toddler's country-of-origin continue to serve as important tools to help children understand their story. Around age four or five, children will begin making comparisons between the characters in the book and themselves. Books about a child's country of origin make his culture and heritage more real, and maps help him to gain some rudimentary understanding of his birth country in relation to his present home. The importance of understanding this aspect of the adoption process was revealed to me when, at age four, Gustavo came home from preschool and announced excitedly that his friend Alex was adopted from Korea. He confidently went to the world map and accurately pointed out Korea, drawing a line with his finger to show the route Alex traveled to come home to Wisconsin, and then compared it to the distance he traveled home from Peru.

At about age seven children's intellectual development makes a quantum leap as they begin to think analytically and sequentially. Parents need to anticipate and help their children prepare to respond to questions and comments from classmates about their adoption, their physical appearance, and their heritage. When children reach elementary school age they begin to grasp the elements of the meaning of their adoption, including the fact that their birthmother, for any of a variety of reasons, chose not to parent them. They may also fantasize about their birthmother, but rarely judge her actions harshly. It is not uncommon for them to extend their budding sense of altruism and sympathy to their birth parents. When he was six years old, Gustavo provided an excellent example of this during a conversation about our litter of puppies. In spite of the fact that the children had agreed before we mated our dogs that the puppies would need to go to new homes when they were four months old, now that they were born my daughter had something very different in mind. She pleaded, "Tasha (mom dog) won't let the puppies leave," to which I reassuringly replied, "Trust me, honey, when the puppies are old enough, Tasha will be happy for them to go to live with their new families." Natalie petulantly responded, "No mama could be happy to have her babies go someplace else to live!" Gustavo quietly but assertively replied, "Yes they can—Mathilde was."

During the middle elementary years parents need to be prepared to respond to factual questions such as, "How old was I?" "How did you find out about me?" along with, "What do my birthparents look like?" An adopted infant's Lifestory usually is less difficult to tell than a toddler's, whose family has to deal with a period of time when they were not part of his life. For many children adopted after infancy, that period of time was characterized by neglect, inconsistency, chaos, or other forms of abuse. The three-year-old can be satisfied being told that his birthmother loved him very much and wanted him to have a forever family. The school-age child wants to know what her name was, all the circumstances of her life, details about the birth father, and why they couldn't take care of him. Many families who adopt internationally have little or none of this information. School age children may experience considerable grief as they come to terms with the circumstances of their early life. They may grieve the loss of their birth parents, empathize with their birth parents' pain, and grieve the fact that their adopted parents did not find them when they were very young. They may also fantasize about their birthparents, but tend not to be very judgmental of their actions.

As children reach puberty, they become capable of more abstract thinking, and thus of handling more sophisticated information about their adoption. Teenagers know how a girl gets pregnant and can understand why someone might not be able to care for a baby. They also understand the concepts of child abuse and neglect, and an obligation that society has to protect children and provide a safe and secure environment for them. Teenagers tend to judge harshly the actions of their birthparents, yet may still fantasize about their eventual reunification.

At any age, children pick up their cues from their parents regarding what topics are safe to discuss. In every family there is a communication climate. It is our responsibility as parents to establish a climate for safe and open communication. In her workshops, adoption educator Patricia Irwin Johnston advises parents that the best way to establish that climate is for a family to model and reinforce the belief that emotions are acceptable expressions of feelings, and that differences in people are appreciated.

It is important to remember to let children take the lead in talking about their early life experiences and their adoption. According to Pat Johnston, it is the parents' responsibility to find a way to meet their child's need to talk about adoption in an atmosphere of openness and safety. Sometimes parents feel so compelled to get that "adoption talk" over with that they provide the right information at the wrong time. Don't expect children to remember what they've been told. The same information will need to be covered again with each stage of a child's growth and understanding. Like all families, adoptive families, too, are forever in transition.

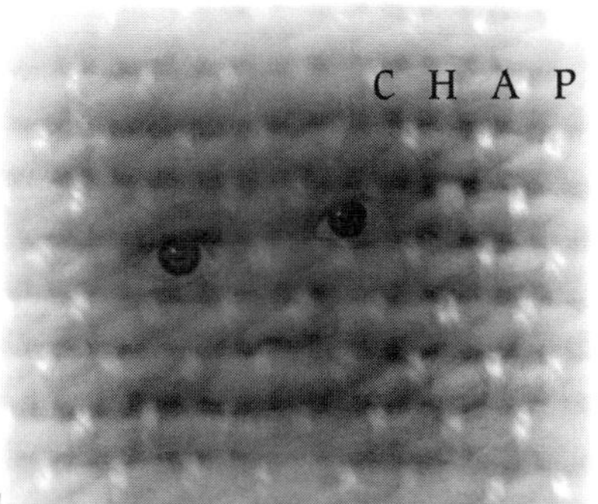

CHAPTER *Five*

Understanding Your Toddler's Development

Orphanage. Institution. Foster care. Neglect. Developmental delays. These words can strike fear in the hearts and minds of parents considering toddler adoption. At eighteen months, Joanna startled at sudden movements and sounds and screamed inconsolably when the family dog barked. Institutionalized during her first fifteen months of life and deprived of stimulation and nurture, she did not know how to calm herself—or how to accept soothing from a nurturing parent.

Jenny, an institutionalized two-and-a-half-year-old, had language skills typical of a child less than half her age. Surprising? Not if you understand that language development requires stimulation and modeling to progress normally.

Eighteen-month-old Gustavo was the size of an average eight-month-old and had the physical skills of a one-year-old when he was adopted.

Neglect, malnutrition, crib confinement and restraints are only some of the factors that contribute to developmental delays.

If a toddler is off to a poor developmental start, do these initial delays signal a bleak future for the child's long-term development? Understanding normal development and knowing how to nurture a child's growth and development helps keep things in perspective.

There are a number of reasons why adoptive parents will want to have at least a rudimentary understanding of the developmental tasks of toddlers. Awareness of the typical sequence and stages of growth, along with the expectation that adjustments will be necessary, helps parents better understand their adopted toddler's development and respond appropriately to their child's behaviors while allowing them to plan activities that stimulate age-appropriate development. Unrealistic expectations that don't take into account the cultural differences and early deprivation common to many adoptions can frustrate both parents and children. For example, some moms and dads reported that they had assumed that their newly adopted two-year-old sons should have achieved bowel and bladder control. Other parents admitted having the expectation that their one-year-old children would be walking independently. A mother of an adopted three-year-old was surprised that her daughter was not interested in sharing her toys with her new siblings and was not able to sit through a movie.

A child's developmental age is not necessarily equivalent to her chronological age. A toddler who has been neglected typically displays behaviors and skills consistent with those of a much younger child. This doesn't mean that she will never catch up to her age peers. But it does mean that she will need to be supported as she progresses through those developmental tasks typically performed by a younger child. Language is a good example. Jenny, an institutionalized two-and-a-half-year-old, arrived home with the language skills of a typical twelve-month-old child. Jenny's parents knew she needed to progress through the normal developmental sequence of first acquiring single words, then composing two-word sentences before she would be able to handle the sentence tasks commonly associated with her chronological age.

A number of parents of toddlers who have been institutionalized indicated that their children's emotional development was typically at the level of a young infant. Normally, an infant learns to self-regulate her emotional response to a variety of stimuli, and learns to accept calming within the first few months. Joanna, who was institutionalized for most of her fifteen months, was at a young infancy level of self-regulation when she arrived home. She startled and cried in response to many common household sights and sounds. She screamed for twenty minutes if the dog barked. Not only did she not have any self-calming skills, but she also would not accept calming by her mom or dad. Unfortunately, many institutionalized toddlers have been so deprived of stimuli and nurturing that they have not acquired these self-regulating strategies, and the absence or inappropriateness of response often confuses or alarms new adoptive parents.

Knowledge of normal toddler development and the potential impact of early experiences helps parents differentiate normal variations in growth from adoption-related issues, environmental factors, and hereditary related concerns. Retardation in physical and psychological developmental milestones or premature development of certain milestones are significant indicators of problems. When Todd arrived home at two-and-a-half, he did not talk. His referral had indicated only that he was a shy and quiet child. He didn't babble, hum, coo, or even cry out unless he was startled. His mother was advised by a number of well-meaning friends and professionals to let Todd develop at his own pace. However, she knew enough about normal development to recognize that Todd's total lack of vocalization was a serious concern. Fortunately, Todd's pediatrician agreed, and referred her to a pediatric speech and language clinician after determining that there was no organic reason for Todd's delayed language development. Todd began vocalizing within six months and had a vocabulary of about two hundred words by age three-and-a-half. His mother speculated that his delayed language was due to both the lack of stimulation in the orphanage, and the psychological trauma of his abrupt move to his new home. Todd's clinician is optimistic that he will continue to close the gap between his and his peers' language skills.

Physical, cognitive, and social/emotional development norms used by pediatricians and other professionals in the United States have limited applicability to many adopted toddlers, especially those adopted internationally. They do, however, provide a frame of reference for thinking about a child's development. While there are some commonly accepted principles or truths about child development, there are a variety of approaches to nurturing children's growth. A pediatrician who recommends adhering to a rigid feeding schedule believes in a behaviorist theory of development. On the other hand, a pediatrician who recommends feeding on demand is probably an advocate of what is called the humanistic theory of development. Pediatricians, adoption social workers, and local preschool educators are wonderful sources of information about toddler development, as are several popular and well respected child development and parenting authors such as T.B. Brazelton, James Dobson, Rudolf Dreikurs, Erik Erikson, William Glasser, Thomas Gordon, Jean Piaget, B.F. Skinner, Benjamin Spock, Burton White and others.

Three Views of Child Development.

Simply put, there are three main theoretical schools on child development. One school holds that the child develops from within, another that the child develops as a result of external conditioning, and the third that the child develops from an interaction of nature and nurture.

The theory that children develop from an internal, natural unfolding of potential encompasses what is referred to either as the psychoanalytical or the humanistic approaches. The psychoanalytical and humanistic approaches represent the "nature" view of the nature vs. nurture controversy. Sigmund Freud is the pioneer of this inner person concept. Proponents of this view believe that children have an internal timetable and motivation to grow and develop. According to this theory, children are inherently resilient, but they suffer serious consequences if they do not have the opportunity to develop according to their inner timetables. Psychoanalytical theorists believe that children who do not have the opportunity to attach to a primary parent figure during the critical first year of life are seriously disadvantaged. Humanistic type therapy for such children may include temporary regression to earlier stages of development, thus recreating the opportunity to develop according to the inner timetable. Proponents of this approach would emphasize a parenting approach which is supportive, accepting, and empathetic as the adopted child struggles to acquire a sense of belonging and self-esteem.

At the opposite end of the continuum are the behavioral/social learning theories, which suggest that children are a product of environmental conditioning. This approach represents the "nurture" side of the nature vs. nurture controversy. Behavioral theorists such as B.F. Skinner view behavior as learned and development as the product of environmental influence. Behavioral theorists would interpret the developmental level of the adopted toddler as a product of his early environment and experiences.

For example, Jeff, who arrived home at age two, was very physically aggressive toward his parents. A behaviorist might interpret Jeff's aggression as a learned response to physical abuse. In contrast, the humanist is more likely to interpret Jeff's behavior as a reaction to not having to learned to trust adults in infancy.

The most widely accepted contemporary theory of child development is the belief that growth occurs through an interaction of an internal drive and external forces: a combination of nature and nurture. Jean Piaget, pioneer developmental psychologist, believed that the environment provides the setting for optimal development of a child's inherent potential. It is important for adoptive parents to recognize and understand the interconnectedness of nature and nurture as they identify different aspects of their toddler's development and make adjustments for it.

The Basics of Child Development.

Even though theoretical approaches to understanding child development differ considerably, there are some areas of basic agreement among most theorists and practitioners that are helpful in understanding adopted toddlers.

There is general agreement that development occurs in a series of stages, each of which is different from those that precede it and increasingly more complex. Each stage of development is associated with certain cognitive, physical and social/emotional tasks which need to be accomplished before moving on to the next stage.

It is also generally accepted that children need to reach a certain level of maturation before they can achieve specific tasks. In fact, levels of maturation are actually better predictors of developmental tasks than is chronological age. Children's maturational levels may be affected by a number of factors, including general health and nutrition, biological development, heredity, gender, and environmental stimuli.

A third generally accepted principle is that development tends to proceed from the head downward, and from the center of the body outward. This can be seen in the development of infants who are able to hold up their own heads before they acquire control over their arms and legs. Children also gain motor control over their arms before their legs, and their arms before their hands.

Most developmental theorists also agree that the process of development involves what is referred to as *discontinuity*. This means that, while a child's development over time is usually represented by gradual and overall growth and follows a similar pattern, development is not a continual and even process of smooth transitions from one stage to another. Child development commonly occurs in spurts and plateaus, with most children narrowly focusing their energies on one aspect of their development at a time. It is not uncommon for a child to regress immediately prior to achieving a developmental milestone. For example, when Maria was focusing on learning to walk, her language skills temporarily regressed. It is also common for toddlers to display irritability and unusual behaviors immediately before acquiring a new skill. For example, Natalie's usual sunny disposition was replaced by crankiness and sleeplessness in the days before she sat alone, crawled, walked, and said her first words. It may be some time before adoptive parents know their new toddler well enough to recognize unusual behaviors. Also, a newly adopted toddler's equilibrium may be disrupted by many factors other than his normal growth and development. For example, changes in schedules, food, or climate are just a few of the factors which may affect the toddler.

Child development specialists use the term *equilibrium* to refer to the emotional state of feeling composed and balanced, and the term *disequilibrium* to describe the feeling of being disoriented and out of sync with oneself. Many child development approaches describe children as alternating between general equilibrium and disequilibrium every six months of their first two years and every year thereafter until adolescence. It is important, however, to recognize that toddlers may be thrown into a state of disequilibrium because of the changes associated with their adoption. Also, adopted toddlers may not be at the same developmental stage as their chronological peers, therefore information about these stages should be used to understand the cyclical nature of growth, not to judge age-appropriate development. For example, while Gustavo's development has been cyclical in nature, his periods of equilibrium vs. disequilibrium have not occurred in six month intervals. Periods of calm, steady development have usually tended to last about three months, frequently followed by about a month of regressive and testing behaviors. Events such as starting school or a change in teachers still tend to trigger a change in his behavior.

Even though all children are more alike than they are different, theorists agree that every child is distinct from every other child in the world. It is essential to remember that all children grow and learn according to their own individual characteristics, styles, and timetables. Each child will progress at his own speed and in his own way. There are a myriad of factors which affect individual differences, including maternal health and prenatal care, temperament of both the child and parents, environmental stimuli, diet, general health, and others. Children adopted as toddlers generally are more like their age peers than they are different. However, they do have unique needs associated with their individual differences, background, and with their adoption. While there is wide variation even among children adopted as toddlers, they do tend to share many characteristics and many have similar needs.

In the following sections of this chapter, physical, cognitive, and social/emotional development are discussed separately as a way of organizing the material. The discussion of general toddler developmental stages and tasks is followed by a discussion of variations common in children adopted as toddlers, along with strategies to enhance the adopted toddler's development. A child who does not fit these patterns and trends is not destined to permanent developmental delays. There are exceptions to every rule. The developmental tasks presented are adapted from Brazelton, 1989 and 1995; Brown, 1990; Linder, 1993; Miller, 1985; Seifert, 1991; Santrock, 1988; and White, 1990.

Physical Developmental Tasks.

The Young Toddler: 12-18 Months

By twelve months of age, the infant's brain has grown to two thirds of the adult size and his birth weight has nearly tripled. In most infants, the period of time from twelve to eighteen months represents a deceleration of physical growth but continuing rapid development of physical capacities. Most children stand alone and take their first independent steps during this phase, creep up stairs, climb up on objects such as chairs or low tables, deliberately throw objects, grasp objects such as crayons and spoons with the whole fist, and further refine willful actions such as putting objects together, taking them apart, or pushing a toy car. Gross motor pursuits such as walking, running, and climbing, as well as fine motor activities such as stacking, nesting, and placing objects in a bucket are favorite activities of this age toddler.

The Middle Toddler: 18-30 Months

An eighteen-month-old toddler is normally a whirlwind of physical activity. By eighteen months most toddlers can deliberately back up to and sit in a low chair, run stiffly, jump down from a step or other low object, walk up stairs with assistance, creep backwards down stairs, and turn pages of a book. By thirty months most toddlers have mastered running, including starting and stopping, jumping with both feet, walking up and down stairs, kicking a ball, throwing overhand, holding a crayon and other objects with fingers, and a variety of fine motor skills such as stringing large beads, folding paper, building a tower of five blocks, and unbuttoning large buttons.

The Late Toddler: 30-36 Months

By thirty months, most children have acquired the physical skill to run around objects and efficiently turn corners; to hop on one foot for a few steps, to draw horizontal lines, vertical lines and circles. By the time they reach their third birthday children can usually walk up and down stairs with alternating feet, climb up and down a variety of structures, catch a ball against the chest, use a forearm rotation to turn objects such as door knobs, put on socks, zip and snap, and cut paper with a child's scissors.

Variations in Physical Development.

Physical development depends on physiological factors, emotional nurturance, and simply having the opportunity to acquire a skill. Therefore it is no wonder that many adopted toddlers arrive home delayed in their physical development. Significantly, most of the toddlers whose families provided information for this book were below developmental age norms at placement. Gustavo is a good example. The sparse information we received about Gustavo's birthmother included the fact that she was four feet, ten inches tall. Because of her economic circumstances, it is extremely unlikely that she received prenatal care or that either she or Gustavo had an adequate diet pre-and post-natally. Due to Gustavo's frequent changes in placement and the lack of a consistent primary caregiver, it is also unlikely that he received much emotional support or encouragement to develop and practice motor skills. Children who have been neglected and who have lacked opportunities to develop motor skills will likewise demonstrate poor muscle tone. Children who have been extensively confined to a crib or other restraints will display delayed motor development also. Gustavo's developmental skills were consistent with these genetic and environmental factors. At eighteen months he was the size of an average eight-month-old according to standard American developmental scales. His physical skill acquisition was likewise delayed, similar in most respects to an average twelve-month-old. He was sitting independently, scooted by pushing with one foot while in a sitting position, and had just begun to stand while holding onto furniture.

Inadequate diet and health care, as well as emotional neglect and abuse, can result also in an underweight child with poor skin clarity, dull hair, distended stomach and emaciated limbs. At placement Gustavo's hair was a dark, rusty brown. However, within six months his hair was the glossy black color that is his birthright.

In extreme cases of neglect, the back of the head may become flattened as the result of lying unattended for long periods of time. Head lice is a persistent health problem in neglectful and crowded environments. Immunizations and screening for anemia and lead poisoning may not have occurred. Inadequate diet and dental care may have resulted in temporary or permanent damage to primary and/or secondary teeth.

Even cultural differences affect a child's physical development. In some cultures, children are routinely carried in a confined position much longer than they are in the United States, thereby delaying their acquisition of motor skills. Many adopted toddlers lack the opportunity to develop the fine motor skills that are associated with being able to manipulate a variety of objects and being able to experiment with art materials.

Sometimes an adopted toddler's physical skills seem advanced because they may be those that were learned because they were necessary for coping and survival. Toddlers who were expected prematurely to take care of their own personal care needs, for example, may display the advanced motor skills associated with dressing and feeding. The toddler who has experienced food deprivation may not know how to handle a spoon or fork, but may have acquired physical skills such as digging and tearing necessary for obtaining food. Gustavo lacked most fine motor skills typically achieved by his age peers, but unlike most children his age, he could drink from a soda pop bottle with one hand. He had obviously acquired that skill as a way to get liquids, an important coping skill in his environment.

Most adopted children eventually catch up to their peers in acquisition of physical skills, although heredity and inherent physical characteristics continue to play an important role in determining a child's size and physical attributes. The goal should be, as it is in all areas of development, to maximize our children's development within their range of potential.

Cognitive Developmental Tasks.

Thought, language, reasoning, and imagination are all examples of areas of cognitive development. Most of a newborn's movements are the result of reflex, but by age one children's movements are very deliberate. According to a special feature on "Your Child's Brain," published in the February 19, 1996, issue of *Newsweek Magazine*, a baby's brain is a jumble of neurons when she is born. While some neuron connections are determined by genetics, trillions more have unlimited potential. According to this article, early experiences are so powerful they can change the way of person turns out. In fact, the infant already has learned half of a lifetime's knowledge in the first year of life. Neurons that form the brain are being produced and massive functional electro-biochemical networks become organized so that the majority of the network is normally in place by age one.

Cognitive development, including language acquisition, is affected by both nature and nurture. Most child development specialists believe that children are born with a potential range of intelligence, but where they actually function within that potential range is determined by the environment. Children whose development is stimulated and nurtured are most likely to optimize their intellectual potential.

The Young Toddler: 12-18 Months

The first half of the second year of life is represented by the acquisition of cognitive abilities that are very rewarding for both children and parents. In the last months of the first year of life, the child normally begins to see the relationship between actions and consequences. This is a prerequisite skill to the exciting event that normally occurs right around the first birthday: acting in a way that deliberately causes something to happen. The one-year-old never seems to tire of practicing the new found ability to control cause and effect. Hitting water to watch it splash can entertain the one-year-old for a long time! Another manifestation of this experimentation with problem-solving occurs when the toddler uses an adult to achieve a goal. She deliberately knocks an object off the high-chair tray and crows delightedly when Mom or big brother retrieve it—over and over and over again.

At about this same age a child may begin linking events in simple combinations. He puts a doll in a stroller and pushes the stroller. During this early toddler stage children normally begin pretend play, mimicking events they observe and/or experience on a daily basis such as rocking, eating, or sleeping. Children become adept at imitating sounds, gestures, and other physical activities. The young toddler's pretend play often reveals the type of care he has experienced. The child who has been hit for spilling his milk will similarly hit his doll. Even preverbal children have an uncanny ability to mimic their caregiver's tone of voice, whether it's soothing or scolding! Children at this age want to do everything they see significant adults or older siblings do. They will try to imitate an older sibling's drawings, but rarely achieve any control over copying shapes, lines, etc. before eighteen months. They earnestly wash dishes, clean windows, and sweep floors. Unfortunately, their interest in such chores far outweighs their skills!

Most children achieve object permanence—the knowledge that something continues to exist even when it is out of sight—by twelve months of age. This skill is observable in a child who removes a blanket that has been placed over a toy. She knows the toy is still there after she sees someone covering it. Piaget identified twelve to eighteen months as the age at which children also acquire curiosity and interest in novelty. The acquisition of language represents one of the most complex cognitive tasks of the developing child. Most children express their first intelligible word sometime around their first birthday, but they have used vocalization and body language to declare their intentions, make requests, respond to and acknowledge others long before that time! Receptive language, or language comprehension, is generally more advanced than expressive language throughout early childhood. At twelve months children understand many words, but most will only be saying a few words. By eighteen months however, most children are saying up to fifty words and are combining two words into sentences. As part of their expanding interest in language, books become increasingly important to the early toddler. Typically, children delight in familiar books and will notice if you try to change or skip any words.

By eighteen months, most children have acquired the ability to discriminate objects by like characteristics such as shape or color. In language, this gross discrimination skill is reflected by categorizing objects according to very broad categories. For example, all four legged animals may be called "doggies," while all treats are "cookies."

The Middle Toddler: 18-30 Months

Consistent schedules become very important to the middle toddler because they give children a sense of some control over their lives. Consistency also provides a foundation for understanding time concepts. Children from this age into their third year become almost obsessive about rituals. For the first time, the middle toddler can begin to imagine or envision actions and the subsequent results without having to try them out beforehand. When this age toddler sees something desirable, he might very well plan a strategy for acquiring it and then act on it. For example, the toddler sees a cookie on the cupboard, purposefully pulls out a drawer to use as a stair, and climbs to the top of the cupboard to retrieve it. Most problem-solving results in physical action. Unfortunately, the toddler's cognitive ability to devise and act on a plan usually does not incorporate safety considerations!

Children's curiosity peaks at this age. They want to actively explore everything. Again, curiosity takes precedence over caution. Children at this developmental age become heady with their developing sense of self and power. "No" becomes a favorite word and is used as much to exert authority as to indicate a choice. In fact, many children go through periods of responding "no" to any question as a way to assert their autonomy.

Children between the ages of eighteen and thirty months continue to delight in pretend play, and their play becomes more complex. Imitation may be delayed for hours or days. For example, the two-year-old might pretend to bake cookies, an activity he enjoyed with Dad a day or two earlier. By thirty months, many children can copy circular and vertical strokes and a simple drawing of a face. Play frequently involves a series of actions or schemes. For example, playing with a toy truck may include loading the truck, driving, unloading, crashing, reloading, and finally parking. Doll play typically includes a complex series of activities such as undressing, bathing, dressing, feeding, and putting to bed. By thirty months the toddler can follow two-step verbal directions such as "Go to your room and get your pajamas."

Quantitative comprehension is just emerging at this developmental age. Middle toddlers will identify "one" of something, and be able to differentiate heavy and light, or big and small items. Differentiation of shapes and colors is also improving at this age. Evidence is provided by the ability to stack nesting blocks, insert different shaped blocks in openings of corresponding shapes, or stack rings by size. The vocabulary of the average two-year-old is around three hundred words, including animals, objects, and parts of the body. It is not uncommon for toddlers in this age group to add new two-word sentences to their vocabulary every day.

Children delight in showing off their language skills by responding to queries such as "What is this?" "Can you point to the dog?" and, "Where is your nose?" By age two most children can identify at least six body parts. As children approach two-and-a-half they begin responding appropriately to "yes/no" questions, and "where, who and what" questions. Children's vocabulary becomes much more sophisticated, adding pronouns, prepositions and modifiers. "Mine" is a favorite word! Negative statements are usually indicated by adding a "no" to a two or three word sentence. "No go bed," means, "I have no intention of conforming to your desire for me to go to bed." Even though adults may not understand the speech of a two-year-old, it is very purposeful. The "babbling" of infancy has disappeared. The toddler gets very frustrated by adults or other children who do not understand their speech. Interestingly, other children are often better able to interpret "toddler talk" than adults.

The Late Toddler: 30-36 Months

According to Piaget, by this stage of development the toddler becomes capable of primitive symbolic thinking. Symbolic thinking refers to the ability to develop a mental representation or picture of an object in his or her head, and the ability to use symbols to represent objects that are not present. For example, the two-and-a-half-year-old may use a scribble to represent a house, and pretend play becomes much more sophisticated. A block might be used as a car and a doll might represent Mommy.

Somewhere in the last half of the second year, toddlers normally start to acquire a rudimentary time concept, understanding that some things happened in the past, and other things will happen in the future. This concept is represented by the addition of *-ed* to verbs to show past tense. Many toddlers use the word *yesterday* to mean any time in the past, and *tomorrow* to mean any time in the future. Time concepts are improving, but are still very rudimentary. Late toddlers associate time with events in their lives, such as, after lunch and nap. Children often attempt to understand when something is going to happen by using activities of daily life as their point of reference. Thus the late toddler will ask, "Will we go camping when I go to bed and wake up and go to bed and wake up and go to bed and wake up?" The concept of past and future remains confusing throughout the preschool years.

By age three, children can match objects that go together, such as shoe-sock, brush-comb, and coat-mittens. This ability to categorize is also represented in language. The three-year-old understands, for example, that the word *truck*, describes a variety of types of trucks, but that trucks are different from *buses*.

Thinking and language become increasingly complex and differentiated. In addition to nouns, speech now reflects an understanding of possessives, verbs, adjectives and function. By age three most children are able to remember and follow three-step commands.

The three-year-old's intellectual curiosity and mastery of language is reflected by the emergence of questions. While the two-year-old may use the word *why*, it is generally used in a rhetorical manner. The three-year-old really wants to know "why, who, when, what and where." It is important to remember, however, to confine responses to the specific question asked. In their book *Real Parents, Real Children*, Holly Van Gulden and Lisa Bartels-Rabb suggest that you talk to your three-year-old about being born and how the woman whose special place

she grew in wasn't able to take care of a baby and how you came to adopt her; but they advise that a three-year-old won't comprehend the details about why the birth parents couldn't take care of her. It is important to discuss the birthmother's inability to take care of any baby, rather than personalizing the birthmother's inability to take care of her. Otherwise your daughter is likely to think that there was something specifically bad about her that caused the birthmother to make an adoption decision. Experts also recommend using anatomically correct language when discussing conception and birth so children don't confuse these with eating and elimination processes. By age three, most toddlers can actually sustain a dialogue beyond a few turns. They are becoming delightful conversationalists.

At this stage of development, children begin to create their first symbols for human beings in drawings. These delightful drawings usually include a circle for the body and lines representing legs and arms. As with all artistic expressions, it is important to encourage a child to tell about his drawing, rather than attempting to give it an adult interpretation.

Variations in Acquisition of Cognitive and Language Tasks.

Children are biologically predisposed to learn, but what, how, and at what rate they learn are influenced by many factors. An enriched environment with optimal stimulation maximizes a child's cognitive potential; children raised in impoverished environments rarely reach their full potential. Stimulation and encouragement for change and growth are major determinants in achievement of intellectual potential. Children raised without a specific, significant caregiver frequently display language delays, problems with abstract concepts, impaired time sense, impulsivity, and difficulty attending to task. Significant delays in language development are a common developmental problem for preschoolers entering foster care. Because the brain normally develops at a much faster pace during the first year of life than any other time, delayed development during infancy may have a life-long affect. According to an article titled, "Why Do Schools Flunk Biology?" published in the January 19th, 1996, issue of *Newsweek Magazine*, the windows of opportunity for learning are different for different skills. For example, the neuron connections which affect the ability to acquire a second language develop during the first nine years of life, while the circuitry related to acquisition of vocabulary in the primary language is normally well established by thirty months of age.

Without adequate early social and environmental stimulation, cognitive delays are to be expected in language as well as other areas of cognitive development. Few children adopted as toddlers have experienced optimal environmental and emotional support. It is important to remember, however, that an environment which may be considered suboptimal by advantaged American standards may be more appropriately described as "different". Child-rearing practices and priorities differ throughout the world. A primary example of how cultural differences may affect acquisition of cognitive tasks is in the area of language development. Societies show vast differences in when and how much caregivers speak to infants, and these differences have important effects on children's cognitive development. On the whole, American and European caregivers emphasize the importance of looking at and talking with their infants, while caregivers in many South American and African societies value physical contact with infants over verbal interaction or direct gazing. Not surprisingly, children who have verbally interactive caregivers during infancy show better language comprehension as four-year-olds and higher competence at solving simple problems involving both verbal and nonverbal reasoning. On the other hand, cross-cultural studies also consistently show that babies fuss more in North American societies than in others, and make more verbal demands for attention.

Internationally and cross-culturally adopted toddlers may experience a change in both their primary language and in their cultural familial language. Parents are typically more aware of and sensitive to the challenge of transferring from one spoken language to another than to the more subtle but also daunting challenge of changing cultural familial languages. The first challenge is represented by the move from an environment in which Spanish is spoken, for example, to one in which English is the only language. The second example might be moving from a culture in which head touching is taboo to a family who communicates love and claiming through head stroking.

A child's first spoken language is typically egocentric, representing a child's primary relationships. First words usually include an abbreviated name to use to refer to Mom, a name for Dad, and a name to call oneself. Names are usually single consonant sounds, which are easier to produce than multiple syllable words. Thus, *papa* or *dada* is more commonly used than *father*. Young children often learn the word for *mama* very early in their language development because they have established a pattern of indicating needs to their primary caregiver.

The primary caregiver responds to the infant's needs, thereby strengthening the bond between the two. Eliciting a response from the caregiver by calling out to her is therefore a very functional skill. Saying *mama* and *dada* is also a result of social learning and conditioning. Parents respond to and reinforce approximations of those two words much more than they respond to other early babbling. When a six-month-old chances upon the "m" sound during normal babbling, Mom reinforces the behavior and announces to the world that her precocious baby is saying *mama*. Parents reinforce their child whenever he chances upon the vocalizations that sound like the words for mom and dad.

By the time children are two months old they have normally acquired skills in attracting and holding adult attention. Infants primarily use eye contact and smiling. Adult attention is both a survival and social skill, rewarding to the infant as well as the person being engaged. As the infant develops, his interest becomes more and more focused on attracting and engaging his loved ones. In fact, a primary motivation of learning to speak is that it provides another way to attract and keep the attention of loved ones. Many adopted toddlers have not had the opportunity to learn the skills associated with attracting positive adult attention. For example, institutionalized children often receive scheduled, rather than on-demand, adult attention. Many have not even experienced the pleasure of social communication with loved ones.

Adopted toddlers who were using a word to refer to their former caregiver, such as using *mama* to refer to a foster mother, will not immediately transfer that designation to their adoptive moms. On the other hand, children who have used the word *mama* to indiscriminately refer to anyone who fed them, will not limit its use to their new mamas for some time.

In addition to external stimuli and reinforcement for acquiring language, children are born with an internal drive, or motivation, to vocalize. Even children who are deaf vocalize early in infancy. Young children seem to delight in the sound of their own voice, and practice varying pitch and volume in much the same way they practice physical movement. This drive seems to be stronger in some children than in others, but adopted toddlers may arrive home with a broad repertoire of sounds which they have discovered and enjoy. It is also possible that the adopted toddler may have acquired an invented language. While most common in twins who are extremely close during infancy and toddlerhood, children who are raised together in an orphanage or other residential setting with little adult interaction or stimulus, may develop their own individual ways of communicating. This may include both vocalizations and other forms of expression that represent meaning to the children involved. The child who is removed from siblings or peers who speak her own language will not only miss the ability to socialize, but will be quite frustrated with your lack of understanding.

As discussed earlier, children's capacity for imitation is amazing. The adopted toddler's vocalizations may mimic whatever she has heard. Many years ago I taught a young boy diagnosed as cognitively disabled who nonetheless displayed precocious vocabulary and grammar. What he said though, was always out of context. His response to, "Did you have a good weekend?" would be something like, "Tomorrow will be overcast with a sixty per cent chance of rain." I finally discovered the reason. While watching a television commercial for a laundry product that "eliminated ring around the collar," it dawned on me that Joel had perfectly mimicked the commercial earlier that day during a reading class. I found out later that since infancy, he had been placed in front of a TV during most of his awake hours at home. Unfortunately, this was the family's coping strategy for dealing with a son who had a significant disability.

Delayed development due to environmental deprivation is further complicated by a change in a child's primary language. For example, an internationally adopted two-year-old from an impoverished environment may be just beginning to speak a few words in her native language, a skill normally acquired at one year of age. It is likely that all intelligible speech will cease for a period of time while the child "regroups" and transfers to the new language. Often children will progress rapidly once they reengage their speech skills, and development will occur in bursts. Gustavo is a good example of this phenomena. At eighteen months his speech was at the developmental stage of late infancy (babbling, but no intelligible speech). He completely stopped using spoken language for a few months, but relied heavily on body language, crying and screaming to communicate. At around age two he began speaking, but instead of speaking in single words for six months as a one-year-old typically does, he was speaking in two word sentences within a few weeks of his first word.

The child's rudimentary language skills may have provided her with a tool by which she was able to get more of her needs met. She may be extremely frustrated by a move to caregivers who do not understand her communications. Her frustration will probably be expressed by physical and vocal raging.

Even if the adopted toddler is experiencing spoken language delays, it is important to be sensitive to other forms of expressive language and the child's developing receptive language skills. The receptive (intake) skills of children adopted across languages are typically far ahead of their expressive (output) skills. All toddlers get frustrated when they are misunderstood. Children have many ways to express themselves, and most newly adopted toddlers will attempt to communicate regardless of limitations in spoken language. An exception to this is the toddler who is displaying severe withdrawal. He may not initially make any overt attempt to communicate even his most basic needs, such as hunger. Withdrawn behavior may be related to the trauma of the loss of a loved caregiver, abuse, fear of the unfamiliar parents, or a child's loss of his language.

The adopted toddler's performance of tasks associated with cognitive development may reflect environmental conditioning rather than intellectual potential. Therefore valid testing results are difficult to obtain until the toddler has fully transitioned to his new home. For example, Katie was tested by a psychologist shortly after arriving home at fifteen months from an impoverished environment and was diagnosed as developmentally delayed. As part of her testing, she was assessed as not having acquired the cognitive task of object permanence because she showed no interest in retrieving a toy which the evaluator showed her, then placed behind a screen (a typical strategy for testing this skill). Yet Katie's mother knew she understood that something continued to exist even when she couldn't see it. Earlier in the week she had removed a cookie from Katie's vision by placing it in a cupboard. As soon as Mom turned around, Katie went to the cupboard and opened the door to retrieve the cookie. Evidently Katie found food more motivating than toys. The ability to recognize permanence of food was a survival skill.

Assessment of intelligence in young children necessarily relies on observable behaviors. Toddlers are great mimics who can be expected to imitate behaviors they observe. When the behavior they imitate is similar to those that might easily be interpreted as evidence of delayed cognitive development, diagnosticians can be misled in their assessment of a newly-adopted toddler. Behaviors such as a shuffling walk, self stimulation, hoarding, and vacant staring are commonly referred to as "institutional behaviors". Some behaviors displayed by the toddlers from residential settings are mimicked behaviors of their younger ward mates. Toddlers would be particularly likely to imitate infantile behaviors if those behaviors were rewarded.

Are the initial learning delays and set-backs experienced by adopted toddlers early indicators that predict problems over the long-term? Yes and no. Some child development specialists adhere to a critical period theory of cognitive, physical, and social/emotional development. According to this theory, there is a critical period, or fixed time period early in development, that exists for the emergence of a skill. If that window of opportunity is lost, the child is permanently disadvantaged. Support for this position is found in studies of the acquisition of language. Generally, individuals over the age of twelve have much more difficulty acquiring a second language and typically will speak the new language with an accent for the rest of their lives. However, there is little evidence that the critical period for acquisition of the cognitive skills described in this section are fixed in the first year of life. In fact, the developmental histories of the toddlers referenced in this book provide evidence to the contrary. Most of the toddlers made tremendous strides in all areas of development in their preschool years. Most of the children did not have significant cognitive developmental delays by the time they were school age, but a higher percentage (than the population in general) of the children participated in speech and language therapy and other supplementary educational support programs. The most reasonable position seems to be one of expecting early life experiences to influence, but not predetermine, our adopted toddler's subsequent cognitive development.

Social/Emotional Development.

In many toddler adoptions, a child's social and emotional development is a primary area of concern, especially in regard to grief and attachment issues. While attachment is primarily a function of social/emotional development, the capacity to form a healthy relationship with the primary caregiver(s) also affects all other areas of development. Therefore attachment issues cannot be divorced from any discussion of the overall physical, cognitive or emotional well-being of the adopted toddler. Two important developmental tasks of the early toddler are to have achieved a sense of trust in others and to begin the long journey toward autonomy. Development of trust and autonomy are both an outgrowth of healthy attachment, and are in turn, related to greater mobility skills, improved language and higher levels of cognitive functioning. Therefore attachment becomes the overriding concern for healthy social/emotional development in all areas.

Attachment theory, characteristics associated with secure, insecure and ambivalent attachment, and strategies to enhance attachment are explored in detail in Chapter 7. Therefore, this chapter focuses only on the developmental tasks associated with attachment and other areas of social/emotional development.

In addition to attachment, social/emotional development is also influenced by physical and environmental factors. Children are born with an inherent temperament, but it is shaped and influenced by what happens to them as they grow and develop. Such characteristics as passivity, irritability, sociability, impulsiveness, adaptability, and activity level are part of a child's temperament.

There is an increasing interest in studying the relationship between inherent temperament and the way in which caregivers react to their children. There is some evidence to suggest, for example, that children who are easily irritated are at higher risk of being physically abused. It is often difficult however, to determine the relative effect of nature vs. nurture on a child's temperament. For example, many children who are physically abused learn passivity as a coping mechanism. Inherent personality characteristics such as irritability and activity level are normally displayed within the first hours of life. However, even then, pre-natal environmental influences such as maternal drug abuse, the circumstances of birth, and immediate post-natal care affect the child's behavior. It is especially difficult to differentiate the effect of nature vs. nurture with adopted toddlers because adoptive parents don't have the opportunity to observe their children's infant behavior and temperament, and the information parents receive about their children's infancy is often sparse to nonexistent. Adoptive parents of toddlers can speculate about their children as infants, but they can never retrieve the opportunity to know them from birth.

Social/emotional characteristics and health are very affected by the style of authority practiced by our children's former caregiver(s). Some adopted toddlers may have been fortunate enough to have had caregivers who established clear parameters of acceptable behaviors but were also empathetic and supportive. This parenting style is associated with optimal social/emotional development.

The Young Toddler: 12-18 Months

The emotionally healthy twelve-month-old is a very social being who is securely and firmly attached to a small number of adults or other caregivers. Cherie demonstrates healthy attachment because she has enjoyed a healthy dependency on her foster mother during her first year of life. Emotionally healthy infants are dependent on their caregiver(s), but the relationship is symbiotic, or mutually pleasurable to both parties. The twelve-month-old who enjoyed a symbiotic relationship should have achieved the developmental task of "differentiation," the awareness of himself as separate and different from his caregiver. The toddler's awareness of himself as separate and different from his caregiver often leads to an increase in separation anxiety around the twelfth month. Distress and anxiety are not pervasive, but do occur when children are separated from their objects of attachment.

Interestingly, at this same age when children are still very attached to their caregivers, their biological clock is also motivating them to become more independent and to explore their environment. During this stage children engage in practicing at being a separate and independent individual where the focus is on the other-than-mother world. The result is that children of this age often simultaneously walk away from Mom while looking over their shoulders to assure themselves of Mom's presence. They are thrilled if Mom gives chase. The chase is a physical enactment of the child's balancing the simultaneous drive for separateness and oneness with the parent. Children of this developmental age regularly return physically to the parent, or check back visually. This "emotional refueling" assures the toddler that the parent is still physically and emotionally available. The securely attached toddler becomes frantic if her caregiver disappears. Even securely attached toddlers experience frustration when their budding desire for independence collides with their dependency needs. Charlie's goal is to reach the very top rung of the jungle gym. He is outraged when Mom plucks him off the second tier of bars. The freedom to explore and try new things must constantly be balanced by the family having reasonable expectations for the child and placing limits which will protect him from serious harm while helping him learn social skills.

Other characteristic behaviors of toddlers at this developmental stage include a growing interest in toys and other inanimate objects, an increased interest in other family members, a growing ability to delay gratification, and the use of transitional objects as "lovies"" to handle anxiety. Lovies may be objects as diverse as the traditional blanket to an article of clothing. Typically the object is made of a material that absorbs smells and can be molded to a desired shape. When feeling tired, hungry, or stressed out for other reasons, the toddler uses the lovie to help himself regain his composure.

Play is truly the work of the healthy one-year-old. Both Sigmund Freud and Erik Erikson stress the social and emotional importance of play in early childhood. Play provides an opportunity to satisfy the toddler's budding need for independence by providing a mechanism for gaining mastery over problems. In fantasy play the child is in charge. Play also provides an outlet for the release of upset feelings and an opportunity to explore cause and effect.

Early in the second year of life, humor begins to develop. At this stage children find humor in incongruous actions toward an object. For example, mom pretending to eat a shoe is sidesplitting!

Joy, exhilaration, pride, fear, frustration and anger are all normal emotions frequently displayed by the healthy young toddler. Their expanding physical and cognitive abilities are a source of joy, pride and frustration. Throughout toddlerhood, the inability to do something "by myself" is a source of frustration and anger. "Me do it!" is a favorite expression for most toddlers. The emotionally healthy one-year-old is very interested in other children, but lacks the ability to really play together with them. Young toddlers frequently engage in onlooker play (watching others play without joining in), or parallel play (sitting next to each other to play but not interacting.) Play may be centered around a single object even though the children are not actually playing together. For example, two toddlers might be climbing on the same box, but they are not coordinating their actions. Young toddlers will commonly grab toys, food, or other interesting objects from each other as they have no understanding yet of "yours vs. mine" or "sharing vs. stealing."

The Middle Toddler: 18-30 Months

The securely attached eighteen-month-old still demands the proximity of familiar adults, but often alternates between clinging behavior and resistance to adults. Children of this age still tend to be more interested in adults than peers, as reflected by a preference for social interaction with adults and a tendency to mimic adults in their imaginative play. Primary caregivers are still the essential base of support, and the toddler is especially needy of close physical and emotional support when fatigued, hurt, or frightened. Jason hotly declares that he can get into the swing by himself, impatiently pushing his father's hands away. However, he scrapes his knee on the swing. Sobbing, he reaches out his arms to be held. Within a few minutes he brushes away his tears, pushes Dad away, and tackles the swing once more. The securely attached toddler's affection toward loved ones is delightfully spontaneous, genuine, and uninhibited! It's not unusual for the two-year-old to exchange sloppy kisses with all her loved ones, including the family dog.

Around the age of fifteen to twenty-two months the securely attached toddler reaches the developmental stage of *rapprochement*, which involves alternating between independence and dependence. Children at this age tend to fluctuate between courting the caregiver's love, attention, and closeness and trying their limits. The middle toddler can be very demanding, particularly when Mom or Dad are trying to focus on something else. Separation anxiety and overt concern for always knowing mom's whereabouts are common at this age. Natalie's first four word sentence, which appeared at this age, was "Where did Mommy go?" For three months that question was what I woke up to, and what I went to sleep hearing.

An exciting development in the journey toward autonomy occurs at about eighteen months: referring to oneself by name! Later in this stage children recognize themselves in recent photographs or videos. Children love to examine photographs of themselves with family, friends, pets etc. at this stage. Pictures of birthday parties and other memorable events will be looked at over and over again. Of course, the toddler doesn't recognize that she is the infant in older pictures or videos, and in fact may very aggressively deny that he is that "tiny baby." Two-year-olds play alone, and independently, most of the time. Parallel, noninteractive play will normally predominate until about thirty months. Children still do not interact much when they play together, except to protect and acquire possessions! The one-and-a-half-year-old will use all the cognitive, language, and physical skills at his disposal to protect the all important, "mine." However, a sign of healthy social development is that positive or neutral interactions with peers should exceed conflicts. Parents of two-year-olds are often dismayed at their children's lack of interest in sharing, however, possessiveness is normal and is in fact, evidence of the emerging sense of self. Children of this age have very little ability to take the perspective of others, therefore their actions are not determined by empathy for another's point of view or feelings. Interestingly, however, studies have shown that children as young as eighteen months may display behaviors which unselfishly benefit another person. Gustavo's behavior at one-and-a-half is a good example. He became very distraught over crying babies and would do his best to console them by trying to put their pacifiers back into their mouths or patting their heads.

The roots of conscience normally emerge in the second year of life. As the two-year-old reaches for something she knows she isn't supposed to touch she may firmly tell herself, "No, no, Sara." In *A Child's Journey Through Placement*, Vera Fahlberg describes this behavior as the beginning step in acknowledging right vs. wrong. This behavior is precursor to the development of a conscience. During the second year some children begin showing remorse when they have done something they know is forbidden. Healthy shame plays an important role in healthy identity formation. According to John Bradshaw, the author of *Healing the Shame that Binds You*, healthy shame is the emotional energy that tells us we made and will make mistakes, and that we need help. It gives us permission to be human. Feeling ashamed of doing wrong is eventually important for healthy social/emotional development. However, this does not mean that toddlers should be "shamed" in ways that humiliate them or make them feel that they, not their behavior, are "bad."

Toddlers are often a study in contrasts. Five minutes after he has screamed and fought to get a toy, he will crawl into your lap and offer you a bite of the cookie he's been clutching in his sweaty little hands! Emotional lability (rapid and frequent mood shifts) is very common in two-year-olds. Mood changes are frequently triggered by seemingly innocuous events. Adam's squeals of delight as his dad carries him to lunch turn to howls of rage when he sees that his peanut butter sandwich is cut into fourths instead of halves. Extremes are also the norm, from dependence to independence, aggression to passivity, helpful to stubborn.

The healthy eighteen to thirty-month-old is going through a normal oppositional, stubborn, egocentric stage which is necessary to the development of his identity. Temper tantrums are a common way of expressing frustration, releasing tension, seeking attention, or trying to achieve a desired goal at both the eighteen-to-twenty-four, and the thirty-to-thirty-six month stages. The two-year-old has difficulty separating pretend from reality. Stories about monsters, bad dreams, or threats about "bogey men" are very real and therefore terrifying to the two-year-old. Her fears should never be trivialized or disregarded.

The Late Toddler: 30-36 Months

A major developmental task usually achieved by the securely attached three-year-old is what is called consolidation of individuation. This is where she is truly, and experiences herself, as an individual. In his popular book, *The First Three Years of Life*, child development specialist Burton White refers to the three-year-old as a relatively complete junior being. Children of this age who are not developmentally delayed due to disruptions or other factors have a strong enough mental image of their caregiver(s) to feel safe and protected even during brief separations.

By age three, temper tantrums are usually decreasing. The three-year-old's expanding language and other cognitive skills provide other ways of thinking about and expressing feeling. By the third birthday children begin to play with, rather than next to, other children. The ability to play with peers is enhanced by their decreased possessiveness, as well as their increased imagination, language, and physical skills. They are still heavily into ownership, but most three-year-olds can sometimes engage in cooperative play in which children consciously form into groups to accomplish some mutually agreed upon activity.

By the age of three, a child's sense of humor is becoming more sophisticated, paralleling increased cognitive abilities. Humor at this age relates to incongruous elements of a concept, such as a cow that barks, or distortions of familiar sights and sounds such as those found in nonsense rhymes.

The three-year-old recognizes gender and racial differences, therefore it is an especially critical age to be vigilant about experiences that might reinforce stereotypic and discriminatory behavior. For example, a three-year-old boy is very interested in his "maleness," and unfortunately takes very seriously a taunt by a playmate that, "Boys can't play with dolls!" Many children's toys and network TV commercials are particularly guilty of reinforcing stereotypes.

Numerous child development specialists assert that the three-year-old is capable of an elementary awareness of ethnic differences based on color and other observed physical and behavioral differences. This awareness represents the beginning of racial attitudes and the knowledge that the characteristics associated with differences are permanent and unchangeable. Children need both to feel like their parents, and have their unique differences reinforced. Ethnic identity is influenced by how a child perceives others, his or her sense of belonging to a group, and reactions of other people. The reactions of others is increasingly important as the child reaches school-age. Accurate and complete self-identification does not usually occur before age seven.

Toddlers at High Risk of Social/Emotional Developmental Delays.

Many children adopted as toddlers display significant social/emotional developmental delays. Insecure or ambivalent attachment is common, which in turn, affects all other areas of social and emotional development.

Social/emotional problems are often a result of an internal battle being waged inside the toddler. His biological clock may be saying that it is time for him to begin his journey toward independence before he has experienced a healthy dependence. He may have achieved the cognitive capacity to accomplish the developmental task of recognizing his or her own "personness" (individuality or "self"). He also may be aware of his ability to make decisions, control the environment, and act on his own desires. However, the healthy acquisition of a sense of individuality evolves from a secure attachment with a primary caregiver. A secure sense of individuality also grows out of the ability to understand and remember that a loved one continues to exist, even when that loved one is not present (object permanence). Finally, even as the emotionally healthy toddler celebrates his emerging personness, he firmly believes that his caregiver will be available to meet his needs when necessary. Unfortunately, many adopted toddlers have not enjoyed a consistent and secure attachment. Others have delayed object permanence because their loved ones have disappeared. And still others have not been able to count on their caregivers being available when needed. Therefore many adopted toddlers arrive home without a healthy sense of who they are as individuals.

In child development lingo, the term *separation* is used to indicate the process of a child first emerging from her dependent and symbiotic relationship with her caregiver. The separation process, which normally begins in late infancy, is evident by the child's interest in exploring everything in her environment. Her actions seem to be saying, "Watch out world, here I come!" In contrast, the toddler who did not experience a healthy symbiotic relationship with her caregiver during infancy tends to become preoccupied and anxious about her relationships, and thus tends not to engage in normal exploration. According to noted child development expert Erik Erikson, a firmly developed early trust and dependence is necessary for a toddler to develop healthy self esteem and independence.

Very few toddlers who become available for adoption have experienced the type of physiological and environmental nurturance needed for optimal social/emotional development. Many have neither learned to love a caregiver, or to love themselves. Many have experienced neglect and other forms of abuse, as well as multiple disruptions. Typically, the physical needs of children in institutions or foster care are met, but not their need for continuity in relationships.

The transition strategies described in Chapter IV are very important. However, even children who have been assisted in transferring their attachment may experience temporary developmental delays. Older children who have experienced the trauma of multiple disruptions and/or significant periods without attachment are often placed in a "transitional" foster placement prior to a permanent family. It is my opinion that because toddlers are at a particularly vulnerable stage for development of attachment, and because they have limited cognitive ability to participate in the traditional grief resolution therapies, that they should be placed in a permanent home as soon as possible, regardless of their attachment status. Adoption specialists agree that when a toddler has never developed an attachment to a caregiver, time is of the essence. Therefore expediting a permanent placement is critical. However, adoptive parents of toddlers with attachment problems must be better educated and supported than has traditionally been the case.

The Importance of the Developmental Age.

Knowing a child's developmental stage at the time of adoption is important. Holly Van Gulden and Lisa Bartels-Rabb assert that the child will not begin the new relationship with his adoptive parents at a developmental stage he has not yet reached under the care of previous caregivers. An adopted toddler who has never enjoyed a healthy symbiosis (dependency) may become even more withdrawn and convinced that she should not trust adults to meet her needs. A child who has never experienced healthy dependency may also demonstrate premature independence. She may use compensatory techniques to comfort herself rather than accept comforting from her caregivers. Such a child has probably given up on adults meeting her needs, so she self-comforts and tries desperately to take care of herself. Common self-comforting routines include self-rocking, head banging, and relentlessly sucking on a body part or inanimate object. For example, she usually perseveres in these activities until eventually falling asleep from exhaustion, without achieving any real comfort. Such a child may also resist being fed, and may act as though he can handle anything.

There is considerable support for the theory that a child who has never experienced healthy symbiosis needs opportunities to regress to that stage before he will be ready to develop healthy attachment. This means that the child needs to go back to the emotional level of a young infant and progress through the developmental processes which he missed. Regression strategies (often referred to as Reparenting) are described in Chapter 7.

The toddler who has experienced healthy symbiosis with a previous caregiver, and has moved into *differentiation* (recognizing himself as a separate being), needs to transfer the trust or bond to the new caregiver(s). If he is in the early stage of differentiation he will probably experience intense separation anxiety. It is thus extremely important that the transition strategies discussed in Chapter 4 be implemented if at all possible to ease the transfer. The previous caregiver must give the child permission to transfer his trust and love. It is important to allow the expected and entirely normal grief process to occur and support it without abandoning the child to her grief.

Children who are in the differentiation stage may also need to regress or repeat parts of previously completed developmental tasks as a way to strengthen their attachment to the new parent. Children moved at the differentiation stage are also at risk of becoming prematurely independent, as indicated by precocious self-parenting or by not using parents as a secure foundation. An indicator of this problem would be the toddler who runs away from his parents without ever looking back over his shoulder or returning to his parents for emotional refueling. Another toddler might demand to do everything for herself and be extremely resistant to seeking or accepting assistance or might strenuously reject being physically comforted, even when tired or hurt. Without associating parents with comfort and relaxation, attachment is inhibited because the positive interaction cycle cannot be completed.

People who choose to adopt a toddler as a way to avoid the dependency stage of infancy may unfortunately encourage premature independence. Likewise, parents who are unfamiliar with normal toddler development may reinforce inappropriate independence. Some parents may even mistakenly interpret prematurely independent behavior as "precocious intelligence" rather than as a warning sign that their child is not attaching. For example, some parents and other well-meaning adults inappropriately encourage a twelve-month-old child to display affection toward any and all adults.

A toddler who is placed for adoption during the developmental stage of practicing his autonomy will also need to transfer the trust and attachment achieved with his previous caregiver(s) before feeling safe to continue exploring the world. A child who does not successfully achieve this developmental stage may get stuck in an earlier stage, or may again demonstrate inappropriately premature independence. If a child does not attach and thus become free to experience the pleasure and self-confidence associated with practicing autonomy, she may become stuck in the stage of separation anxiety, become increasingly withdrawn, and/or use extreme aggression as a response to frustration.

Children who are in the developmental stage of *rapprochement* (alternating between dependence and independence) have a particularly difficult time attaching to new parents. This is probably due to the fact that the child's greatest fear—that she will be abandoned by the person she is attached to—has been realized. A child placed during this stage is very resistant to attaching to a new person whom she fears may also disappear, and typically displays her rage and fear through excessive aggression, poor impulse control, and intense resistance to authority.

The child who is placed during the developmental stage of *consolidation of individuation* (truly becoming his own person) may also feel very vulnerable to the potential loss of another loved one, and therefore be very fearful of falling in love with his new parents. As the parent of a child at this developmental level, it is more reasonable initially to help a child accept love rather than expect love to be reciprocated. The child who experiences a disrupted placement at this stage may believe she did something wrong which caused the loved one to abandon her, and subsequently she may internalize feelings of being bad. It is extremely important for the child at this stage to be given permission (and even encouragement if possible), from his former caregiver, to transfer his attachment.

Common Reactions of Children Who Have Been Neglected and Otherwise Abused.

Toddlers who have experienced trauma, neglect or other abuse, abandonment, or disruption, may use extreme withdrawal as a coping mechanism. Sam, a sexually abused toddler, frequently retreats into himself and turns his anger and frustration inward. Such children may appear autistic-like in their behavior and appearance, manifesting such behaviors and characteristics of withdrawal as rhythmic self-stimulating behaviors, lack of eye contact, severe temper tantrums, downcast eyes, glazed expression, hypotonic (rag doll behavior), slack mouth and drooling, and little or no reaction to visual or auditory stimuli. Withdrawal may also be characterized by physically hiding or retreating to inconspicuous locations. Withdrawal may have been a learned behavior, a defense mechanism to avoid punishment, or as a way to escape the reality of an abusive world.

Infants and toddlers who have been severely neglected may also resort to self-stimulating behaviors for arousal or comfort. While some rhythmic and self-stimulating behaviors are common in toddlers, prolonged or self-destructive head banging, rocking, or meaningless perseveration is not normal. Self-stimulating behaviors such as chewing on fingers or head banging may even become self-abuse.

The neglected or otherwise abused toddler may display obsessive-compulsive behaviors as a way to establish some control over his life. As discussed earlier, control is an important issue for all toddlers, but the abused toddler may become obsessed with control. If the toddler has learned that he can't stop Dad from hitting, he may redirect his control needs to compulsively arrange objects. Food is also a common obsession of malnourished toddlers or those from environments in which withholding food was used as punishment. Stealing, hoarding, and gorging are all examples of food obsessions.

Toddlers who have been severely punished for displaying oppositional behavior which are normal for their age may suppress healthy defiance and resistance to avoid further punishment. If the child does not experience opportunities to display normal oppositional behavior her sense of self as worthwhile and capable may be jeopardized and she will have difficulty learning appropriate independence.

A child who has not enjoyed secure attachment typically does not acquire the self-control that develops from an internalized values system. He may however have learned self-control as a defense mechanism to avoid punishment. For example, if he has been punished for crying, he may have learned to hold back his tears, even when he is hurt. Unfortunately, because oppositional behavior can be very frustrating to adults, the poorly informed adoptive parent may unwittingly continue to reinforce unnaturally compliant behavior, further suppressing the normal development of conscience.

Adopted toddlers may display abnormal aggressiveness for a variety of reasons. Aggression may have been a coping mechanism useful for acquiring food or other essentials, it may have served as a defense against older aggressive children at an orphanage, it may be modeled on aggression displayed by adults, or aggression may be an external manifestation of the internal rage and hurt experienced by children who are not securely attached.

We know toddlers are wonderful mimics. Much of their social behaviors reflect behaviors of caregivers and others in their immediate environment. Therefore inappropriate behaviors such as hitting or biting may have been learned through role-modeling.

Neglected toddlers may have delayed or distorted self image or sense of themselves as individuals. This may be reflected by such things as a lack of identity of themselves in pictures, not using their own name, and lack of appropriate assertion of personal needs and desires. Children's early identification of themselves is a reflection of how their parents see them and their experience. The child who has internalized the message that he is good, worthwhile, loved, capable and an important person in his own right will display a healthy self-esteem and self-concept. Many adopted toddlers neither received nor internalized that message. Therefore their view of themselves might be distorted and delayed.

The notion of the extended self is reflected by the healthy toddler's frequent declaration that everything within his reach belongs to him. "Mine," he declares with impunity. The notion of the extended self may be delayed for the adopted toddler who had no personal possessions or caregiver attachment prior to adoption. For example, Gustavo had no sense of anything being "his," because he had never had blankets, toys, or even clothing that were exclusively his. Even sadder, because Gustavo had not experienced a caregiver as an extension of himself, he had not learned to declare, as an attached toddler does, any claim on his caregivers. Gustavo finally began claiming us at thirty months of age. One day when I was holding a friend's daughter, he walked over, stuck his face in the little girl's face, and emphatically announced, "Dis is *my* mama!"

When You're Faced with Developmental Disabilities.

All of our children are special, and all have unique needs. As discussed throughout this book, adopted toddlers also have special needs due to caregiver disruptions and other life experiences, subsequently most adopted toddlers have developmental delays in some areas. However, most of the adopted toddler's differences diminish considerably by school age.

There was a group of children among the families interviewed for this book whose special needs continued or even intensified in the years following placement. Some of these children arrived home with diagnosed physical disabilities or other characteristics that appeared unrelated to environmental conditions or to their adoption, but most manifested conditions that seem to be directly correlated with their early life experiences.

Parents may knowingly or unknowingly adopt a toddler who has a chronic disease, disability, or other special need. Of the twenty-six children referred to in this book, by the time their parents were in contact with me, nine had been diagnosed with physiological, sensory, cognitive, learning, emotional, and/or attention deficit special needs that were serious enough to require special medical, therapeutic or educational interventions.

Domestic adoptions are more likely than international to include accurate data regarding the child's health, inherited risk factors, the birthmother's prenatal care and health status, etc. With international adoption this information is often not available and/or may be complicated by language differences or differences in resources or practices.

Sometimes referral information is misleading or inaccurate. Friends of ours accepted a referral of a five-year-old boy who, according to the referral information, was minimally developmentally delayed. They reasoned that minimal delays would be expected given the circumstances of his first five years, and subsequently traveled to South America fully intending to proceed with the adoption. The lack of any common language or a translator delayed for two days their realization that Andre had no intelligible oral communication. He repeated a limited number of sounds over and over. Further autistic-like behaviors manifested during those two days and the inability to control Andre's physical aggression resulted in their decision to terminate the adoption proceedings. When they returned Andre to the orphanage, a staff member did admit that they had minimized Andre's disability in the earlier report.

In the United States, adoptive parents have successfully sued adoption agencies for failing to disclose, for concealing, or for misrepresenting information about a child's disability, adoption circumstances, or background information. Failing to disclose or misrepresenting information is referred to as "wrongful adoption." While a family history may not be available in cases of abandonment, most adoption professionals now feel that full disclosure of background information should occur whenever possible.

Some developmental disabilities are identifiable at birth or by toddler age, while others are not manifested until later in life. In some cases, a toddler who does not display a particular disability such as mental illness may be ascertained to be at risk due to his genetic and environmental influences. In still other cases, there are no predictive physiological or environmental factors but a person develops a disability anyway. There are no guarantees in adoption just as there are none with birth children. Within this book's contributing families, five of the nine children with developmental disabilities were diagnosed after placement. In each of these cases, the parents were the first ones to suspect that their child had serious developmental delays and/or behavior problems. Most commonly, pediatricians and preschool or primary teachers then confirmed the suspected special needs and the children were subsequently referred to specialists for a specific diagnosis. The federal government mandates that assessment for suspected exceptional education needs be provided by local educational agencies free-of-charge, but many parents choose also to obtain independent evaluations.

Many physical conditions and severe cognitive disabilities are displayed within the first two years of life, but frequently behavioral and learning problems may not be evident until school age or later. Of course, neither our children nor we are immune to the potential of acquiring a serious health condition or other disability at any time in our lives!

Chronic Diseases, Physical and Cognitive Disabilities

Most disabilities caused by genetic or chromosomal abnormalities are apparent prenatally or at birth in the baby's phenotype (physical appearance) and/or in their genotype (genetic profile.) For example, amniocentesis and chorionic villus sampling can provide pre-natal evidence of conditions such as Down's syndrome, sickle-cell anemia, muscular dystrophy and cystic fibrosis. Ultrasound can detect physical abnormalities such as spina bifida or hydrocephalus. Disabilities caused by prenatal trauma or toxins are also usually apparent at birth. Many serious childhood diseases are also apparent by age one, and should be reported during adoption procedures. While it is impossible to delineate all possible physical and cognitive diseases and disabilities, the more common ones that can affect adoptable toddlers are described here.

A chronic disease which is not uncommon in situations where there is poor sanitation is Hepatitis B, an infection of the liver caused by a virus. Endemic to Eastern Europe, it is not uncommon for toddlers adopted from orphanage settings to have been infected by their birthmothers during birth or through blood transfusions and contaminated needles. The acute phase occurs just after infection, but in the chronic phase the virus remains in the liver and blood and the person becomes a "carrier." Over time, an active chronic infection can destroy the liver and a small percentage of infected people die from liver failure. A vaccine does exist, so family members and others who are in regular contact with a child who has Hepatitis B can be immunized. Although the risk of transmission is extremely low, many families experience stigma associated with Hepatitis B similar to that of having a family member who is HIV positive. Some Hepatitis B infected children and their families are subjected to discrimination and rejection by neighbors, teachers, and friends.

A variety of disabilities may result if the birthmother contracted rubella during pregnancy, especially during the first trimester. While rare in the United States, it is still a high risk factor in developing and third world countries, potentially resulting in cognitive disability, skull deformities, blindness, deafness and heart abnormalities. Obviously, related physical disabilities would be apparent at birth or in early infancy, but mild cognitive delays would probably not be diagnosed prior to school-age.

One of the leading causes of cognitive disabilities is Fetal Alcohol Syndrome (FAS), a condition that has only been officially recognized within the last decade (it has obviously been present long before that, however!) Fetal Alcohol Syndrome results when damage is done to the developing fetus by alcohol consumption of the mother. Typically, an individual with FAS has an IQ range of 65 to 80, although diagnosed cases of FAS range in IQ from 15 to 105. The physical characteristics of FAS include a low nasal bridge, short upturned nose, small head circumference, generally smaller stature, small midface, wide set eyes and narrow eyelids. Effects can include severe cognitive disability, cranial, and skeletal anomalies. Individuals with FAS display poor social judgment and disjointed thought patterns. They often lack motivation and may appear lethargic, impulsive, and disorganized. Learning and behavioral disorders are typically increasingly displayed as the child grows, particularly attention disorders and hyperactivity. The manifestation of these signs and symptoms vary from very subtle to extremely severe, sometimes making an accurate diagnosis difficult. The amount of alcohol necessary to result in FAS is unknown at this time, which is why pregnant women are advised to abstain from alcohol and other drugs during pregnancy. The birthmother's alcohol consumption may be difficult or impossible to ascertain, particularly in cases of abandonment. However, FAS is usually evident by toddler age due to the physical characteristics and associated behavioral and learning disabilities.

More difficult to diagnosis and typically not diagnosed until school-age is Fetal Alcohol Effect (FAE). FAE does not include documentation of the full syndrome but relates cognitive and behavioral disabilities to the birthmother's alcohol consumption during pregnancy. FAE may be suspected but impossible to confirm in toddlers due to incomplete prenatal history.

An accurate diagnosis of children born to cocaine-addicted mothers should also be possible before toddler age. The effect of cocaine use during pregnancy is tragically, on the increase. Equally tragically, the vast majority of mothers who abuse cocaine abuse a variety of other chemicals as well. Effects, ranging from minor to severe depending on the amount and timing of drug use, include decreased gestational age, weight, length, and head circumference. Other common abnormalities associated with maternal cocaine use include genital and urinary tract malformations, kidneys distended and obstructed, undescended testes, and the absence of muscles in the abdomen. Physical malformations are twice as likely in infants of cocaine using mothers. Infants exposed to cocaine cannot focus on voices or faces and avert their gaze. They have extreme difficulty making the transition from sleep to a waking state, and lack the ability to calm themselves or achieve an alert state. They frequently startle and cry hysterically. By the age of two, most have caught up in body size, but the head circumference remains below average, so brain growth has been undoubtedly compromised. Cocaine-exposed children typically demonstrate a short attention span, disorganized behavior, distractibility, a lack of playful thinking, and attachment problems.

Poisoning from ingestion of substances containing lead is permanently and progressively toxic to the central nervous system. Lead poisoning is associated with seizures, cerebral palsy, and cognitive disabilities. Blood tests can be used to diagnose lead poisoning. Children who live in substandard environments where they may have ingested lead by chewing/mouthing lead based paint, lead pipes or have been exposed to air polluted by lead smelters or lead gasoline are at high risk.

The number of infants and children with Human Immunodeficiency Virus (HIV) and Acquired Immunodeficiency Syndrome (AIDS) increases every year. The vast majority of infants and children with HIV or AIDS acquired the infection from their birthmothers. The Human Immunodeficiency virus attaches to the cells that coordinate the body's immune system. More and more viruses are produced and the body is unable to fight off disease. HIV positive individuals are diagnosed with AIDS only if they develop one of the serious diseases associated with a deficient immune system. AIDS is a devastating disease at any age, but children who test positive for HIV or AIDS are not only subjected to the physical deterioration associated with the disease, but many are also abandoned by birth families and are extremely difficult to place with adoptive families. Potential families need to carefully consider their ability to knowingly adopt a child with this or any life threatening disease.

Learning and Behavior Disabilities

The term *learning disability* refers to a disorder in listening, thinking, speaking, reading, writing, spelling, and/or math. It does not include children who have problems in these areas due to a cognitive disability, emotional disturbance, or environmental deprivation. There are more school-aged children diagnosed as learning disabled in the United States than the next three most commonly diagnosed disabilities (speech disorders, cognitive disabilities, and behavioral disorders) combined. There are a variety of theories as to the cause of learning disabilities, including brain dysfunction, biochemical factors, genetic factors, and environmental factors.

Children diagnosed as having a learning disability typically display underdeveloped learning strategies, time concepts and physical abilities; attention disorders; perceptual, memory, and spatial disorders; and an inability to follow directions compared to their peers. Some types of learning disabilities have specific labels, such as dyslexia which refers to a reading learning disability. Children are rarely diagnosed as learning disabled prior to school age. A number of researchers have identified a correlation between children who were adopted and are diagnosed as learning disabled. However correlation does not establish cause and effect. There are many possible reasons for the correlation, including the theory that teachers are predisposed to expect adopted children to have learning problems, effects of early nutritional deprivation, poor prenatal care, an increased tendency for parents to be alert to learning difficulties, and self-concept factors.

Attention Deficit Disorder (ADD) and Attention Deficit Hyperactivity Disorder (ADHD) are sometimes considered to be types of learning disabilities, but the movement is toward identifying these as separate disabilities that often occur in tandem with learning disabilities. The assessed incidence of ADD and ADHD has increased dramatically since the late 1980s. Characteristics of ADD include the inability to focus on the task at hand and paying attention to the wrong features of a task compared to peers. These children may fixate on certain objects or activities and have difficulty transferring their attention. ADHD includes those characteristics plus extreme impulsiveness, inability to control behavior and excessive movement compared to peers. In retrospect, parents of school age children identified as ADHD often describe their infancy and toddler years as being characterized by extreme irritability. For example, they were very easily wakened, upset by minor irritations, and very difficult to calm. Children diagnosed as ADHD may demonstrate selective attention. For example, the ADHD child may display the ability to play a favorite computer game for an extended period, but be unable to attend to a manipulative task for more than a few minutes. One of the most controversial aspects of diagnosis and treatment of ADD and ADHD is the frequency with which behavior-altering drug treatment is prescribed, with Ritalin being the most commonly administered drug. Both ADD and ADHD have been directly related to metabolic abnormalities. However, it is usually difficult if not impossible to "sort out" the physiological and environmental factors associated with ADD and ADHD. Many children with these disorders are blamed for getting into trouble, that is, it is often assumed that they could sit still and pay attention if they wanted to. Therefore, by the time ADD is diagnosed there is typically a long history of social problems and negative experiences with parents, caregivers, teachers and peers that influence the child's self-concept and behaviors. Pre-school age children may be diagnosed as ADD or ADHD if their behavior is at great variation with their peers, but it is much more commonly diagnosed at the primary or elementary level. Characteristics of ADD and ADHD (attention deficits, irritability and activity level disorders) may be related to other factors. Children have a limited repertoire of coping mechanisms or behaviors which they can display in reaction to what's going on in their environment. It would not be unusual for a child who is experiencing stress due to any number of factors to display these characteristics. For example, as I discussed earlier, Gustavo had a very effective coping mechanism of withdrawing when he was overwhelmed with what was happening to him during the transition to his new family.

An important element in the diagnosis of ADD and ADHD is how chronic and persistent the behaviors are. In other words, have the behaviors continued over a period of time? Do they occur in multiple environments? Are they resistant to behavior management strategies?

Emotional disorders are generally categorized according to whether the characteristics are manifested through externalizing (acting out) or internalizing (withdrawal) behaviors. Conduct and oppositional disorders are often first observed at the pre-school age, but it is important to remember that in diagnosing any exceptionality, a comparison with the peer group is essential. For example, toddlers lie as part of their fantasy play and because they have immature socio-moral reasoning abilities. Preschoolers often react physically when frustrated or angry, but the child who chronically assaults others and reacts with physical aggression when any limits are imposed may be showing early evidence of externalizing behavior problems. Children of any age, even infants, can experience depression. Toddlers who are grieving the loss of a primary caregiver may display depression. Other examples of internalizing behaviors would include children who do not speak (but no known organic reason can be determined), excessive and unexplainable fears, and excessive withdrawal.

A toddler may be diagnosed as displaying Reactive Attachment Disorder in infancy and early childhood if he displays symptoms associated with severely pathogenic care and frequent changes in caregiver, including failure to thrive, developmental delays, failure to make eye contact, feeding disturbances, hypersensitivity to touch and sound, failure to initiate or respond to social interaction, indiscriminate sociability, repetitive non-functional behaviors, self-stimulation, and susceptibility to infection. It is important to remember that most adopted toddlers do not immediately attach to the adoptive parents and that not all children who experience attachment problems following adoption will end up being diagnosed with Reactive Attachment Disorder. The severity and resistance to efforts to establish attachment are both taken into account in the diagnosis.

There are a number of clinical mental health diagnoses that may be applied to children and youth, including but not limited to childhood schizophrenia, gender identity disorders, or post-traumatic stress disorder.

What about Long Term Developmental Problems?

The future of children adopted as toddlers is bright, but not without shadows. While most of the adoptive parents of toddlers whom I've interviewed reported that their children were functioning within the normal range of cognitive, physical, and social/emotional development by school-age, many children did have ongoing developmental needs. It is important for parents to realize that there are potential continuing developmental delays and problems associated with the prenatal conditions and experiences of infancy which are common among children placed for adoption during the toddler ages. Some children continued to be of small stature, although many children considered unusually small by the American norms for height and weight are not unusually small for their own races and cultures. Children who display severely delayed language development or who experience a complete change in their primary language as an older toddler are often involved in speech and language therapy well into their school age years.

There is contradictory research related to the mental health of adopted children. While many people believe that adopted children are at risk of developing mental health problems, research from the Search Institute indicates that overall, children adopted before the age of two display similar mental health as birth children during the teen years.[5] Research purporting that adopted children are more likely to be involved in professional therapy than birth children is often misrepresented as evidence that adopted children and their families are destined to be maladjusted. Adoptive families may be more willing to seek professional assistance. Perhaps adoptive families have become comfortable with and aware of the benefits of professional counseling during their infertility assessment and treatment, home-study, and placement! According to the National Adoption Information Clearinghouse publication titled "Adoption and School Issues," adoptive parents tend to be extremely watchful of their children, and tend to seek professional help at the slightest sign of a problem.

There is a relationship between the conditions experienced by many toddlers who are available for placement, and subsequent need for professional intervention. Lack of stimulation, maternal deprivation, and/or maternal abuse are all known to be related to psychological deficiencies. Memories during the first two years of life are stored according to sensory and movement input. After age two, children's brains undergo a tremendous explosion of interconnectedness and

5 Benson, P., Sharma, Anu and Roehlkepartain, E. (1994) *Growing Ip Adopted.* Minnesota: Search Institute.

they move into a new stage of memory retention. Because early life memories are stored in an essentially different system, it is very challenging for the individual or the therapist to access those early life memories. Thus, an infant's deeply held conviction that other people are dangerous, and that survival can only be ensured if others are not allowed to have any control whatsoever is very resistant to change, and has life long implications.

The potential diagnosis of specific learning disabilities and/or attention disorders needs to also be considered when looking ahead to the school age years. Adoption itself is not a causal factor, but conditions which children experienced before or during their adoption may be related to learning and attention disabilities. According to the National Adoption Clearinghouse publication "Adoption and School Issues," one theory is that there is a genetic component, that is, people who choose adoption for their children or whose parental rights are terminated may themselves have learning problems. People whose learning problems are associated with problems of impulsivity are more likely to become pregnant at an untimely point in their lives. According to that same publication, prenatal influences such as inadequate nutrition and chemical abuse are also risk factors. Severe sensory deprivation during infancy is known to be related to subsequent cognitive delays. Therefore children who were not physically, auditorialy, or visually stimulated, intentionally, or because of benign neglect, are at risk of learning and attention problems.

Services and Treatment for Developmental Disabilities.

The families with whom I have spoken have obtained assistance and support from a variety of sources. Virtually every family stressed the vital role informal support networks played in their lives, including those provided by extended family, adoption support groups and "buddy" families. Many of the families have also accessed professional services and treatment. One mom recommended making an appointment with a counselor the day your toddler arrives, explaining that she believes their services will be needed at some point so you might as well start working with them right away. Another dad cautioned, "Don't wait to get help, the problems our children have don't usually just go away by themselves."

At the time this book was written the most common outside sources for family support included continued involvement with the family adoption agency and social worker, early childhood education for language and other developmental delays, and counseling from spiritual leaders. Five of the twenty-six families who provided extensive information had been or were currently working with professional counselors or psychiatrists other than their social worker.

Locating Services

Obtaining treatment or support services for chronic health problems and/or physical disabilities is often more straight forward than seeking treatment for a child's learning or behavioral/emotional needs, for a number of reasons. Physical and medical needs are usually quite obvious, while learning and behavioral problems are often more elusive. Some diseases are life threatening and require immediate attention, whereas behavioral problems may be attributed to a "phase" that the child will outgrow. Perhaps most significant, there is typically much less perceived or real "stigma" associated with seeking treatment for health related or other physical conditions (with the exception of communicable diseases) than for learning and behavioral needs.

There is no simple way to determine when and where to get help. Many factors come into play, including the child's age, family's financial status, insurance, knowledge of resources, religious affiliation, availability of services in community, etc. Parents may seek outside assistance for their adopted child when other factors such as a divorce, job loss, or other stresses compound the family needs. Parents are generally in the best position to determine when to get help, but advice from relatives, family physicians, teachers, and others in a position to know the family should be carefully considered.

Services for children with special needs are provided by a variety of professionals. A physician—pediatrician or the family practitioner—is usually the place to begin. Families may be referred to a neurologist for a thorough assessment and diagnosis of neurological functioning (related to cognitive or learning disabilities, seizure disorders or other central nervous system problems). For specific communication difficulties families may consult with a speech and language therapist, while a physical therapist would develop a treatment plan to enhance motor development. A rehabilitation technologist or an occupational therapist prescribes adaptive aids or activities of daily living. Early childhood educators specializing in working with children with special needs may be called a variety of titles, including head start teachers, early childhood education exceptional education needs teacher, or early childhood specialist.

Early Educational Intervention

Toddlers and preschoolers who might have a physical, sensory, cognitive or emotional disability are guaranteed the right to a professional assessment under federal Public Law 99-457, Amendments to the Education of Handicapped Children Act of 1986. Parents, preschool teachers and pediatricians are among the people who can appropriately refer a toddler for assessment. Parents should contact their local school administration office to find out to whom a referral should be submitted in their particular district. Parental consent must be provided to proceed with the assessment. The focus of child assessment at this age is on developmental delays rather than on specific disabilities. The process normally includes an assessment of the child's cognitive, physical, speech and language, and psychosocial development in relation to peers. The assessment data is generally generated by the child's pediatrician and/or medical specialists, parents, early childhood specialists, and child development specialists. A family assessment is also part of the process. A number of family needs are usually addressed, including but not limited to information needs, support systems, support services, financial needs and parenting strategies.

A team which includes professionals and parents reviews the assessment data to determine if the child and family have exceptional needs. If an exceptional need is identified, an Individualized Family Service Plan (IFSP) is developed which specifies the family's needs in regard to enhancing the child's development; goals for the child; services to be provided and by whom and when; and a plan for transitioning the child to other services and regular education. PL 99-457 emphasizes that parent participation is integral to identification, planning, and the delivery of services. For example, the speech and language therapist might work with the child and train the parent to follow-through on language stimulation activities in the home. Children and families may be served by professionals coming to the home, at an early childhood program, or by a combination of home/center based services.

Medical Intervention

While PL 99-457 mandates early intervention for special developmental and educational needs, it does not cover medical interventions. Some domestic adoptions involve subsidies for ongoing professional medical services, while other families rely on private insurance or other resources. There are a multitude of medical services that may be indicated depending on a child's special needs.

I am not going to attempt to delineate all the possibilities, but instead propose the following considerations for selecting service providers: 1) they support toddler adoption, 2) they do not subject the newly adopted toddler to standard developmental norms (most newly adopted toddlers are developmentally behind their peers due to a variety of causes), and, 3) they either have expertise in, connections to those who do, or will refer families to experts in the type of unique needs the adopted toddler may have. Referral to other specialists is especially important for toddlers adopted internationally who may have conditions that are rare in the United States.

Psychotherapeutic Services

The legally mandated early intervention and special education services discussed in this chapter may include child and/or family counseling provided by social workers and/or school counselors, but they do not cover services provided by psychiatrists or private practice therapists. Families may choose to access these service providers before, during or after adoption for a variety of reasons. It is essential that any therapy begin with a complete assessment of the child and family situation. This may include home visits, observations of child-family interaction, interviews with other family members, asking parents to keep a journal, observations and discussions with the child alone, and a review of the family case history.

There are a variety of considerations in selection of a therapist. Some families are connected to a mental health facility through their insurance provider. Others select a service based on recommendations of friends, teachers, etc. Most families seek a therapist who has had specific training and experience working with adoptive families. The child's reaction to the therapist is also an important consideration in the selection process. Because psychotherapeutic interventions associated with attachment problems are frequently associated with adopted children, specific attachment therapies are discussed in Chapter 7.

Fostering Healthy Development.

All children need a stimulating and safe environment in which they can develop, practice, and expand their physical, cognitive and social/emotional skills. Toddlers deserve the opportunity to experience toys and activities appropriate to their level of development rather than their chronological age. Toys and activities that are beyond a child's developmental level are more frustrating than stimulating. Most of all, toddlers need intensive, rewarding and sustained interaction with their caregiver(s).

The Importance of Parent-Child Interaction

Children learn when they interact with and impact their world. While toys play an important role in psychomotor, cognitive and social development, parents assume a major role in enhancing growth through interacting with children and structuring their environment. Many adopted toddlers have learned not to expect or desire adult interaction and appear perfectly satisfied to spend long periods of time simply watching or playing quietly alone. Unfortunately, in the United State's majority culture, "good children" are often interpreted as children who don't seek adult involvement in their play. In fact, many toys and other gadgets are marketed on the promise that they will "keep children entertained for hours!" While all children need to learn to be comfortable with their own company and should gradually acquire the capacity to be self-directed, parents will want to spend as much time as possible with their new toddler.

One of the advantages of a toddler adoption is that the child can be immediately involved in most home based daily activities. Anything can be an adventure to the toddler! He enjoys riding in a back-pack while Mom mows the grass. She can sit on the sorting table and help Dad throw socks into the washing machine. He can sit on the cupboard and add ingredients to the bowl or take pots and pans out of the cupboard while Mom is cooking.

Even if a child initially rejects direct interaction, parents can get involved in her activities. They can sit next to her as she eats or plays. Parents can verbally reinforce what both are doing and invite closer involvement with comments such as "I'm having so much fun with the blocks." "I love the way you lined up your cars." "Would you like to use this car?" "I need someone to help me taste this cookie dough." Interaction enhances the attachment between parent and child.

Accommodating Individual Learning Styles

Some children enjoy intensive bouts of very physical play, others enjoy quiet activities and calmer interactions. A child's attention span is both a function of developmental age and temperament. Careful observation of how a child reacts to various stimuli provides valuable information about style and temperament. Most toddlers learn best through whole body, multi-sensory modalities, however some become easily overstimulated by a lot of activity, noise and visual stimuli. Many children become increasingly agitated and active when they are in fact becoming fatigued and/or over-stimulated. Some children enjoy physical contact such as light strokes on the forehead while others need to regroup without physical contact. Some fall asleep to music, others need quiet. A challenge faced by new parents of toddlers is dealing with the expectation others often have that they "know" their children's temperament, preferences, learning style, and developmental level.

Communication Strategies

A major priority for many adopted toddlers is to build speech and language skills in the context of normal interaction. Regularly talking to toddlers is much more important than the content of the conversation. Grocery stores provide rich opportunities for language and social skills training. Place the toddler in the cart-seat so that parent and child are at eye level, face to face. Discuss the color, temperature, texture, size, and quantity of the food. Ask questions such as, "Can you help me count out three grapefruit, 1, 2, 3? Should we pick Cheerios or Corn Flakes? Can you help me put the bag of marshmallows in the basket?" Car trips provide another rich opportunity for language development. Talk about the weather, point out interesting scenery, discuss the destination, sing along with the radio. Even toddlers can participate in car games such as finding a cow or looking for something blue. Parents can use photographs and magazine pictures to reinforce language skills and strengthen attachment. Simple games can be developed with family pictures. For example, Dick and I would hold up a photograph and say, "This is our dog Tasha, can you say Tasha?" After Gustavo learned to name the dog, we would lay a few pictures on the floor and say, "Can you find the picture of our dog Tasha?" Independent thought and decision making can be encouraged by asking questions such as, "Show me a picture of something you like to eat."

There are also a vast array of computer programs and educational TV shows such as *Sesame Street* which are intended to enhance language acquisition and development. Books are essential tools for language, cognitive and social/emotional development. Picture books printed on board or cloth are appropriate for children who are developmentally below the twelve month stage or have never been exposed to books. Books that depict simple, familiar themes are appropriate for toddlers. Avoid fairy tales with frightening themes such as people being eaten by wolves or children being abandoned in the woods because the young toddler does not differentiate pretend from real, and especially for children whose lives have been unstable, such images may create fear.

The young toddler doesn't care if parents read the text word-for-word. In fact, he will often get impatient and want to turn pages before Mom or Dad finish reading a page. Toddlers frequently memorize their favorite books. When Gustavo was two years old, I once suggested that we "eat" the cookies depicted on a page in one of his storybooks. He laughed delightedly as I pretended to pick the cookie off the page, nibble it, and say, "Yum, now you have some." Every time we looked at that page for the next year we had to repeat the same ritual! One day when he was four years old, he brought that same book to me and said, "Eat the cookie like you used to!"

The toddler is advantaged in acquiring receptive language skills more quickly than an infant because she has the cognitive abilities to better understand body language and contextual clues. The toddler who is adopted after acquiring speech may or may not continue to use her original language as she acquires the language spoken by her new family. If family members are bilingual, the child should retain her original language and acquire the new language. However, sporadic attempts to help a toddler retain her primary language were not effective in the families I interviewed. One family arranged for a Spanish major from the local university to spend one evening a week with their three-year-old adopted from South America. In spite of their hopes to the contrary, the toddler stopped speaking Spanish as she acquired English. In fact, for a couple years she adamantly rejected attempts to be "retaught" her native language, and told her mother to "Stop talking like that!" when she attempted reading in Spanish. Finally at age six, she agreed to attend a summer session Spanish class, but did not regain fluency in her native language. Several adoptive parents reported that their post-lingual toddlers stopped talking altogether for a period of time as they regrouped to learn a new language. Sean stopped talking for nine months following his adoption at age three. He worked with a speech and language therapist from the time he was three-and-a-half until catching up with his age mates when he was eight years of age.

Play, the Work of Toddlers

Play is truly the work of young children. Through play, children learn about and learn to enjoy their environment. Children do not need toys or any other special equipment to play. Even in environments bereft of such traditional resources, children use a stick for a doll, a rock for a marble, and leaves for toy dishes. To be free to play, what children do need, however, is an environment in which they feel loved and safe.

Many adopted toddlers had limited opportunities to explore the environment and fully develop all of their senses. Mud provides an opportunity to explore body movement, tactile sensation, sounds (squish, slurp) and language concepts (wet, cold, brown). Playing together at the beach encourages sensory exploration, large and fine motor development, and social skills. Finger painting (with a homemade solution of one part laundry starch, three parts soap flakes and one part cold water colored with food coloring) in the bathtub encourages creativity, body awareness, and large motor development. It's also easy to hose down!

Mastery of physical skills such as walking, catching a ball, and climbing stairs, represent exciting milestones for both children and parents. Most toddlers are inherently motivated to expand their repertoire of physical skills and therefore even the most reluctant toddler is usually less rejecting of parental intervention in acquisition of physical skills than other areas. One wonderful aspect of helping a young child acquire physical skills is that it usually provides a vehicle for positive touch, an essential factor in attachment.

Another child-directed activity that reinforces the toddler's emerging sense of self and provides an opportunity to exert positive control over her own life is any "stop/start" game. This can be used with any pleasurable activity such as rocking, swinging, gentle wrestling, etc. but the beginning and ending are determined by the toddler. In *A Child's Journey Through Placement*, Vera Fahlberg described two such activities that delight many toddlers: being lifted high in the air until they yell "stop," or gentle tickling in which the child says when to start and stop. Gustavo's particular version of this game was to be bounced on our knees until shouting, "Drop," at which time we were to extend our legs and let him slide down our legs, while holding firmly to his hands. He would shout, "One more time," and the game would be repeated! Toddlers need to practice their emerging sense of autonomy and control within safe and reasonable parameters.

Manipulative toys and apparatus play a role in supplementing play, but should never be used to supplant direct parental involvement. Parents and children can use manipulative toys together. Examples of developmentally appropriate manipulative and large motor resources which facilitate physical development are described on the next page.

Developmental age less than 12 months:

foam blocks and balls
push/pull walking toys
cradle gyms
boxes and containers for filling and emptying
activity boards
low climbing apparatus
pop-up toys
toys with dials, knobs, etc. to manipulate

Developmental age of 12-18 months:

stacking and nesting toys
pots and pans
large blocks and balls
nonbreakable mirrors
low sturdy climbing apparatus
rhythm instruments (drums, tambourines, horns)
tub toys (unbreakable funnels, cups, sponges, squirters) shape sorters
toddler swing
low slide

Developmental age of 18-30 months:

sandbox with digging and filling toys
3-5 piece puzzles with knobs to facilitate manipulation easel with large crayons and brushes
large threading beads
small wagon and foot-propelled ride-on toys
sturdy small vehicles without small parts
building blocks
rubber or plastic animals
non-toxic modeling dough and finger paint

Developmental age of 30-36 months:

blunt scissors
large interconnecting blocks
tricycle
sewing cards
large boxes to crawl in and out of

Dramatic or pretend play is very important to toddlers. In fact, toddlers often have much better imaginations than do older children, and especially, they have better imaginations than do many adults! The healthy toddler is uninhibited and unselfconscious in his pretend play. Dramatic play serves a variety of functions. It provides a vehicle for trying on or exploring a variety of roles. For example, the toddler often imitates responsibilities observed in her daily life such as cleaning and food preparation. Dramatic play provides a way for children to practice appropriate roles such as nurturing behaviors. The securely attached toddler reenacts her mother's nurturing behavior through the cuddling and feeding of her dolls. Dramatic play stimulates many aspects of cognitive development, including imagination, problem solving, recall, and understanding cause and effect. Dramatic play is sometimes used by trained professionals as a strategy for investigating trauma experienced by a child, or within Play Therapy, as a therapeutic strategy for resolving traumatic experiences such as abuse or abandonment.

To encourage imagination and gain insight on how a child is experiencing her world, dramatic play should be open ended and child directed. Very simple dramatic play emerges between the twelve to eighteen month developmental level. At that age, dolls, blankets, bottles, play telephones, hats, doll carriage, toy lawnmower, etc. are appropriate for dramatic play. Dolls of his gender and race are especially good for toddlers. A child who has developed the expectation that his needs will be met lovingly and consistently will mimic those care-giving functions with his dolls or even with other children. Pretend play becomes more sophisticated after the developmental age of eighteen months, but is still dominated by simulation of familiar daily activities. The doll might be fed, then tucked into bed. Parents might be assigned to "take care of baby" for a short while, or if they're lucky, they might be served a delicious lunch of bath water soup! At this age, children should have access to nonbreakable dishes, pretend food, or empty food containers such as egg cartons or jello boxes, cleaning equipment such as a rag and small broom, toy dolls and animals, and easy-on-easy-off dress up clothes. A costume box is a wonderful addition. Garage sales and cast-off adult clothing are great resources for building the costume-box. Toddlers love grown-up items like purses, wallets, office equipment, briefcases, and big shoes (avoid high heels that can cause falls). Also check out after-Halloween sales for staples like wigs, fake noses, and outlandish ties, but avoid costumes that represent frightening characters.

As children reach the developmental age of three, they become delightful partners in pretend games and love to reverse roles. For example, they play the mom and Mom is the baby, or they serve the food and Dad is the customer. This is a wonderful way for young children to practice independence in a safe environment and to feel empowered, because they are in charge. Children also use pretend play to confront and assume some control over their fears. That is why playing doctor and being the one to give the shots is so popular with children. Child-controlled play can reinforce specific cognitive tasks such as object permanence. Children engage in various forms of appear-disappear play beginning at about the developmental age of six months as a way to explore issues of attachment and develop object permanence. Favorite examples include watching Dad put a scarf over his face then quickly pulling it away, or doing the same thing with baby while saying, "Where's Baby? There she is!" The games become more sophisticated as the child grows. Such games allow young children to confront their fears of parents disappearing and to assume some control over people's coming and going. The game of peek-a-boo, which infants love, can still be used at the toddler level to reinforce that Mom and Dad are permanent, even after disappearing momentarily.

The toddler also loves to hide and be found under a blanket, behind a door, or even behind their own hands (young children do not understand that you can still see them even when they can't see). The older toddler loves large cardboard boxes that they can crawl into and hide. The rules of the game include pretending you don't know where your child is, talking loudly so she knows where you are and you don't surprise (scare) her, and "looking" until you find her or she comes out from hiding. Toddlers love the game of hide and seek, but invariably hide in the same location time after time, or they hide where the last person hid. A game both my children loved at the developmental age of two to three was crawling into a box so I would loudly proclaim, "Oh a present for me, I wonder what could be in it?" I would slowly open the box, the child would jump up and I would exclaim, "Oh, it's Gustavo! What a wonderful present!" They would happily repeat this sequence until I finally called it quits.

Summary.

Toddlers are delightful works-in-progress. Parents will want to learn as much as possible about toddler development so that they can better understand their child s stage of development, and respond appropriately to their child s behavior. Even though many adopted toddlers arrive home with physical, cognitive, language, or physical delays, there are many things parents can do to foster their child's development. Nurturing a child's growth by providing developmentally appropriate activities is one of the great joys of parenting.

CHAPTER *Six*

Parenting the Grieving Toddler

Sharon, who had lived with a foster family for twelve months prior to adoption at eighteen months, spent her first month at home gazing out the front door.

LouAnn was often startled awake by the eerie sense of someone being in the room. Someone was...her newly adopted two-year-old, standing in the dark... just staring at her.

Mariel, described by the orphanage staff as a competent, verbal three-year-old, clung to her adoptive mother and demanded to be carried everywhere. Supposedly toilet trained, she regressed to routinely soiling her clothing and bed.

Many people believe that toddlers are incapable of realizing loss and experiencing acute grief. Not so. In fact, a toddler's experience of grief is complicated by the way in which he thinks. Left unacknowledged and unattended, grief can block development and attachment to the adoptive family.

Human beings of all ages grieve the loss of a significant other, even though manifestations of grief vary depending on the person's age, culture, and individual personality. Toddlers are no exception. A toddler who has experienced a strong attachment to one or more former caregivers will grieve the loss of those relationships. The loss of a parent is a young child's greatest fear. To be abandoned, whether through termination of parental rights, voluntary relinquishment, death, or any other means, is a child's worst nightmare come true. As hard as it may be for adoptive parents to accept, even children who have experienced abuse can be strongly attached to the abuser.

Unfortunately, many people believe that toddlers are incapable of realizing loss and experiencing acute grief because of their unsophisticated stage of language and cognitive development. As a result, caregivers and professional support staff may deny or seriously underestimate the severity of the effect of loss. Indicators of grief such as changes in behavior, eating habits, and sleeping patterns, or illness may either not be recognized as indicators of grief, or may be attributed to other causes. In some cases, adoptive parents may be reluctant to acknowledge their child's deep attachment to a former caregiver and grief over the loss of that relationship. However, as painful as it may be to acknowledge a child's love for other parents, it is absolutely essential to support this loss. Left unacknowledged and unattended, grief can block development of attachment to the new caregiver(s). Even when given good support, losses and separations may leave vulnerabilities that can be triggered by new developmental tasks, new relationships or achievements, or any other significant changes occurring in the course of a lifetime. Children who are provided the opportunity to grieve and are assisted through their mourning experience fewer short and long term consequences and are able to attach more effectively to new caregivers.

Children who fail to attach to a former caregiver are much less likely to grieve the loss of that relationship. Also, children who have experienced multiple disruptions are much less likely to display grief at the loss of one more caregiver. When a toddler feels only tenuous connections, even with a birth relative, her grief is likely to be short-lived and simple when that relationship is disrupted. Unfortunately, however, as discussed throughout this book, these never attached children are frequently more resistant to attachment than are children who are grieving actively the loss of a caregiver.

Understanding how toddlers think about loss is also important to understanding and supporting their grief. The older toddler will tend to personalize everything and believe that his own thoughts, wishes, or actions are responsible for whatever happens to him and to others. She thus believes that she did something which caused the former caregiver to leave. Toddlers also interpret everything they hear literally and have a great deal of difficulty differentiating reality from fantasy. The toddler who is told, "You are going to fly home to your new mom and dad," visualizes herself flying like a bird. A toddler who is told, "Your birthmom couldn't take care of you," may internalize that she lost her mother because she was such a bad baby.

Indicators of Grief

While no one reacts to loss in exactly the same way, several common reactions to a significant loss have been identified. About half of the children whose families provided anecdotal information for this book reported that their children displayed acute grieving behaviors during their first weeks and months at home, although not all recognized the source of these behaviors. Depression and grief are often manifested by crying, but also in such ways as lethargy, poor appetite, or infantile behaviors.

Despair

During the early stages of grief, the toddler typically protests and displays overt signs of despair. A number of parents reported that their newly adopted toddlers cried inconsolably. Sad crying is very different from crying associated with rage or terror. When grieving, the child's body is typically limp or curled into a fetal position, and there are a lot of tears. Anger and/or fear on the other hand, is indicated by a stiff, tense body, protruding blood vessels, perhaps few tears, and a high pitched cry. Not surprisingly, the children who had no preparation or transition help displayed especially intense grieving behaviors. Sabrina, adopted at sixteen months from long-term foster care, often awoke sobbing and calling out to her former caregiver for months following her placement. Fortunately, even though she had not been prepared for a change in placement, her parents used postplacement transition strategies and supported her grieving process, so instead of emotionally detaching, Sabrina began transferring attachment to her mom and dad.

Seeking Behavior

Seeking behavior is very common in the grieving toddler, even after the child's overt protestations and sorrow have subsided. Children who experienced an abrupt change in placement are the most likely to continue searching for their birth or foster parent long after placement.

Shortly after Lisa arrived home at nineteen months she saw a picture of herself sitting on her foster mother's lap. When Lisa saw the picture she pointed to it and began crying uncontrollably and arching her back. She squirmed to get down from her mother's lap, then began banging her head on the floor. Another family described how their daughter cried out for "Eba," her name for her foster mother, for months after placement whenever she was hurt, frightened, or overly tired. A four-year-old boy who had been adopted from South America at age two pointed to a Hispanic woman in a grocery store one day and said, "She looks like Mommy." His father pointed out how different she looked, and his son responded, "No, I mean she looks like my mommy-all-gone." Another mom described how her Korean daughter ran, arms outstretched, to an Asian American she saw in a store. Sharon, who had been with a foster family for twelve months prior to adoption at eighteen months, was often found gazing out the front door for weeks following placement. Her parents believed she was watching for her foster mom.

Sleep Difficulties

The vast majority of the adopted toddlers in families who shared their stories with me experienced sleep problems. While most acute during the first days, weeks, and months following placement, some children experienced years of night terrors and other sleep problems. Parents described their children's extreme difficulty going to sleep, sleeping peacefully, and/or waking up, especially during the first months. However, Carl resisted going to sleep and for years would wake up every hour screaming. Other children reverted to old patterns of sleep disturbance when there was a stressful situation in their lives. Many toddlers become increasingly active as they get tired, but some children seem so desperate to avoid falling asleep that they push themselves beyond what the human body should be able to endure. Perhaps children who have experienced what they perceive as a life-threatening loss may be so distrustful that they cannot let down their guard enough to fall asleep. Perhaps other children have been comforted by a bedtime ritual followed by a former caregiver and are so disoriented by the absence of that ritual that they cannot program themselves for sleep. Still others may avoid falling asleep in the new caregiver's home because they are expecting their loved ones to return for them. They fear that if they are sleeping they may miss their loved one.

Grieving toddlers may experience sleep disturbances called sleep or night terrors. Night terrors differ from nightmares in terms of the child's awareness, their duration and their intensity. The child's eyes are usually open but unfocused. He often walks about and speaks, albeit in a very disorganized manner. He is not responsive to any attempts to communicate and often violently rejects attempts at physical comforting.

Waking has also caused problems for a number of adopted toddlers. Some children are very frightened and sad upon waking during the first weeks at home. One mother reported that her daughter woke up crying nearly every day in the first months. Parents speculated that perhaps their children were dreaming of being in a different place with a former mom and dad, and were confused and frightened to find their new adoptive parents there upon waking.

Unconscious memories seem to revisit many toddlers during their dreams. Sharon, adopted at eighteen months, was six years old before she stopped waking up at night because her leg hurt. For some time, her parents were at a loss to explain this behavior. There appeared to be nothing wrong with the leg, although x-rays revealed an old fracture line. Her parents didn't find out until Sharon was four years old that her leg had been broken when she was six months of age by abusive birth parents.

Separation Anxiety

Separation anxiety, a phenomenon experienced by almost every child whether born into a family or adopted, showed some unusual patterns in the group of adopted toddlers whose stories were shared. About half of the participating parents reported that their children showed acute separation anxiety after their arrival home, while most of the others reported that their children initially displayed no separation anxiety at all. Professional therapists affirm that extreme reactions to separation are common in grieving children as well as children with anxious attachment.

Children who were the most securely attached to a birth parent or foster parent prior to their adoption display the earliest and most overt separation anxiety. Two moms reported that they found it necessary to quit work because they couldn't handle their child's hysterical screaming when they tried to leave them with a caregiver. For other children, however, the extreme fear of being abandoned again goes well beyond the normal definition of the term "separation anxiety". A number of families described their children's terror and despair if they even left the room to go to the bathroom. Most of these same children also had sleep problems which some parents attributed to the real fear of sleeping alone and the imagined fear of being abandoned during the night.

It is not at all unusual for toddlers who experience extreme separation anxiety also to display anger and aggression toward their parents. Grieving children who are unable to express their anger to the one who left may lash out at those who remain. This may also be due to the immature nature of a toddler's ability to differentiate and regulate intense emotions. Fear and anger, therefore, may become confused, and a child may lash out at a parent who they really fear may leave them.

Some children show little or no reaction to their parents' comings and goings at first. While the lack of separation anxiety may seem easier to deal with on the surface, it often indicates a lack of secure attachment which can be more problematic in the long run. Most of these children have had no consistent early caregiver or were in neglectful/abusive environments prior to placement. A parent of one previously institutionalized toddler described her daughter's indifference to her presence, her willingness to go to any adult, and her indiscriminate crawling onto the laps of complete strangers. Another parent described her son's behavior in terms of wandering away from his parents and not responding to them when called.

Anger that tends to be pervasive, intense, and not necessarily associated with parental separations may also be an indication of grieving. Rage is characteristic of children who are experiencing attachment challenges. Some children may convert sadness into rage, releasing their sorrow as hostility, irritability, annoyance, or complaining. Other children may have used tantrums as a strategy to obtain attention. Still others have learned to behave in ways that draw negative attention and punishment, which then appears to provide them with an excuse to release the tears and anger they are having trouble releasing.

Unusual Fears

About a third of the children whose parents contributed information were reported to have unusual fears or fears for which parents knew of no rational explanation. It is likely that these fears were associated with their children's prior experiences or the loss of a loved caregiver. Because toddlers do not differentiate fantasy from reality, their fears may seem illogical to parents, but they are none the less important to acknowledge and support. Not all fears are necessarily associated with grief and loss. Some may represent a fear of the unknown or unfamiliar. Regardless of the possible source, all fears should be handled empathetically.

The fear most commonly described by families is the fear of bathrooms or toilets. Some of these toddlers had never seen or used flush toilets, so perhaps the sound and action was frightening. Unfortunately, others had punitive toilet training which may have resulted in their fear of anything associated with elimination. Two children were reported to be afraid of pictures of older men, especially if the pictures were dark or the men had beards. Another little girl who had been adopted at fifteen months still cried a year later if her mother used an electric knife. Three children became hysterical over hair and fingernail cutting. Another boy was very afraid of any loud noise.

Some parents were able to determine the underlying causes for their children's fears. One fifteen-month-old screamed if anyone tried to hold her so that her head was over their shoulder. Her parents finally realized why this was so when they visited their daughter's orphanage and observed children being restrained in that position while their heads were shaved. Lonny's parents were surprised about his fearful reaction to walking barefoot on grass until they learned that he had spent his first nineteen months totally confined within his orphanage with its tile floors and a paved, grassless outdoor play area. Another recently adopted toddler struggled to escape when her parents tried to place her in their blue car. Too young to explain her fear, she was reacting to having moved from her foster family in a blue state car, and in her magical thinking, the car had the capacity to wrench her again from her family. In our family Gustavo has always been fearful of dolls or masks without facial features or with distorted features. At age two he happened to see a Hallmark poster that portrayed a craft-type doll with no nose or mouth. Slowly he backed away from the picture. When he had put a safe distance between himself and the picture he turned and ran to me, saying, "Bad baby hurts Gustavo." For years he continued to fear and avoid any dolls or masks without facial features.

Developmental Regression and Delays

Many families indicate that their toddlers regressed from the reported levels at which they had been functioning prior to placement. This is a common phenomenon in most placements regardless of the age of the child. Regression is an expression of grief. When faced with a loss, children may react by reverting to old, comforting behaviors. Regressive behaviors may occur immediately after a disruption or may resurface at a future time when a child is reprocessing grief.

A child's language skills are especially likely to regress. It is no surprise that internationally adopted children have set-backs in their language acquisition as they change languages. It seems likely that many children who appear to be regressing in language are actually using their developing receptive language skills even while their expressive skills seems lost. Three internationally adopted children who had already acquired some spoken vocabulary but were not yet fluent in their native language stopped talking altogether for several months. They then started over in English, gradually increasing their vocabulary to where it had been prior to adoption.

For families contributing to this book, toileting was the next most frequently reported area of regression. Many parents were told that their children were fully toilet trained prior to placement, but in reality they were not. Some of the children had been forced to spend long periods of time on small chamber pots or had been left undiapered to urinate and defecate on the ground. Anna, reportedly trained when adopted at two, showed no interest in using the toilet until after her third birthday, but then made the transition within a few weeks. Most of the children were over three before becoming independent in their day toileting and were four before staying dry at night. To avoid creating problems over this issue, many adoptive parents simply chose to diaper their children from the start, thus avoiding accidents and confusion until a child was clearly ready to be toilet trained.

Grief issues may also cause developmental plateaus in toddlers. Because of the toddler's magical thinking, she may connect a loss to a particular developmental task such as oppositional behavior or toilet training. A two-and-a-half-year-old who believes the loss of her caregiver is associated with her behavior can become stuck in negative, controlling patterns of acting. Another toddler may become extremely anxious about toileting if he thinks his former caregiver left because she was mad about his soiling and wetting. Claudia Jarratt counsels parents and professionals never to underestimate how strong the need is in many children to blame themselves rather than to think that life can hurt them randomly and with no warning, making them feel overwhelmingly vulnerable and helpless.

Withdrawal, Indifference, and Despair

Becoming distant and unapproachable is a coping mechanism humans use in situations where they feel helpless and powerless. As a reaction to loss, older children often withdraw by physically escaping or changing the subject. Approximately half of the families I've interviewed described withdrawal behaviors in their toddlers. These included lack of eye contact or averted eyes, a lack of facial expression, and unusual body posture such as limpness when held or reverting to the curled up fetal position of a newborn. When Laura was adopted at sixteen months, she showed little apparent interest in her surroundings and had what her parents described as "an orphanage look.". Kim Su, adopted from an orphanage at fifteen months, was described by her parents as being emotionally indifferent for the first six to ten months after her arrival home. In retrospect, Laura's father realized that their daughter's initial placement was too calm and easy. Instead of the anticipated crying and pleading to stay with her foster mom, Laura left willingly. However, once home, she made no eye contact, initiated no physical contact, and asked for nothing of her new parents. While she was easy to be with because she caused no difficulties and had no outbursts of behavior, she seemed indifferent to people and to her new surroundings. Another mother of a girl adopted from Korea at age three reported that her daughter spent the first week lying on the floor in the fetal position staring into space. In one extreme example of selective withdrawal, a child adopted from an orphanage at age two-and-a-half had been diagnosed as deaf, but gradually indicated that he could, in fact, hear in the months following adoption.

In pessimistic resignation to the bleakness they experience, despairing children often lack motivation or energy. While intense despair generally lasts from ten days to a few weeks in toddlers, severe withdrawal that continues to be unresponsive to intervention from caring parents is often an indication that professional help is needed. However, without the benefit of a full and accurate history, it is easy, even for a professional, to misdiagnose such children as severely disturbed rather than grieving their past.

Supporting the Grieving Process.

The grief associated with a toddler's separation from caregivers with whom he has had a strong attachment is unavoidable. To try to deny or avoid displays of grief is magical thinking on the part of adults. Acknowledging and supporting their child's grief is one of the first acts of love adoptive parents can give their new son or daughter.

The more directly involved toddlers are in the preparation and transition process, the less confused they will be about what is happening to them and the less they will rely on magical thinking to explain the loss of former caregivers. The more concrete the transition and placement processes are, the more able toddlers will be to process what is happening and the less fearful they will be. Talking to toddlers during the preparation for and adjustment to a change in placement is intended to support grieving by confronting their magical thinking and assuring them that they are not responsible for the loss. Toddlers need to be told who will take care of them and be assured that someone will be with them at all times during the transition. Other messages that support the toddler's grieving include: "It was not your fault that you moved. You didn't do anything bad. It's OK for you to cry and be mad. I'll be right here to take care of you."

Children who are tricked or ignored during the transition and placement process are likely to suffer the most intense and prolonged grief. One adoptive mother told how her two-year-old daughter's foster mother drove them to the airport for their trip back to the United States. Even though they had engaged in specific transition strategies during the adoptive mom's two week stay in Brazil, Maria still clung to her foster mother. The foster mother dropped them off at the gate, telling Maria, "I'll go and park the car." Instead, she left, and Maria never saw her again. Maria was denied the opportunity to physically participate in saying good-by, to receive the blessing and best wishes of her beloved foster mom, and to experience the actual separation. Not surprisingly, Maria strongly resisted getting on the airplane, was extremely distraught, and continued to search for her foster mom long after coming home to America. It is not hard to imagine the type of magical thinking that must have haunted Maria, imagining her former caregiver lost forever in an airport, searching for her in similar-looking cars. The energy she could have devoted to attaching to her new parents was diverted to coping with the pain and searching. One can only imagine the terror Maria might experience the next time a loved person drops her off while they go to park the car.

Crying is therapeutic.

Most people can relate to the calming and stress reducing affect of a "good cry". Grieving children should be supported in their need to cry. Unfortunately, children sometimes suppress their tears, thinking that they can control their pain if they control their crying. Parents may find their child's pain very stressful or threatening and may therefore knowingly or unknowingly suppress natural expressions of grief. They may try to distract the child by promising a treat if he stops crying; cutting the feelings short ("Hush, hush"); minimizing the feelings ("You're OK now"); contradicting his reality ("You're going to love it here"); criticizing ("Stop making such a fuss"); embarrassing ("You're too big to act like such a baby"); or threatening ("Stop it right now or I'll give you something to cry about").

Crying should be supported with empathy and nurturing. It might be helpful to say something like, "I can tell that you are feeling very bad. Maybe it is because we were just looking at pictures of Nana, and you're thinking about her now and missing her. Let's sit here together for a while and I'll rub your back." Don't rush the toddler's grief before she is ready to let go of it. When the crying has subsided, offer a cold glass of juice or a walk outside. Oftentimes children are more receptive to being cuddled, making eye contact, and other attachment strategies after an episode of acute sadness.

Sleeping and Eating Strategies

Two extremely important life functions for toddlers are eating and sleeping. Anxious children relax and feel more like eating when they are offered their usual diet, including special "comfort foods" such as those they are used to eating when upset. As an adult, I am still comforted by eating the special casserole my mother made for me when I was ill as a child. For toddlers, comfort foods may vary by culture.

One parent reported that her daughter was drinking out of a cup at adoption, but frequently tried to breast feed during the early months. Karina, who had lived with her birthmother prior to adoption, enjoyed playing "bebe" and being carried and rocked while she pretended to nurse. Her brother, who was from an abusive birth family, showed none of those behaviors. Karina was attempting to recreate the warm, satisfying relationship she had once known, while her brother had no memory of positive relationships on which to draw. Two parents reported that their children wanted to return to bottle feeding although they were already weaned. All of these parents accommodated their children's needs to be cuddled and held while eating. While none of the mothers I interviewed reported breast feeding their toddlers, La Leche League does assist adoptive moms who want to attempt adoptive nursing.

Grieving children often experience sleep disturbances and typically need more sleep than families might first expect. Therefore, it is a good idea to plan ways and rituals that support a child before, during, and after sleeping. Soft, warm, textured garments such as blanket sleepers or sweat suits or sleeping between flannel sheets may help toddlers feel cozy and secure and better able to face the night. Because grief often precipitates feelings of being cold, children should wear soft warm clothing during the day as well. Sleeping with a security object may also provide comfort.

A number of families reported that their children had previously slept with adults or other children, either out of necessity in orphanages or because family beds were the norm in the native culture. Families dealt with this in a number of ways. None left a child alone in a new bed and room during their first nights home. Roberto's parents realized that sleeping in a bed in a separate room would be difficult after sleeping with his foster parents, so Roberto was allowed to sleep in his parents' bed. Many parents sat with their children until they fell asleep. Some slept with their children for a period of time, then gradually transitioned them to their own bed and bedroom. Gustavo and his daddy shared the one double bed in their hotel room for the three months they were in Peru before coming home. Some parents let their children fall asleep in the parents' bed and then moved them. Others made a bed for the child on a quilt or sleeping bag next to the parent's bed, and still others bunked siblings together. Some toddlers arrived from settings in which they slept on the floor. Parents initially placed mattresses on the floor to prevent their toddler from falling and to provide a measure of familiarity. Children may fall asleep more readily when they can hear the reassuring sounds of grown-ups talking, the television, or soft music. The bubbling of an aquarium in their room creates both soothing noise and soft light to provide comfort.

Combining a gentle awakening with a predictable morning routine is also reassuring to a grieving toddler. Some children need time in the morning to regroup and prepare themselves to face the day. With such children, a gentle back rub and comforting talk, followed by a few minutes to be alone again might be effective. Some families recommended quiet activity surrounding, rather than aimed directly at, their toddler as a wake-up strategy. For example, speaking or singing in a quiet voice while getting the day's outfit ready, or quietly moving about, turning on a soft light and straightening the room allows a child to wake up to the reassuring sounds of routine family life without having to interact immediately with others.

Children who experience nightmares or night terrors need special comforting. Toddlers should never have to tough it out alone. Children who wake up from a nightmare are usually more responsive to immediate comforting than is a child in the throes of a night terror. However, toddlers may call out to their former caregivers, and be disoriented and distraught when the new mom or dad responds instead of the expected caregiver. Even a child who seems securely attached to his new parents during most day-to-day activities may revert to calling out to his former caregiver in times of illness, fear, or other crisis. Try not to surprise a toddler child in the middle of the night, especially if she is still disoriented by her new home and family. It is better to begin speaking softly when approaching her bed. Having a soft night light lessens the chance that she will be startled when the light is turned on.

When a child is in the midst of a night terror, he will not appear responsive to voices or physical contact. Speak in a low, calm voice and reassure him that he is safe. Say his name and frequently ask him to respond as a way to tell when he starts to come out of the night terror. If he allows, gently stroke his forehead, arm, etc. Sometimes standing him on his feet, gently wiping his face with a cold wet washcloth, carrying him outside, and other physical strategies to break into his consciousness are effective. Other times parents simply have to wait it out. Children are usually receptive to being comforted after a night terror. In fact, as frightening as they are, offering comfort after a night terror is a wonderful opportunity to enhance attachment. Sometimes it is one of the earliest opportunities for parents to provide comforting to a child who is normally distant and rejecting. Discuss the frequency and intensity of night terrors with the family pediatrician or family therapist. While night terrors are not uncommon for toddlers, expect the frequency to diminish as your toddler acclimates to his new family and home and to fade altogether as he reaches school age.

Supporting Regression and Fears

Not only is regression perfectly normal, but it can also represent a positive, healthy way to respond to feeling overwhelmed. Accommodating a child's need for being fed or comforted in a manner usually reserved for infants provides a wonderful opportunity to develop attachment. Activities such as rocking and feeding a toddler before putting him to bed can be rewarding for parents and child. It is important, however, that parents not unwittingly discourage their toddlers from progressing developmentally even while they are supporting their need for temporary regression. Parents should seek professional assistance if their toddler seems immobilized by grief, shows no interest in developmentally age-appropriate tasks, or loses all initiative to grow and develop.

Attempting to understand and being appropriately accommodating to the fears of a toddler conveys respect and builds trust. Parents help their children overcome fear by modeling appropriate responses to fear as well as by supporting them while they confront those fears. Gustavo's fear of featureless faces mentioned earlier in this chapter did not interfere with his activities of daily living. We accommodated his need by avoiding having craft dolls or pictures of featureless faces in the house. Until Gustavo turned three, when he was confronted with such a doll or picture in someone's home we quietly mentioned it to the host and asked them to remove it. After that, we quietly pointed the object out to Gustavo so he wouldn't be startled and could avoid being near the offending object. Then, when he was five, we enrolled him in an art class that inadvertently provided the mechanism for him to confront and overcome his fear of masks. While in this special art class, Gustavo painstakingly created a clay mask of the very face that had so frightened him as a toddler. I was startled when I visited his class one day and he proudly showed me the mask which would have terrorized him a few years earlier. His teacher reported to me that he had devoted unusually intense attention to creating the mask. Gustavo, she went on to explain, would become so engrossed in his work that he would become oblivious to the chatter and activity surrounding him as he worked. This unplanned bit of art therapy allowed him to conquer that clay mask in more than one way. It is now proudly displayed in our sun room, and Gustavo's fear of masks has vanished.

Providing Structure and Predictability

Toddlers are reassured by familiar routines, regardless of their nature. When the environment prior to placement is a healthy one, the use of transition objects that link the former caregiver's style and schedule to the present provide the sense of structure that is important to the toddler's developing sense of security in his new home. A consistent schedule is also important to the child who is experiencing separation anxiety. Parents should be absolutely reliable about returning when expected. It is important to help children anticipate their schedules by talking through the day's routine. Because toddlers cannot tell time, use concrete, regularly scheduled events to help them mark time with events such as mealtimes or the timing of a favorite television program such as *Sesame Street*. Parents should make every effort to delay making additional major life changes following a toddler adoption such as moving to a new home, adding another family member, divorce, or marriage until new routines are firm and secure.

Responding to Withdrawal

When a child withdraws emotionally from new parents, it is crucial that they do not, in turn, react by withdrawing from him. This can happen when parents withdraw to protect themselves from the emotional pain of feeling they are ineffective in parenting an unresponsive toddler. Gentle and persistent efforts are necessary to connect gradually with the child, along with the understanding that all things happen in their own time. Strategies to enhance attachment described in the next chapter are useful for establishing the foundation of trust essential to lure children from their self-imposed haven of solitude. It is important to note that children are rarely as unaware of their environment as they appear to be during withdrawal. In fact, many adopted toddlers have amazing insight and memory of people and events, and are astute observers, even when they appear oblivious of their surroundings. Therefore, it is important not to stop giving comfort, support and structure. Those efforts are received and processed on some level even if not immediately apparent in the child's overt behavior. During the early months when Gustavo was extremely resistant to any physical contact from me when he was awake, I would often sit beside him on his bed and stroke his forehead when he appeared to be sleeping. While Gustavo never reacted noticeably to this routine, a year later he quietly walked up to me when I was ill and appeared to be sleeping on the couch and stroked my forehead in exactly the same way as I had done so many times for him.

Looking Ahead.

Resolving the grief over a major loss is a milestone that is never achieved completely. Children need to revisit their grief experiences and their feelings as they grow and develop. Sometimes their behavior or recurring concerns will signal that they need help. Children deal with loss differently as they mature and as their intellectual capabilities develop. They understand their own life story differently as their thinking becomes more sophisticated. While a toddler may accept at face value that his birthmother was very sick and couldn't take care of him, that same child is likely to ask more sophisticated questions about his birthmother's illness, the quality of care she received, why no one helped his birthmother, how long he was with his birthmother, and other issues as he gets older.

Children experience significant cognitive developmental changes at around the age of six or seven, again at puberty, and once again at adolescence, and each stage precipitates new questions and understandings. Confronting difficult facts about one's birth and infancy may cause grief issues to resurface or may precipitate new sensations of loss. Children who did not react to a disruption when they were toddlers because they were not securely attached to the caregiver may have a delayed grief reaction when they learn the facts of their early life experiences. At that point they may grieve the lost potential for a relationship that was never achieved more than for the actual loss of the relationship. John Bowlby addresses this phenomenon in his book *Loss: Sadness and Depression* in which he reports that even though children's efforts to attach to a caregiver wane if their needs are not met, the need is never completely abandoned, and under various conditions may be reactivated anew. Feelings of yearning or pining for a real or imagined family of origin may recur in some adoptees throughout their lives.

Times of family difficulty, major developmental changes, visits to the country of origin, a new loss, or other life changes can also affect a child's sense of loss of his birth family or of key caregivers to whom he was once attached. Grief can often be cyclical with anniversaries, holidays, changes in season and the day length, a return to old places or familiar situations, and the recombining of families reawakening bereaved feelings. Sounds, sights, and even smells can trigger feelings of loss and despair in young children. A family reported that almost exactly to the day, every six months their four-year-old who was adopted at age two-and-a-half becomes very demanding and uncontrollable. They believe his behavior reflects an inner time clock that was established when he experienced three consecutive disruptions after six months with a caregiver.

When children move during the toddler years, it is nearly certain that as they mature they will need information to help them in understanding the reasons for these moves. Parents and professionals should expect and be prepared to provide satisfactory answers to their children's questions as their age and or experiences cause grief to resurface.

Summary.

It isn't pleasant or easy to confront a child's grief. Parents want to protect their children from pain, but adopted toddlers often bring pain with them to their new homes. As difficult as it is, adoptive parents must acknowledge and support their child's grief.

The prognosis is optimistic for adopted toddlers who are provided the opportunity to grieve and are assisted through the process by loving parents. While issues of grief may resurface at various times in the child's life, he is likely to develop normally and form a strong and healthy attachment to his parents.

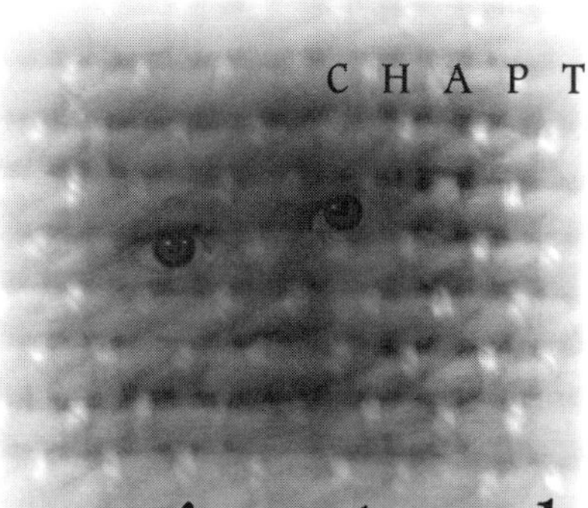

CHAPTER *Seven*

Becoming Attached

Five-year-old Juan reached under his bed and drew out a brightly colored Nike shoe box and placed it on his bed to show his mother. "It's my stranger box," he explained matter-of-factly. Among other survival and protection items, the collection included a length of rope for tying up a stranger, a whistle to scare the stranger off, and a toy farm implement to be used in self-defense.

When Michael failed to get off the bus at his sitter's home, she knew something was wrong and immediately drove to his home. When no one answered her calls, she went back to her house just in time to see Michael's mother drive up. A quick call to the bus company verified that her son had, in fact, gotten off the bus at his home instead of at the sitter's. It was dark when his mother entered the house, turned on the lights, and called out to her son. She finally found him curled in a fetal position under his parents' bed. He gave her a chilly smile, and in a low, growling voice said, "Go away! I don't need you! I'll never need you again!"

Toddlers who did not enjoy a healthy attachment with a loving and consistent caregiver during their infancy learn to fend for themselves. Hopeless situations? Not necessarily. Attachment behavior can be learned and there are strategies which parents can use to encourage it.

Attachment, the affectionate relationship between a child and caregiver that endures through time and space, is critical to healthy human development. In the 1940s, John Bowlby demonstrated the importance of attachment to all areas of development. Mary Ainsworth studied the development of attachment and indicators of healthy attachment beginning in the early 1950s. Since this pioneering work, numerous other researchers have found a strong link between a child's development and a healthy relationship with his caregiver(s). A child's secure attachment to her parents creates the base of security from which she is free to grow and develop. Children who form secure attachments in the first three to five years of their lives are more likely to be trusting, confident, competent, and resourceful. Attachment has been demonstrated to be essential to positive self-esteem. A secure attachment between child and parent also provides a foundation for the development of conscience, self-reliance, and the ability to cope with fear, anger, and other stressful emotions. It provides the groundwork for future relationships.

Because of the important role attachment plays in all areas of development, a basic understanding of the attachment process is critical for adoptive parents of toddlers. Attachment issues are central to literally every toddler adoption. If the adopted child has previously enjoyed a secure attachment, the parent(s) must support her through the grief associated with the loss of that relationship and the task of transferring her attachment to her new caregivers. If the adopted toddler has not been fortunate enough to have experienced a secure attachment, the parents will be confronted with the challenging task of building attachment by re-creating the attachment cycle. Either responsibility is demanding, but one to which adoptive parents of toddlers must be committed.

How Attachment Occurs.

Attachment has two components, parent-to-child and child-to-parent. Attachment is based on reciprocal relationships, although the parent-child relationship is very different from the give and take inherent in the attachment between two adult partners. Adult partners are equally responsive, but, in the parent/child relationship, from the beginning, it is the parent who assumes the responsibility for responding to the child's needs.

Parental attachment to a child normally occurs as the parent consistently meets the infants needs and is rewarded by the infant's smile and recognition of the parent. An infant normally attaches through a process of having basic needs met by a consistent and loving caregiver. The child experiences a need: pain, hunger, or discomfort. The need creates a rage reaction and the child expresses that rage. In response, a loving caregiver responds to gratify the need. It thus becomes the caregiver's role in this interactive process to recognize the displeasure, identify the need, and satisfy it so the baby can relax. Gratification strategies include the essential elements of food, touch, eye contact, smiling, and motion. Attachment researchers have called this cycle of need, displeasure, response, and gratification many names, including the arousal-relaxation cycle, first-year-of-life cycle, the trust cycle, the bonding cycle, the attachment cycle, the soul cycle, and the love cycle. After many cycles of need and gratification have been completed, the child develops a sense of security and learns to trust that the caregiver will meet her needs in a consistent and loving manner. In this way, attachment occurs. Thus created, attachment eventually allows the child to develop the ability to tolerate delayed gratification and accept controls imposed by the caregiver because she trusts the caregiver to meet her needs. Gradually the role of primary caregiver(s) in meeting those needs is differentiated from the role of people in general. Developing this trust and recognition is the most important developmental task of the first twelve months of life. When this attachment cycle does not consistently occur, or when it is disrupted, instead of trust, the child learns not to trust and develops a desire to protect himself from further pain.

Some child development specialists believe that it is difficult if not impossible to recover or regain attachment if the moment was lost during infancy. They allege that children moved after infancy may have extreme difficulty transferring or establishing a bond with adoptive parents. Not surprisingly, adoption counselors and others who adhere to this belief discourage parents from adopting the unattached or insecurely attached child who is past infancy.

Others believe that children are inherently resilient and capable of recovering from trauma at any age, and thus assert that early experience has little influence on later emotional development and behavior. A child development specialist who believes this theory might suggest that attachment problems can be attributed to a similar environment at different times rather than the effect of early deprivation. Proponents of this theory point to individuals who overcame early neglect, abuse and other trauma to become secure and successful adults. This position would be represented by an adoption counselor who assures prospective adoptive parents of an insecurely attached toddler that, "Love is enough to overcome any bad start in life."

Most child development specialists and adoption counselors now advocate a modified theory of attachment somewhere between these extremes. They believe that attachment is possible but more difficult to achieve with toddlers and older children who are insecurely attached or unattached. Therefore they believe that time is of the essence when adopting a child who has never developed an attachment to a caregiver. They believe that most children who attached insecurely in the first year and are later provided a secure, loving, nurturing environment supplemented by professional help when necessary, can overcome the effects of early deprivation and form healthy attachments.

Causes of Attachment Difficulties

Lack of attachment or insecure attachment results when an appropriate social bond does not occur between a child and caregiver. There is no exact formula for how this happens. The attachment cycle is affected by the caregiver's response to the child, the timing of inadequate care or disruptions in care, and by characteristics of the child. Breaks in the cycle in the first year cause severe and predictable childhood psychopathology, but the extent of such pathology depends upon the age of these children, when the cycle was blocked, the length of time that the cycle remained broken, the inherent ego strength of the child, and his genetic make up.

Attachment problems usually occur in situations where a child's needs are not met in a consistent and loving manner, or when food is not accompanied by touch, smiling, eye contact, and motion. For example, even if food is provided, if it is not accompanied by human contact, attachment will not occur. Examples of such incomplete care are common in understaffed institutional settings. Inadequate or inconsistent care may occur in cases when a child experiences multiple disruptions in care or in instances where a parent is chemically dependent, cognitively disabled, mentally ill, emotionally unavailable to the child, or physically abusive. Children who have experienced inconsistent parenting often develop an ambivalent love/hate relationship with their caregivers. This type of unhealthy attachment is represented by a child simultaneously seeking and rejecting her parent, as in the case of a child who avoids eye contact and hits at the same time he is clinging to the parent. Children who have been severely neglected typically display no attachment behaviors rather than ambivalent attachment. This is often the case in overcrowded institutions where staff do not or cannot meet the emotional and physical needs of the children. Children of neglect usually display a lack of attachment, whereas children of abuse usually display insecure attachment. A rare, but possible caregiver behavior affecting a lack of attachment is overindulgence. This occurs when the caregiver always anticipates a child's needs and never allows the child to experience frustration or express rage. The caregiver over-gratifies both needs and wants, and in fact, appears unable to differentiate the two. If the child never experiences need and subsequent distress, they never associate the caregiver with gratification of need. This may happen to an institutionalized child who becomes the "orphanage pet" and is showered with staff attention and affection.

Timing is everything. As discussed earlier, the first year of life is critical for the normal development of attachment. Every moment counts for the toddler who has not enjoyed healthy attachment during the first year. The number of disruptions endured by a child and their timing has an effect on subsequent trust and attachment, therefore adoptive parents have to be particularly watchful for potential attachment problems and committed to fostering attachment.

Another important aspect of timing is for parents to recognize that transfer or establishment of attachment does not occur overnight. Some toddlers may not display attachment behavior toward them for months, or, in some cases, for years after adoption. This can be very painful to the new parent who immediately expects reciprocated love. Parents feel more in control if they can focus on their role in fostering attachment, develop a long-range perspective on reciprocated love, and celebrate progress toward healthy attachment, no matter how slow it seems in developing.

While children have their own internal time clocks, sometimes events occur which seem to speed up or slow down the process. One mother reminisced that extended hospital stays during her daughter's first months home actually speeded up attachment because her daughter only tolerated physical comforting during painful treatments. Other parents reported set-backs or delayed attachment due to such things as family moves, the addition of another child to the family, or parental illness.

The number of disruptions in caregivers and the manner in which those disruptions occurred have significant effects on the toddler's resistance or responsiveness to attachment strategies. While there is obviously not a perfectly predictable relationship, parents consistently found that the more disruptions their children had experienced, the longer it took and the more difficult it was to build attachment.

The way in which disruptions are handled also affects a toddler's adjustment. Children who are abruptly disrupted without any preparation or transition typically experience the most difficulty resolving their grief and trusting their new parents.

Another aspect of timing involves how long and when children experienced inadequate parenting. Sasha, adopted at age two-and-a-half, had experienced inadequate parenting all of her life. Weighing only nineteen pounds, she was extremely resistant to her parents' efforts to help her attach to them. Toddlers who experienced a healthy attachment cycle in infancy, but for some reason, experienced neglect after the age of one, will have a better foundation for attaching to the adoptive parent than children who have never experienced attachment at all. On the other hand, children who experienced severe neglect in early infancy but have been in a responsive foster family prior to transfer to the adoptive home, may have already begun to develop trust.

Prenatal conditions and individual characteristics of the child are also important considerations in understanding the strength and security of a child's attachment to his caregiver. Unwanted pregnancies, violence and illness during pregnancy, premature births, poor (if any) prenatal care, and chemical abuse during pregnancy have all been linked with personality disorders, attachment problems, and other special needs. Childhood schizophrenia and autism create tremendous challenges to attachment. Less obvious, but also detrimental to the attachment process, are conditions characterized by chronic pain. If, for example, a child has an undiagnosed chronic ear infection, the child experiences a constant distress which the parent cannot relieve and attachment isn't achieved. The child's expectation that the parent should be able to fix it is not met, so, despite the parent's best attempts, the child feels no trust or confidence in the parent.

A child's personality, temperament, and intelligence all affect how she indicates her needs, how strenuously she indicates distress, how easily she is comforted, how adaptable she is, and how she responds to having her distress relieved. As previously discussed, some children appear to have inherent resiliency which affects their ability to attract others and allows them to thrive in spite of neglect.

Characteristics of Children with Attachment Problems

It may be helpful to clarify some terms used in child development literature and by therapists to discuss attachment problems. Infants, toddlers or children who are not securely attached may be referred to as *insecurely attached, anxiously attached, resistant, avoidant,* or simply *unattached.* Often a distinction is made between children who 1) demonstrate some attachment to their caregiver, albeit hidden or unhealthy, 2) those who defy a relationship, and 3) those who appear totally devoid of attachment. The first group are often referred to as ambivalently or insecurely attached, while the second group are often called resistant or avoidant. The third group are usually considered to have an attachment disorder.

To a parent whose child is having difficulties involving attachment, the clinical explanation for the child's problem can seem secondary to finding a workable solution for that problem and its symptoms. Parents are concerned primarily that their children develop a healthy, secure attachment to the people who love and care for them, and thus become secure and happy family members. The following overview of characteristics of toddlers and children who have attachment problems does not differentiate between different types of attachment difficulties. These indicators are provided to assist parents in recognizing the need to focus specifically on parenting strategies that foster attachment, and to seek assistance in deciding when professional help is called for. It is when these characteristics are extremely resistant to change in spite of parenting efforts to develop attachment that they become indicative of a chronic and pervasive problem. Because attachment problems become more resistant to change as the child grows, early intervention is essential.

The characteristics associated with attachment problems can be viewed as coping mechanisms, or protection against further anxiety and pain. Sometimes these coping mechanisms are seen in aggressive acting out behavior, while in other cases, children draw inward to avoid additional possible pain. No single profile of characteristics fits all children, but the following patterns of behavior are representative of children who are not securely attached, as described by attachment specialists such as Bowlby, 1988; Cline, 1992; Delaney, 1993; Fahlberg, 1991; Hage, 1995; Van Gulden and Bartels-Rabb, 1994; Jewett Jarratt, 1994; Magid and McKelvey, 1988; Rossi and Rossi, 1990; and Watkins, 1987.

Characteristics of Attachment Problems

Late Infancy Through Toddler

Developmental delays unexplained by known disabilities
Unusual patterns for eating and sleeping
Resistance to being comforted and cuddled
Ambivalent behavior toward parents
Selective rejection of one parent while accepting the other
Scarcity of distinction between parents and strangers
Raging and aggressive behavior
Extremely negative and controlling behavior
Unorganized behavior and poor impulse control
Missing or extreme separation anxiety
Premature independence
Unnaturally positive behavior

Parents who contributed information for this book provided numerous examples of their children's behaviors which were consistent with the previously listed indicators of attachment problems.

Developmental Delays

Developmental delays are strongly associated with attachment problems. Healthy attachment is the foundation for social/emotional, physical and cognitive growth. It is often difficult to differentiate the effect of attachment difficulties from other potential causes for developmental delays, therefore it is also difficult to predict whether the adopted toddler who is delayed will experience any long-lasting effects. Almost all of the toddlers described by those who contributed to this book displayed developmental delays at adoption. Many were six to twelve months delayed in their physical, language, and cognitive development.

Sleep Disturbances

Unusual sleep patterns were reported by the vast majority of families of adopted toddlers whom I've interviewed. Since sleep disturbances are associated with both grieving and attachment problems, it may be difficult to differentiate the relative extent of each. Many of the toddlers were exceptionally resistant to going to bed and also very angry upon awakening, often screaming and lashing out at anyone within striking distance. One little boy was so resistant to falling asleep that he would lie awake for hours. When his body could fight sleep no more, he would fall asleep but his eyes would remain open, as if in watch. Occasionally toddlers would hide in closets or under beds and eventually fall asleep there, but would resist sleeping in their own beds. Others actively fought being put to bed for naps or nighttime, resisting falling asleep in any location at all. Many were disoriented when they woke and required some quiet time before being ready to join the family.

Resistance to Being Comforted and Cuddled

Securely attached young children "conform" to their caregiver's body when held. In other words, they relax and mold their bodies to that of the caregiver in order to maximize body surface contact, as well as to reduce the likelihood of falling. Securely attached children routinely seek their parents for comforting, but especially do so when they are tired, afraid, or hurt.

In contrast, children with trust and attachment problems hate being held by a caregiver. Even securely attached toddlers hate being confined by someone they don't trust, so it is common for toddlers to reject being held by their new parents initially. Many toddlers resist close physical contact, even when frightened or hurt. However, continuing rejection of physical contact is an indicator of attachment problems. About half of the adopted toddlers whom I'm familiar with passively or aggressively resisted physical contact with their parents. One parent described her child as being like a "prickly pear cactus," another like a "pole" that just slipped between the parent's arms. Other parents described their attempts to hold their children as comparable to trying to hold a slippery eel or wet noodle. Mara's mom reported, "She just slipped out of my arms." These same children even rejected the kind of physical contact that is extremely pleasurable to most people, including back rubs and head stroking. In contrast to their response to human contact, all but a few toddlers seemed to enjoy physical contact with animals and family pets from the beginning.

Some parents were amazed that their toddlers seemed to be oblivious to pain, while others described various self-comforting behaviors in which their toddlers engaged, such as rocking back and forth when hurt, while at the same time rejecting being rocked and comforted by their parents.

Ambivalent Behavior

It is not unusual for some toddlers to alternately—or even simultaneously—seek and reject their new parents. Some parents told how their children seemed ambivalent toward them from the beginning, while others reported that their children vacillated as they started to show signs that they were bonding to them. Such ambivalence is clear in this description by one mother of the behavior of her son, adopted at eighteen months. "In the beginning, he wanted nothing at all to do with me. In fact, he would scream if I even came near him. Then, after a few months, he would sometimes reach out to me if he was tired or hurt, but then withdraw his arms as soon as I came near. He would cry out, 'Mama, Mama,' when he woke up in the morning, then scream and turn away when I came into the room. He would run toward me, and then, as if he had run into an invisible wall, he would stop right before he got to me and rock back and forth. I could actually see him fighting with himself. Even after he began tolerating my physical touch, he would often cling to me with his arms while kicking at me with his feet. As he developed language he would hold me tight while screaming, 'Go away, go away.' This went on for years whenever he was really mad because I had done something which upset him. I just knew inside of me that he both loved me and hated me at the same time. Maybe what he really hated was that he loved me. Maybe that was just too scary."

Selective Rejection of One Parent

The majority of parents who provided information for this book reported that initially, their toddlers reacted much differently to one parent than to the other, with seventy-five percent of those children overtly rejecting Mom and twenty-five percent overtly rejecting Dad. There was no obvious pattern in terms of the child's gender or prior situation, but most of the toddlers had been cared for and separated from women prior to their placement.

Rejected parents suggested various reasons why their children preferred one parent to the other. If toddlers had previously experienced a disrupted attachment to one or more women, they may fear attaching to another woman or may vent their rage for the disruption on the closest available woman. Some parents theorized that their children distrusted Mom because they had been abandoned by women. One couple thought that their two children adopted two years apart both preferred Dad because he carried them everywhere while they were in Guatemala. Another couple suggested that perhaps their son intuitively felt one parent's anxiety and clung to the other more calm and reassuring male parent.

The less common pattern identified by the families was for the toddler to aggressively reject Dad and cling to Mom. One family suggested that this might have been due to the fact that the only experience their institutionalized son had had with a male was with a male doctor who swooped in periodically to inflict pain. Another family sensed that their Asian child was simply terrified of the strangeness of her very large, bearded, dark-skinned father.

The rejection behaviors were very similar among the children, while behaviors toward the "preferred" parent ranged from constant clinging to mere tolerance. Tari's mom reported, "She was clearly dependent on me and stayed very close to me at all times, but did not want to be touched for anything beyond the basic necessities. Her first smile was for her eight-year-old sister, and I believe the next-door neighbor's dog got the second!"

Many children reacted toward the rejected parent in the way Mara did, physically attacking her target in every way she could and screaming at the sight of her. Carl's parents reported that not only did he display an immediate and intense dislike for his new mother, but for many months he was extremely fearful of any young to middle-age Caucasian woman. Another toddler's behavior included spurning all physical contact with Mom, physically pushing her away if she got close to Dad, and avoiding all eye contact with Mom.

In some cases, physically aggressive behavior was displayed only if the rejected parent was alone with the toddler, making it difficult for the other parent to fully appreciate the intensity of the rejection. One eighteen-month-old boy became openly hostile toward his mother, pinching, hitting and biting her when Dad left the room. It was as if Mom were being blamed for Dad's absence. Another mom described how, when she reached out to her son or initiated other physical contact, "He covered his head with his arms and screamed." She further reported that if Dad left the room, even to go to the bathroom, "He tried desperately to follow, pounding and kicking the door" to gain access. However, while this little boy stayed within a five foot radius of Dad, he rarely sought physical contact.

Adopted toddlers may form a bond with a sibling before they show any attachment behavior toward Mom or Dad. Mara's mom reported that, "Mara first accepted her older brother Nathan, then Dad, leaving me and her older sister out in the cold for months." Two parents expressed regret that there wasn't an older sibling for their adopted toddler to bond with and use as a role model. A number of parents reported that their toddlers seemed instinctively to trust a sibling before adults. Frequently siblings are less nervous and anxious about a new brother or sister's behavior and mental health, and simply respond to them as they would a handy playmate.

In some cases it was months before a toddler was ready to respond positively to the rejected parent. It took months for Carl to put his arms and legs around Mom when she carried him and a full year before he said he loved her. But even then, she became *persona non grata* when Dad was available. It was also a year before Kim Lee tolerated physical affection from Mom, and another six months before displaying any affection. It took over six years for Joey to begin bonding with his dad, and that attachment is still fragile, with the relationship regressing whenever his father has work-related travel that takes him away from home for a few days.

Scarcity of Distinction between Parents and Strangers

While not as common in toddlers who have attachment problems as it is in older children, some toddlers are inappropriately affectionate toward strangers. Parents of six children who were older toddlers at the time of their adoption engaged in frighteningly precocious displays of affection toward total strangers. Three of these children responded most affectionately to people who seemed to remind them of their former foster parents. Joey's behavior at a convention illustrated this well. His parents reported that he was charming and vivacious, working the crowd, winning friends, and crawling into stranger's laps. At the same time he openly rejected any advances by his mother. Mara's case was similar. She preferred strangers to Mom and Dad, especially men. Her parents lamented, "No one believed what a difficult time we were having at home because she was so charming and affectionate to everyone else!"

Shelly was so frustrated by strangers positive' reaction to her previously-institutionalized son's physical overtures that she had cards printed with the message, "Please do not respond to my son's behavior. It is inappropriate." She handed these cards to people whom her son tried to engage in inappropriate physical contact.

Children who were described as being inappropriately affectionate toward strangers were unattached or insecurely attached prior to adoption. None of the children who enjoyed a secure attachment to a former caregiver displayed this behavior.

Rage and Aggression

Over seventy-five percent of the parents who were interviewed reported that their adopted toddlers initially acted out rage and aggression far beyond typical toddler temper tantrums and willfulness. Three families described their children as the stars of their orphanages because they were playful or assertive. These same parents felt that their children's volatile and aggressive behaviors were partially a reaction to their no longer being able to get away with such behavior. Other parents felt that the lack of consistent and loving discipline had a strong influence on their children's behavior. Most felt that the children were justifiably and understandably filled with rage because of their life experiences. The majority of the toddlers who acted out aggressively did so toward one or both parents, but fewer initiated aggression toward other adults or peers.

Parents generally agreed on what constituted aggressive behavior in their new toddlers. "He hit everything and everyone for the first four to six months." "She would scream feo (ugly) at us as though she were screaming four letter obscenities." "He bit and kicked when he had a tantrum." "His extreme tantrums lasted up to ninety minutes." "She bit, kicked, pulled my hair, scratched." A number of parents told of tantrums occurring up to ten times a day and lasting up to an hour.

Grace Sandness eloquently describes the anger of these children and the ache parents feel for their children in her poem, "my angry son."

my angry son

I ache to understand you
the need in you
-the driving
torturing force
erupting
lashing out
(lashing inward?)
I ache to understand
the rage in you
imprisoning
your vibrant spirit
barring you
from that sure love
you must be seeking...
talk to me!

Grace Sandness

Extremely Negative and Controlling Behavior

Approximately ninety percent of the children whose parents were interviewed appeared to have an extreme need to be in control at all times. This was evident is what they chose to eat, what they played with, when they were held, and when they went to sleep. While all toddlers resist authority at times, most are able to relinquish some control to Mom and Dad. The toddler with attachment problems displays an extreme fear of not being in control and has an excessively hostile reaction to being out of control. One mom described her daughter's willingness to carry on for hours in order to win in all cases! Parents described temper tantrums triggered by a simple refusal on the part of the parent to allow them to walk into the street or by something seemingly insignificant such as being given the "wrong" cereal spoon. Many children were extremely volatile, with severe tantrums and aggression erupting in a matter of seconds. One mom reported ruefully, "Often I didn't even have time to protect myself before he would gouge skin out of my face as the tantrum came on so quickly." Healthy toddlers display more emotional lability than do older children, but those struggling with attachment issues can shift moods and behaviors with lightning speed.

Perhaps adopted toddlers show such a strong desire to control their world because they have experienced the ultimate loss of control for a young child, that of not being able to control being appropriately nurtured by their birthmothers. To experience the disruption from former caregivers must create a terrible sense of loss of control. No wonder they often try to gain whatever control over their lives that they can. Individual temperament and personality cannot be discounted, but Dustin's mom speculated that while she believed his personality was related to his independent nature, it seemed more than likely that his life experiences prior to adoption also contributed to his demanding style.

Unorganized Behavior and Poor Impulse Control

As with the desire for control, disorganized behavior and poor impulse control are characteristics shared by all toddlers. Their level and intensity, however, are more extreme in toddlers struggling with attachment issues. Typical examples provided by parents included falling apart when sweets or toys were not given on demand, aimless wandering and limited attention span, the inability to tolerate any wait for a desired food or object, and the inability to prevent playful behavior from becoming frenetic and out of control. Disorganized and impulsive behavior often precede the temper tantrums described earlier.

Children who are not securely attached are not free to grow and learn. Rather than displaying normal curiosity and determination to acquire new skills, they often wander aimlessly, picking at one thing after another, easily distracted and lacking the ability to display sustained attention and energy. They may spend considerable time in self-stimulating behaviors such as head-banging or rocking, or may seem completely in a world of their own and have difficulty connecting with others for any significant amount of time. Children who have not learned to trust adults have no reason to rely on parental support to help them control their impulsive behaviors. One mom lamented, "It's so difficult to keep up with a toddler who flits from activity to activity, frantically following every whim that seems to occur to him." The ability to delay gratification is an outgrowth of the attachment process. In describing their three-year-old, his parents said, "He became so hysterical if food was not provided on demand that he couldn't eat when the food was produced." Toddlers who have not gone through the attachment process have not acquired the ability to expect that their needs will be met, and therefore, delay gratification.

Missing or Extreme Separation Anxiety

Interestingly, both extreme separation anxiety and the absence of any show of anxiety at all are indicative of attachment problems. Children whose anxiety was great were most often described by parents as children who had been strongly attached to at least one former caregiver, regardless of the quality of care received. I watched as one eighteen-month-old girl, adopted less than a month earlier, sobbed hysterically when her mother let go of her hand briefly to shake hands with someone to whom she had just been introduced. Her daughter literally crawled up her leg while screaming uncontrollably. This child had lived with her birthmother until being deposited into the arms of her new adoptive parents the day they arrived in South America. Her birthmother carried her to them, set her down, turned, and walked out of her life forever. No wonder she became frantic when her new caregiver let go of her.

Toddlers who had not enjoyed any secure attachments prior to their placement with their adoptive family were more likely to display a lack of separation anxiety. While most toddlers enjoy escaping from Mom and Dad, they typically check back physically and visually to make sure their secure base is still there. The toddler with insecure attachment may never look back as he wanders off, apparently oblivious to Mom or Dad's whereabouts. One dad reported following his son one day, certain that he would eventually look over his shoulder to see if he was being followed. "He never did," reported the father, "so I finally stopped him a couple blocks down the street because he was about to walk out into traffic."

Premature Independence

All parents strive to build a sense of independence and competence in their children. However, growing independence is a developmental task of childhood, and premature independence should be viewed with concern. Two parents who each adopted three-year-old toddlers reported that their children acted more like miniature adults than children. One had been the oldest child in the orphanage and the other had been in a foster home and was adopted along with an eight-month-old infant. Both toddlers displayed unusually mature care-giving behaviors toward younger children and had uncharacteristically serious demeanors.

When observed at play, Maria devoted herself to giving and retrieving toys for her infant brother and never smiled or engaged in any playfulness herself. At the dinner table she willingly surrendered any food which her brother grabbed. While this behavior may appear helpful to parents, each child needs to experience his own childhood to its fullest. As Maria became more securely attached to her parents, she gradually relinquished responsibility for the baby and allowed herself to be the child she was. In fact, her parents were relieved when she had her first temper tantrum!

Other children not only appeared fiercely independent when they arrived home; they also showed little regard for their own safety or concern for their parents' presence. This characteristic was seen most frequently by children who had no prior secure attachment. Lonny, who was removed from an abusive birth family, would hide from his parents and not respond when they called for him frantically. While all toddlers struggle with the desire for independence in the face of the need for dependence, some adopted toddlers reject all offers of assistance and comfort during their early months home. Carl, for example, calmed himself by sucking his finger and sniffing his blanket but rejected physical contact with Mom.

Unnatural Positive Behavior

It is fairly common for children over age three at the time of their adoption to display unusually good behavior for a short period of time following placement. During this so-called "honeymoon period," the child may keep herself and her room immaculate, and be unusually polite, cooperative, helpful, and studious. Sometimes this is simply the replication of what was expected under rigid orphanage rule, but it also is a striking characteristic found in older children who have attachment problems and appears to be a controlling mechanism. Just about the time the astonished parents begin to relax and congratulate themselves on their excellent parenting, all hell breaks loose! Most toddlers with attachment difficulties do not display such model behaviors, although a precocious older toddler may. In fact, one striking difference between adopting an older child and adopting a toddler is the lack of a honeymoon period.

Parental Strategies that Foster Attachment.

Many parents either are told or convince themselves that love alone will be enough to overcome any attachment problems which their newly adopted toddler may have. Unfortunately, without addressing the underlying problems for the unhealthiness of the attachment, love alone is not sufficient.

The attachment cycle must be recreated along with supplemental strategies used to reinforce trust and a sense of security. Adoptive parents must begin where the child is developmentally, not chronologically. Healthy dependence must be recreated for the child who is not attached to the adoptive parent, regardless of the child's age.

Strategies to foster attachment to the new parents are as important for children who were securely attached and need to transfer their attachment as they are for insecurely or unattached toddlers. In some cases, parenting strategies need to be further supplemented by professional assistance, as described later in this chapter. All of the strategies recommended here are based on the assumption that the parent is focusing on building trust.

Grace Sandness' book, *Commitment, The Reality of Adoption* (1984) was my lifeline during the early months with Gustavo. Her poem "Love Will Grow" served as a constant reminder to me that my primary job was to earn my son's trust. There is still a framed copy of this poem, adapted for a boy-child, hanging on Gustavo's bedroom wall. The poem is reprinted here with the author's permission.

love will grow

do you trust me
little girl?
when your merry eyes
seemed dimmed with dreaming
do you grieve?
in their troubled depths
lie memories
of other mothers-
this I know
do you trust me

little girl
realize that after me
there will be
no other mothers-
that for this human measure
of "forever"
I am yours?
trust me first
my darling...
love will grow

Grace Sandness

In many cases, a child's reasons for not trusting have taken quite a while to form, so parents shouldn't expect to see an immediate change in his behavior. Two of the adoptive couples I interviewed advised new parents, "Plan that developing a strong attachment will take at least as long as it took for your child to develop attachment problems." While all toddlers test their parents, parents of newly adopted toddlers should expect to be severely tested over and over again through physical and verbal rejection, outrageous behavior, and withholding of affection. It takes perseverance and incredibly hard work to build attachment but the rewards are extraordinary.

The Basics: Recreating the Attachment Process

Recreating attachment is an intrusive process. It does not involve ignoring inappropriate behavior or segregating children for displaying behaviors characteristic of attachment problems. It involves staying in their faces and imposing the care-giving role upon the (often resistant) child.

The first step is to differentiate the toddler's *needs* from the toddler's *wants*. While all of an infant's demands are basically needs, toddlers demand both what they want and what they need. The toddler who has not had his needs met may be particularly confused about wants and needs. Both are likely to create a rage reaction.

To recreate the attachment cycle, the adoptive parent should initially provide for the child's needs on demand in the same way that the appropriately responsive parent meets the needs of a newborn on demand. Gratification of needs is gradually and periodically delayed as the attachment cycle is completed, but delayed gratification of needs is not appropriate with the child who is not displaying attachment behavior. Toddlers with attachment problems should have their needs met as quickly as possible.

Healthy food and drink are needs if they are used to satisfy hunger and thirst and to reinforce the attachment cycle. Sometimes a child who has experienced malnourishment or has been subjected to food and drink being used in abusive ways (to taunt and deny) has lost the ability to recognize hunger and thirst. Such a child may gorge until throwing up and may need to have food regulated. A child who is extremely anxious about the availability of food may be relieved by accessible small quantities of healthy food. One mother of an eighteen-year-old adopted from an impoverished orphanage at age two-and-a-half told me that her daughter still cannot go to sleep without a plate of crackers next to her bed as insurance against the possibility of waking up hungry.

A child who has been deprived of physical affection may have learned inappropriately to substitute food for affection. If that is suspected, such as in the case of a toddler who continues to scream for food after eating so much that he vomits, the parent should provide physical comforting in response to the rage reaction. Therapeutic foster parent Deborah Hage recommends physical cuddling accompanied by reassurance such as, "Let's see if a hug can fill you up." Of course, in cases of inappropriate gorging or other eating problems, a complete physical examination is indicated.

Providing food during physical comforting and gradually providing comfort before offering food may help the child differentiate what needs to be satisfied. Several small servings of food could be provided instead of one large serving to children who gorge huge quantities of food. Candy and other treats on the other hand, are wants, and should not be provided on demand.

Always assume that a request for parental contact and comforting represents a need for a toddler struggling to develop attachment and meet that need on demand, day or night. Parents need to reframe their thoughts about getting up at night with a new toddler as a wonderful opportunity to build attachment rather than a dreaded chore. Do *not* leave an adopted toddler alone crying at night as often recommended by many parent discipline specialists. The techniques of temporary segregation and isolation are for children who are securely attached, not for toddlers learning to trust that their parents will meet their needs in a loving and responsive manner.

On the other hand, constantly demanding undivided attention is a want, and can hinder developmental progress. The anxiously clinging child needs to learn to trust that her caregivers will not abandon her, but her parents do not need to be constantly interacting with her. The anxious child can be helped to learn to deal with separation gradually. Dad can call out to her from the other room where he is fixing dinner. Mom can alert her to the fact that she has to go upstairs for a few minutes but will be right back. Parents can accommodate the clingy child's need for touch by letting her stay close and touching her often as they play or go about their necessary work.

Parents should *not* accommodate the touch-phobic or resistant toddler's want to avoid contact. That is an inappropriate want, and instead must meet his unrecognized need for touch.

Children need the opportunity to play and be children, but they don't need expensive toys. Parents should *not* accommodate the wants of a raging toddler who is clinging to an expensive toy at the store, but should respond to the need of a child for play and interaction with you.

Children *need* food, comforting, shelter, touch, smiles, eye contact, and the opportunity to play and grow up strong and healthy. Meet the new toddler's needs on demand, and she will gradually learn to delay gratification and become more and more able to be responsible for meeting some of her own needs as she grows and develops.

In considering the essential elements of the attachment cycle, food is first and foremost. Parents must establish themselves as the providers of food: the ones who respond to the child's need for food and alleviate the subsequent rage associated with that need. Unfortunately, many adopted toddlers are extremely resistant to accepting being fed by their new parents. It is equally unfortunate that some parents never establish the essential relationship between themselves and the feeding of their child, instead allowing the child to eat independently with no involvement of the caregiver other than as a distant and disconnected entity who buys and cooks the food. While this may be convenient, it's missing an important opportunity to recreate attachment. There are two approaches to breaking down a toddler's resistance to accepting being fed by her parents: gradual intervention and intrusion.

With gradual intervention, the child is gently encouraged to accept a parental role in feeding. The following sequence illustrates what might occur with the child who refuses to accept food from the parent: food is placed on the table and the child picks it up whenever he wants; food is made available when the rest of the family is eating and the child is expected to pick it up in the presence of the parent; the parent places the food on the plate while the child is sitting at the table; the parent hands the child a drink or food; the child allows being held in the parent's lap while eating; until finally, the parent places food in the child's mouth. Using this approach can take years with the resistant child.

In the intrusive strategy, the child must accept being fed by the parent if he wants to eat or drink what is offered. The intrusive strategy is often accompanied by deliberately regressing the toddler to the bottle-fed stage of development. Deliberately regressing the toddler to bottle feeding accommodates the incorporation of the other elements of the attachment process: eye-contact, smiling, physical touch, and motion. A mother of an adopted fourteen-month-old described her very successful regression strategy. Even though her daughter had been weaned, she decided to return her to bottle feeding before going to bed. At first her toddler refused to accept the bottle from her, then grabbed the bottle but pushed her away. In frustration, the mother asked her therapist for advice. Following the therapist's advice, she firmly held onto the bottle while her daughter sucked, refusing to have it pulled away. Then she removed the bottle whenever her daughter broke eye contact, and finally removed the bottle if her daughter was not reclined in her arms while they rocked. Mom reported, "I am convinced that our nightly bottle feedings and rocking while we gazed into each other's eyes did more than anything else to build our attachment, her to me, and me to her." Regression to parental feeding is a well-established technique for enhancing the development of attachment advocated by attachment specialists such as Foster Cline. Cline advises that while the Reparenting feeding technique will not reverse a child's experiences, it can help heal old wounds and facilitate attachment to the new parent(s).

When regressing to bottle-feeding, select a private place and time away from the mainstream of family activity or other distractions. Use cold milk, warmed milk, or juice in the bottle, depending on the toddler's preference. Treat the experience very positively, and under no circumstances allow anyone else to tease or taunt your toddler about being a baby because he's bottle feeding. Do not allow the toddler to bottle feed himself as many toddlers in our society do. To do so would be missing the entire purpose of the strategy. In fact, other than when using bottle feeding for attachment purposes, toddlers should be encouraged to learn to drink from a cup. Select a comfortable rocking chair that is large enough to accommodate parent and child. While the child is feeding, maintain eye contact, and woo her with words and smiles. Parents can speak of their joy in his arrival, assure him of their continuing presence in his life, tell how they waited for him, speak of the completeness of their family now that he is home. Sing songs or play soft music in the background. Maximize physical contact during the feeding. Stroke his forehead with a free hand. If it's warm enough, feed him in nothing but a diaper so his arms, hands, legs, and feet can be stroked. Rock rhythmically. Even when not bottle feeding, parents can use all of the accompanying strategies for a soothing break during the day, a way to recover from a night terror, or as a way to prepare for a nap. Make the rocking chair a haven, a place to concentrate totally on each other and on the developing bond.

Parents must be as assertive and persistent as necessary to strengthen attachment through appropriate touch. Parents claim their children, communicate their love, and manage their young children's behavior through touch. I touch my children the first thing in the morning and the last thing at night. Yet, many parents of adopted toddlers described how their children literally cringed from their touch before they had established an attachment. Children who have been sexually abused are likely to be particularly touch-resistant. Parents need to model loving and respectful touch. Parents may need to help the toddler who has shut down his sensory receptors develop tactile awareness. Provide him with luxurious bubble bath. Rub him briskly after his bath and wrap him in a soft clean towel. Cuddle him in flannel pajamas and tuck him into a soft, warm bed. Rub his back and run your fingers through his hair.

Toddlers cannot be allowed to physically assault others. The aggressive toddler may need to be restrained, but while Mom or Dad are restraining, they can speak of their love and determination not to leave him alone. A child should never be punished for resisting being touched. To do so simply reinforces his sense of isolation and abandonment. It is not only touch that is essential to the attachment process but *when* and *under whose control* it is given. Children with attachment problems may be very controlling in their use of touch to manipulate their parents. Accommodating their manipulation does nothing to build trust and attachment.

Martha Welch recommends a very assertive approach to physical contact in her book, *Holding Time* (1988). Dr. Welch contends that systematic and protracted holding, originally used as a therapy for childhood autism, if practiced in the correct way can connect or reconnect parents and unattached children.

Unlike *rage reduction holding therapy* which is described later in this chapter, the holding technique advocated by Welch acts on the parent and child, rather than the therapist acting on the child. In her book, she details the following holding procedures: the *confrontation stage* where the parent holds the child face-to-face on her lap with her arms firmly over the child's; the *rejection stage* where the parent verbally expresses her feelings (frustrations, anger, affection, etc.) and the child struggles and rejects the parent verbally and/or physically and the parent intensifies the contact while preventing the child's withdrawal; and finally the *resolution stage* where the rejection dissolves into tender intimacy characterized by intense eye contact, touching and gentle conversation. Dr. Welch contends that holding increases secure attachment and serves as a foundation for growth in other areas of development. Dr. Welch presents numerous case studies in her book where the strategy worked very effectively with children who had attachment problems. According to Foster Cline, for children with severely disturbed attachment, therapeutic holding managed by trained professionals should be done as a family therapy under the supervision of a therapist, not just at home.

Smiling, often the first reciprocal reward parents receive for their efforts at parenting, is another important element of the attachment process. Unfortunately, many adopted toddlers who have experienced neglect or multiple disruptions in their short lives seem unable to smile and laugh spontaneously. Parents can help their toddlers regain their capacity to express pleasure while enhancing their attachment to each other by using the same type of activities which infants find so pleasurable. While it is essential to be predictable in meeting a child's needs, infants and toddlers are amused by parents who are spontaneous and unpredictable in their play. For example, when dressing the toddler, surprise him by blowing raspberries on his tummy and nuzzling his neck. Don't give up even if he's unresponsive at first. At first he may try to camouflage his pleasure by turning his face when he smiles or trying to hide his laughter. Lift him high in the air while proclaiming, "Look at what a big boy you are!" Twirl around while holding him firmly. Holding his back and head securely, quickly do a knee drop. Dance together. Gently wrestle. Smile and laugh while doing all of these things so the child associates pleasure with spontaneous laughter and smiling.

Motion is probably the most commonly overlooked facilitator of attachment. As infants are provided food, they also typically are given other sensory input which will be forever associated with the sense of being loved and cared for.

Even though motion is a subtle input, experts advise that the importance of labyrinthine stimulation (the part of the inner ear associated with motion and position) cannot be overemphasized. As evidence of the importance of motion, Foster Cline reminds us that millions of dollars are spent in amusement parks each year on rides that produce labyrinthine stimulation. Many parents unconsciously provide motion through rocking, jiggling, walking, and gentle bouncing. All of these techniques and others can be used with the toddler. Dick provided wonderful labyrinthine stimulation to Gustavo during their first weeks together as he walked the streets of Cusco each day with Gustavo securely tucked into his backpack.

Another wonderful labyrinthine stimulation strategy for the toddler is swinging in a bucket-seat-type toddler swing. Mom or Dad should stand in front of, rather than behind, their child as they push, so they can incorporate smiles and tactile stimulation, into the motion activity. The child can be hugged or even kissed each time he swings toward her parent. Most toddlers also enjoy pretending to be "caught" by their parent with each swing. Another version of swinging can be done by both parents together, with one behind and one in front.

Supplementary Strategies

Even while parents are recreating the attachment cycle, they need to foster their toddler's continuing growth in all developmental areas. This requires a delicate balancing of the need for dependency and independence. During the toddler years, an attachment disruption interferes with the development of the healthy balance between dependency and autonomy. Some toddlers may be afraid to show any autonomy while others will try to be completely independent. While parents need to meet their children's need for comfort and food, they certainly do not want, for example, a child who is already independently toileting to return to diapers. Even while attaching, our toddlers are motivated by an internal clock that drives them to become more independent and autonomous! A challenge under the best of circumstance, adopted toddlers need special help finding appropriate declarations of independence. We have to surround our children with love that claims, but doesn't repress appropriate development.

Every toddler loves routines and rituals, but structure and consistency are also absolutely essential for the newly adopted toddler. Children form a concept of the world partially through the patterns of their lives, and they tend to try to reenact previous patterns in their new homes. If they lived in chaos before, they will expect and try to recreate chaos in their new home. If there was no consistency in caregiver or the care provided, they will expect and attempt to recreate inconsistency in their new home. It is up to the adoptive parents to change the patterns of their children's lives so that they develop positive expectations and are thus free to grow and develop attachments.

Children who have experienced disruptions and chaos must learn to expect that good and consistent things will happen to them. Establishing a consistent routine for Gustavo was especially critical because he had had no consistency in his life before. A child should not have to wonder where or when he will eat or sleep. Because food and sleep are such critical aspects of the toddler's life, establishing routines associated with eating and bedtime are the first order of business. A daily schedule worked well with Gustavo and allowed him to have a feeling of control in his life by being able to anticipate and participate in daily events. In fact, within six months he started anticipating these routines and corrected us if we did not follow them properly. When we both had to return to work, we arranged with Gustavo's sitter to follow the routine we had established in our home. While this isn't always possible for everyone, it is important to work with sitters to maintain as much consistency as possible.

Talking about upcoming events to children helps them develop positive expectations. In the morning, talk about going to the grocery store later in the day. At night, highlight some of the next day's events. At a year of age, children have difficulty anticipating anything beyond the next day or two, but children's time perceptions gradually increase. Favorite events are especially fun for children to anticipate. The two-year-old begins questioning when it will be her birthday again the day after the celebration!

Children with attachment problems are especially vulnerable to feelings of abandonment when they are beginning to attach, but they are still insecure and often test how trustworthy we are. Parents should not leave when their child is sleeping and might wake to the presence of a stranger. Even waking up to find a well-known baby-sitter can be disconcerting to the child who expects to find Mom or Dad there. If parents have to leave very early before their child is normally awake, they should talk about it the night before.

Even the unexpected presence of parents can upset the child who is trying to establish expectancies. One day a year after Gustavo's arrival, I came home early from work and parked my van in the garage. Gustavo and his sitter had gone to the store, so I waited in the house for them. They soon came home and parked at the side door where they did not see my van. Gustavo came running into the house. I walked into the room saying, "Mommy's home!" He took one look at me and threw himself on the floor in a major tantrum. When he could finally speak an hour later, he shouted, "I thought you were a ghost!"

Children with attachment problems need structure in their environment as well as in their schedules. Deborah Hage recommends that an important part of the structure needed by kids who have come from chaotic backgrounds is to have a place for everything, and everything in its place. It is reassuring for toddlers adjusting to a new home, family, and routine to have both consistent routines and consistency in their environment. It is reassuring to find teddy on the bed every time it's time to go to sleep or to put toys away at night and know that they will be there in the morning.

Attachment specialists are increasingly recognizing the role of family traditions and rituals in building attachment and creating a sense of belonging in healthy families. Traditions are those rituals or practices that come to be associated with certain events. As adults, we bring some traditions from our own childhood, modify others, and create new ones of our own. Participating in these traditions will ground your new child in the family and contribute to his feelings of security and trust. It is particularly appropriate to develop new rituals that incorporate the adopted child's heritage and celebrate his addition to the family, such as celebrating the country-of-origin's independence day or the child's arrival day. One of our favorite rituals is celebration of "brother-sister" day, commemorating the day of Gustavo's placement. On that day, we focus specifically on Gustavo joining the family, but also on the fact that he and Natalie became siblings on that day. Each year they receive a gift that they can share such as an aquarium or a puppy. Other sacred traditions in my family include sledding on the back pasture on Christmas day, and Christmas Eve with the extended family that includes an impromptu children's program.

Traditions are much more than once-a-year events. Other important rituals in our family include Thursday-night-pizza, jammy-rides (wearing PJs for a car ride) which end up at the Dairy Queen on warm summer nights , campfires in our backyard on cool nights, and reading to our children every night before bed. An interesting incident happened the summer Gustavo was three years old that provided evidence of the importance of our backyard campfire ritual. On the first warm spring evening, I announced, "Who wants to have a campfire tonight?" Gustavo immediately ran to the kitchen and retrieved the tray we always use to carry the s'more supplies out to the fire pit, shouting, "I do, I do," all the time he was getting the supplies. The interesting thing was that we had not used that tray during the intervening seasons and he remembered both the tray and its location from the previous summer.

The toddler's main task is to attach to his family, so it is best to limit his interaction with a lot of other adults for a while after arrival. Don't invite everyone in the neighborhood to visit at once and request that other adults show a friendly but not familial interest in the newly adopted toddler. Parents will want to discourage inappropriately intimate physical affection with strangers or even casual acquaintances.

Limiting the amount of stimuli in the child's environment will help a toddler focus his energies on attaching to his family. A new culture, new family, and new home are overwhelming enough for a toddler without also meeting a lot of new people or adjusting to many new environments. Attachment routines are best established at home while meeting the child's usual daily needs.

Professional Interventions.

Sometimes parenting strategies to promote attachment need to be supplemented by professional interventions. Parents may choose professional assistance because their child is not progressing and/or because of the severity of the attachment problems. While it would be impossible to report all of the possible professional interventions that could be appropriate in dealing with attachment, a brief introduction to the therapies most commonly used and accessed by the families who provided information for this book follows. Obviously, a family would want to obtain much more information than this before selecting an appropriate therapy.

Play Therapy is one of the most frequently used individual therapies for young children or older children who do not easily verbalize their feelings. Older children who are able to express themselves more typically participate in individual talk-based therapy. Play therapy is considered an individual therapy because it involves only the child and therapist, not the parent. Play therapy involves the use of dolls, drawings, sand play, or other manipulatives which allow children to reveal their feelings through the play modality. For example, children who cannot or will not verbally describe abusive experiences may act out their experiences with dolls. A child grieving his abandonment by his birthmother may be able to express that grief through drawings or role playing. Play therapy provides an opportunity to try out or try on different feelings, reactions and behaviors in a controlled and safe environment. The most important aspect of play therapy is the establishment of a trusting relationship with another adult. It can also be useful as a way to obtain another adult's opinion on the child's attachment behaviors and problems. The therapist can consult with the parent regarding referral to family therapy if attachment problems are revealed during the play sessions. If play therapy is going to be used to address underlying attachment issues of abandonment or neglect, it will involve a very long process.

Family therapy involves looking at the whole picture of how family members react individually and interact with each other. Family therapy often accompanies the individual counseling provided through play therapy. The therapist looks for unhealthy patterns of interacting and helps the family replace those with healthy ones. Sometimes family subsets (such as birth mom, adoptive mom, and child, or just the siblings) may be involved for periods of time. Unfortunately, traditional family-systems theory may not be useful in adoption situations involving attachment problems caused by preadoption experiences. Traditional family-systems based therapy emphasizes how an individual's problems relate to larger problems in the family. In other words, the child's problem is assumed to be related to a family problem. While there is no question that adoption of a child with attachment problems creates stress and difficulty in the family, traditional family-systems theory assumes that there is an inherent problem in the family. This oftentimes is not the case in adoption, where the healthy family may become dysfunctional due to the introduction of the adopted child and his problems. The traditional systems approach overlooks the effect of a dysfunctional individual upon the family as a whole. Eventually, family problems—predictable, dramatic and often fatal to the placement—unfold. Under the traditional model, the mother is often erroneously viewed as causing the attachment problems due to her own over- or under-controlling behavior or due to being emotionally reactive. Many mothers who started out optimistically committed to the adoption are presented as discouraged and emotionally reactive by the time they seek family therapy. To then be "blamed" for the attachment problems her child is having is devastating. A mom and dad who attended one of my parenting workshops described a family therapist who told them their three-year-old son's attachment problems were due to their ineffective communication patterns. After six frustrating months of family therapy they felt their son was even more severely unattached than he was prior to treatment.

Another traditional therapy used with children with attachment problems is *behavioral therapy*, one of several operant conditioning approaches to changing behavior. In this approach, children are introduced to an established reinforcement schedule and the environment is consciously manipulated by the professionals and parents. For example, a toddler may be rewarded with small pieces of candy for sitting in Mom's lap. However, the traditional behaviorist approaches are often ineffective in dealing with attachment problems. While targeted behaviors, such as acts of aggression, may be temporarily affected by reinforcement schedules, these techniques do nothing to alleviate the *underlying causes* of the acting-out behavior or other behaviors associated with the attachment problem. One mother described her frustration with the counselor's insistence on using behavior modification when her son's rejecting behaviors continued to escalate even as he accumulated gold stars on the refrigerator for not spitting food. Children with attachment disorders often learn while very young to manipulate behavior modification approaches to their own advantage.

Group therapy, in which several families or children meet together, is not commonly used with preschool age children. However, it may be used in conjunction with play therapy or family therapy as a support function for parents. For example, several families who are struggling with attachment challenges in their children may meet together with a therapist. In some cases, young children may meet together to work on the play skill difficulties frequently related to attachment problems. However, verbal counseling strategies would not be incorporated into group therapy with toddlers.

Parent training may be provided by professional counselors, educators, or therapists to assist parents in learning strategies to foster attachment. Examples of parent training topics could include suggestions for specific attachment strategies, child development information, positive parenting skills, conflict resolution and mediation strategies, and relationship development. Parent training is frequently provided by social workers, psychologists, or family therapists. In some communities, school staff such as special educators or school counselors provide helpful parent education in these areas.

A type of therapy which relies extensively on training parents to carry out therapeutic strategies at home is referred to as *brief therapy*. During brief therapy, which is, as the name implies, a very short-term, intensive series of meetings with the therapist, the parent is taught specific attachment or grief supporting strategies to use at home. Typically, brief therapy is supplemented with a referral to ongoing parental support groups and readings.

There are several therapeutic strategies specifically intended for children with attachment disorders. *Intrusive therapy* involves physical and verbal provocation to bring out the child's feelings of loss, pain, rage, helplessness, and hopelessness in a setting and in a manner that encourages resolution of those feelings through genuine acceptance, love, and understanding. As described by Foster Cline in *Hope for High Risk and Rage Filled Children*, confrontation is the hallmark of intrusive therapy. *Rage reduction holding therapy* is an intrusive strategy intended to be used with children whose internalized rage is severely interfering with their ability to develop meaningful relationships and whose abusive behavior toward others reflects a lack of socio-moral values. In the controlled environment of the therapeutic relationship, painful events which caused the child's rage (such as abandonment by the birth parents, neglect or other forms of abuse) are brought to the conscious level and confronted. Rage reduction holding therapy involves the therapist, parent(s) and other body holders physically restraining the child while provoking the child verbally and physically until he verbalizes his hostility and anger and finally admits that he is not in control. During the entire process, the designated body holders restrain the child to emphasize that they are in charge. Following the rage reaction, the therapist and parent take advantage of the child's receptivity to recreating the attachment cycle. The critical elements in rage reduction holding therapy include the safe expression of rage and working through of anger; a relinquishment of control; a development of trust; working through of loss and separation; and the building of attachment and bonding. More detailed descriptions of these strategies are found in the writings and work of Foster Cline, Rick Delaney and Frank Kunstal, Vera Fahlberg, Ken Magid and Carole McKelvey. A description of a family's involvement in holding and reattachment strategies is provided in Linda Mansfield's and Christopher Waldmann's book *Don't Touch My Heart,* published by Pinon Press in 1995.

Theraplay, a technique developed by Ann M. Jernberg, focuses on meeting the child's earlier unmet dependency needs through a playful format structured to empower the therapist and parent to provide the needed nurturing. Its goal is to enhance attachment, self-esteem, trust in others, and joyful engagement. Theraplay replicates natural, healthy interaction between parents and young children through structured play. One or more of the following elements are incorporated into all of the structured play activities: structure, challenge, nurture, intrusion/engagement, and playfulness. Structure involves the therapist and/or parent being in charge. Activities are selected that are challenging and therefore enhance self-esteem. Intrusive activities are selected which require child involvement and offer adventure, variety, stimulation, and a fresh view of life, allowing a child to understand that surprises can be fun and new experiences enjoyable. Sessions always include soothing, calming, quieting, caretaking activities such as foot rubs that make the world feel safe, predictable, warm and secure, and provide the child with evidence that the adult provides comfort and stability.

Selecting a Therapist.

Just as there is a confusing array of professionals who provide support services for a toddler's special physiological and cognitive needs, their are a number of professionals who may provide psychotherapeutic support for toddlers and their families who are having difficulty attaching. An *adoption social worker or counselor* who holds a Master's degree in Social Work (MSW) commonly works with families of adopted toddlers. Oftentimes the same social worker who conducted the family homestudy and worked with the family through the adoption process provides post-adoption support services. MSW trained counselors who are not working for adoption agencies may have special expertise in working with families who are dealing with adoption-related attachment issues or other adoption issues.

A *clinical psychologist* is a master's degree level person extensively trained in assessment and diagnosis of social/emotional and cognitive developmental problems, including the use of intelligence testing and projective personality assessment. The *school psychologist* is a master's level person trained in assessment and diagnosis, with special emphasis on educational interventions. Both the clinical and school psychologist's training also includes preparation in counseling theory and processes, but less so than the family therapist or psychiatrist. The clinical or school psychologist frequently employs the consultation model, working with parents, school personnel, and other support service providers to develop and implement an intervention strategy based on the psychologist's clinical diagnosis.

A *marriage and family therapist*, who should hold a graduate degree from a program accredited by the American Association of Marriage and Family Therapy, is trained to provide a variety of individual and group counseling strategies and family-systems based family therapy. Some may be trained additionally to provide play therapy or specific attachment therapies.

A variety of other counselors provide services to individuals and families, including individuals holding degrees in Mental Health Counseling, School Counseling, or Rehabilitation Counseling. While all of these programs typically include a strong counseling theory and processes component, the specific applications of counseling which graduates have been prepared to assume are rarely adoption-related. Many families choose to receive counseling from their clergy person. Pastoral training may or may not have included counseling theory and processes, but most clergy persons acquire extensive counseling experience in the course of their duties.

A *psychiatrist* is a medical doctor who has received additional training in the diagnosis and treatment of psychiatric disabilities, including the provision of psychotherapy. In addition to assessment and psychotherapy, the psychiatrist is extensively trained in the biomedical aspects of psychiatric disorders, and biomedical-related disorders such as depression and childhood schizophrenia. Of the professionals described, only the psychiatrist can prescribe medication. An assessment by a psychiatrist is generally used to rule out the possibility of biomedical related causes for attachment disorders. A *psychiatric nurse* may work in conjunction with a psychiatrist, or may provide ongoing psychotherapy alone.

In selecting a therapist, parents will have certain personal criteria that are important to them, including, but not limited to availability, distance, insurance coverage, cost, and a "gut feeling" about the person. There are other factors that should also be considered when selecting a therapist to assist a family in dealing with adoption related attachment difficulties. The following recommended questions are adapted from a presentation titled "Choosing an Adoption Therapist" made by Sharon Kaplan Roszia at the 1995 Adoptive Families of America Conference in Dallas, Texas. These questions are intended to assist parents in assessing the appropriateness of a therapist for their particular family:

* Has the counselor had specific training and/or experience in current adoption related issues?

* Do the counselor's words and actions provide evidence of being an advocate of adoption?
* Is positive adoption language used?
* Are all parties involved in the adoption triad treated with empathy and respect?
* Has the counselor been personally "touched by adoption"?
* Has the counselor had specific training and/or experience in working with toddlers?
* Has the counselor had specific training and/or experience in attachment- and grief-related issues?
* Is the counselor connected to a larger support service network and therefore able to make appropriate referrals or to consult with professionals with specific expertise in attachment and adoption issues? Is the counselor willing to consult with professionals who have specific expertise in adoption-related grief and attachment problems if he or she does not have specific expertise in those areas?
* Is the counselor creative and flexible, and willing to use a variety of techniques? Does the counselor use just one technique or is the therapy individualized for the unique needs of each family and child?
* Does the counselor have a strategy for keeping the family informed and involved, as the goal is to have the child attach to the family, not the counselor?
* Are parents treated as the experts, and a source of strength, rather than the source of the problem?
* Are expectations of parents clearly defined?
* Is the counselor problem-oriented and goal-focused? Is there a specific plan for how counseling will be terminated?
* Last and most important, are parents personally comfortable with the counselor?

Indicators of Attachment.

The instinct or drive for attachment is present in newborns. In fact, it usually takes months of neglect or a disruption in caregivers before an infant begins resisting attachment. However, once a child has become resistant it takes considerable effort and time to recreate attachment. Children who are grieving the loss of a former attachment, or are displaying ambivalence or resistance toward their adoptive parents do not suddenly bond. Attachment doesn't just happen, it grows. How quickly depends on a number of factors, including the number and quality of prior attachments; individual temperament; parenting strategies; age; and severity of pre-placement neglect or other forms of abuse. Any prognosis is at best an educated guess.

However, attachment is not an all or nothing issue. Attachment ranges on a continuum from the very rare child who displays no attachment behavior, and may be diagnosed as having reactive attachment disorder, to the strongly and securely attached child. In a conversation with Vera Fahlberg on June 7, 1995, she likened the continuum to a teeter totter, on which secure attachment was represented by the center fulcrum, and resistant and insecure attachment represented the two ends. Thus the goal becomes helping the child stay centered at the fulcrum. Any given child may progress and regress on the attachment continuum as his age and circumstances change. Even the securely attached child may display attachment problems if he experiences a loss of caregiver or other serious trauma. However, children who did not experience the attachment cycle during their first twelve months of life are more vulnerable to resistant and insecure attachment than children who enjoyed secure attachment in infancy. Indicators of attachment problems have already been discussed. On the other hand, how can we tell when our children are moving toward attachment?

Many adopted toddlers initially display behaviors which are ambivalent toward their parents, but move in the direction of secure attachment. In other words, the children show early indicators of a budding attachment that precede the more traditional attachment indicators. These indicators are important milestones in the attachment process and are reassurances to parents that the bonding process is progressing, albeit more slowly than we oftentimes wish. Examples of these early indicators as described by parents include the following.

* Children were described as displaying subtle indicators that they noticed and differentiated parents from other adults by behavior, expression etc. At this stage, the child did not react noticeably to the parent's presence or absence, but careful observation revealed that the child was tracking the parent with his eyes, and subtle changes such as a widening of the eyes indicated a reaction to the parent's presence.
* Parents reported that their children began to display a healthy interest in parental and sibling activities and location before joining in or seeking parent(s). This overt, relaxed watchfulness is very different from the child who is defensively watching adults so as to get out of the way of an angry word or fist.
* Transient eye contact, especially in a moment of shared mirth or when receiving something pleasurable, was described as preceding consistent eye contact.
* Parents described that their children typically demonstrated a seeming tolerance or passive acceptance of physical contact before seeking physical contact, especially in conjunction with pleasurable activities such as eating or "reading" books.
* Similarly, parents described children as accepting verbal and physical indicators of affection long before initiating expressions of affection.
* Acts of kindness toward infants or peers such as retrieving a dropped baby bottle, were reported by parents as typically preceding displays of empathy toward parents.
* Some parents reported that their children displayed kindness and consideration toward animals, and accepted affection (licks, cuddles) from their pets long before they appeared comfortable with such overt displays of affection with parents.
* Parents reported being vastly encouraged by rudimentary indicators of sympathy and empathy, such as looking distressed when someone else gets hurt, even though these indicators of a developing conscience were typically displayed later in adopted toddlers than in children who experienced healthy attachment in infancy.

* Parents reported that an early indicator of a budding attachment was when their children first displayed a preference for them over other people, in spite of the fact that it was often rather obliquely displayed.
* Children were described as gradually accepting parental controls.
* Because developmental delays are so commonly associated with attachment problems, physical and cognitive development is a positive indicator of attachment potential.
* Parents described an early indicator of emerging attachment as being an appropriate sense of humor and playfulness.
* Some children were described as beginning to display attachment behaviors when they stopped being obsessed with food. These toddlers were described as being able to attend to something other than their compulsive need to eat once they seemed to feel reassured that food wouldn't disappear.
* Interestingly, a number of parents described that their children became more testing as they started to display attachment behaviors, and seemed to overreact to seemingly minor frustrations such as a schedule change or when parents went out for the evening.

Over a period of time, hopefully the fleeting eye contact, laughter, acceptance, and giving of affection happened more and more frequently. Finally the toddler was connected more often than disconnected among those families I surveyed. While most of the toddlers who displayed attachment problems at adoption were described by their parents as continuing to have some residual affects of attachment problems, the majority were reported to be displaying a strong attachment to their parents within three to four years following placement. The following behaviors and characteristics are indicative of healthy attachment at the toddler and preschool age. These are adapted from the work of Bowlby, Cline, Delaney, Fahlberg, Magid and McKelvey, and Watkins.

Attachment Indicators

* Seeks positive interactions with caretakers by eye contact, touch, vocalizations, etc.
* Maintains appropriate eye contact

* Shows caution of strangers but develops trusting view of the world as time passes
* Smiles and looks at other people and is interested in the environment, but retains contact with parent(s) as her base of security
* Explores the environment but retains visual contact with parent as the secure base and frequently returns to parent for reassurance and to "touch base"
* Is able to become comfortable in another environment after a safe exploration period with parent
* Age appropriately tests limits but shares control with parent(s)
* Seeks autonomy and sense of self but seeks reassurance and sometimes "retreats" to the security of parent(s) care
* Exhibits generally age-appropriate behaviors
* Initiates and welcomes affection from family members and other close relatives or friends but is not indiscriminately affectionate with strangers
* Develops age-appropriate signs of conscience, such as beginning to share, remorse over wrongdoing or when parent is angry, difficulty making eye contact when lying
* Develops age-appropriate interpersonal skills, such as beginning to share and show empathy toward peers' feelings
* Manages age-appropriate impulse control
* Demonstrates positive self esteem through such behaviors as proudly displaying artwork, confidently contributing suggestions, stating personal opinions
* Expresses genuine and spontaneous expression of joy: belly laughs, sparkling eyes etc.
* Eats and toilets normally if no known physiological reason for disorders
* Exhibits normal language development if no known physiological reason for speech/language delays
* Plays normally and is not preoccupied with gore, fire or aggression
* Generally avoids extreme physical aggression toward self, others, and animals

- Seeks assistance and support from parent(s) when in danger, hurt, etc., but not excessively needy or whiny
- Spontaneously seeks out parents in a crisis
- Presents physical and cognitive development within normal range, assuming there is no physiological or cognitive impairment
- Engages in symbolic attachment play: cuddling dolls, putting stuffed animals "to bed," etc.

- Displays separation anxiety consistent with developmental age and circumstances, e.g. more intense in new situations, or when staying with a new sitter
- Is spontaneously affectionate with family and friends

A couple of weeks before his fifth birthday Gustavo drew the picture displayed here. This picture, originally drawn in beautiful rainbow colors, is Gustavo's depiction of his family holding hands together under a rainbow, surrounded by symbols of love. This is a picture by and of a child finally displaying strong attachment.

Looking Ahead.

The experiences of the families surveyed for this book support the belief that most toddlers adopted into a loving and consistent family can and do form a strong attachment. However, the majority of parents who described their toddlers as exhibiting serious attachment problems indicated that their children continued to display some attachment-related challenges as they aged, even after they displayed most of the signs of secure attachment most of the time. The parents also reported that the route was strewn with set-backs and plateaus. A number of parents described that attachment process as lengthy and uneven.

Early life experience may permanently alter the individual's threshold and duration of emotional stress reactions. In other words, the adoptive family can "replace but not erase" the child's early experience.

Almost all of the children described as very aggressive during their first weeks and months home acquired better control mechanisms as they matured and settled into their new families, but their parents reported that they continued to display very strong personalities and tempers. Three families indicated that their children were still the type to push everything to the limit and then one step further, even after they were clearly attached to their parents. Two families described their children as still being the type to initiate physical fights with other children, even three or more years after adoption. The vast majority of parents who had indicated that their toddlers had attachment problems reported that their children continued to struggle with power and control issues long after placement. They reported that behavior management of their children continued to require a great deal of emotional energy. The strategies recommended by Mary Kurcinka in *Raising Your Spirited Child; A Guide for Parents Whose Child Is More Intense, Sensitive, Perceptive, Persistent, Energetic* and by Foster Cline and Jim Fay in *Parenting with Love and Logic* were strongly endorsed by these parents.

According to their parents, the children who were initially described as prematurely independent when adopted as toddlers continued to be independent and persistent, perhaps because their early need for survival skills permanently influenced their temperament.

Three of the children who were over age four when their parents provided information about them were still reverting to their earlier survival behaviors when in real or perceived danger or in the midst of other emotionally intense experiences. This was often noted in a cold indifference or attitude of independence when angry or emotionally hurt. The children's parents thought that they were pretending this indifference, and that they were reverting to their aloof behaviors as a defense mechanism.

An interesting example of such reverting to the "survival mode" could be seen in Gustavo's reaction to our dentist. Both of my children required major dental work when they were three. As the dentist descended on Natalie's mouth, she locked eyes with me and didn't avert her gaze during the entire procedure. Consistent with the securely attached child's use of parents as the base of security, she depended on me for her support during that frightening experience. If I had shown fear or distress, or even averted my eyes, she would have panicked. She trusted me implicitly. Gustavo was taken to a pediatric dentist who specialized in working with children who had difficulty with dentists. Because we agreed that the experience of being worked on while awake would be traumatic, we decided to sedate him during the procedure. Gustavo had been soundly sleeping for ten minutes when I laid him in the dental chair. The dentist and assistant began placing restraints on his arms and legs so he would not involuntarily move during the procedure. With just one of Gustavo's arms remaining free, the dentist suddenly and unexpectedly found his throat grabbed by a little fist. The determination and strength of that clenched fist, not to mention the pain, rendered the dentist speechless for a full minute! The dentist had never encountered a child whose flight/fight response was strong enough to enable him to roose himself from a drug-induced sedation. Under the same circumstances, Natalie would have called out for me rather than try to defend herself.

A number of parents have told me that as their adopted toddlers grew older, they still tended to revert to the same misguided survival behaviors they displayed as young children when they were in new or otherwise stressful situations. Three behaviors commonly reported were lying, stealing and hoarding food. At a recent workshop I conducted, a mother and father of a young adult adopted as a toddler reported that their son still tends to lie as his first reaction to a question which he perceives as at all threatening, even when the truth is seemingly non-threatening. For example, if mom says, "I tried to call you on Sunday, but you must have been out," the son is likely to reply, "I was home all day, you must not have called on Sunday," when in fact he was at the grocery store. A father of a girl adopted at age three recently told me that he and his wife had placed their twelve-year-old daughter with the paternal grandmother for a year. He went on to explain that because she continued to be overtly aggressive at home, his wife wanted a reprieve from her for a period of time. Unfortunately, the family was not involved in any joint counseling, the grandmother lived a long distance from the parents, and the parents did not appear to be actively parenting (making decisions, talking frequently with the daughter, etc.) during the out-of-home placement. It came as no surprise when, in response to my question as to how the daughter and grandmother were getting along, the man replied, "I don't think my ma is going to put up with this for long because Ayla is stealing her blind."

A mother of an eighteen-year-old daughter adopted at two-and-a-half told me recently that her daughter got in trouble with her new college roommate because she had reverted to her old pattern of stashing food in her room. She didn't just hoard college staples like chips and candy bars, she was stashing entire meals in closets and drawers. The roommate was understandably upset about the resultant odor. Through counseling, her daughter was able to identify the source of her compulsion to revert to food hoarding as a reaction to the sensation of emptiness her homesickness was creating, which resurrected her anger and pain over her early life abandonment. With the cooperation of her mom, she developed a plan to regularly call home for emotional refueling, and to keep a small quantity of non-perishable food in her dorm room.

Many of the children who had early severe attachment problems continued to have problems displaying appropriate emotions for a number of years. Instead of responding to situations normally eliciting sadness, jealousy, fear, or other emotions, these children tended to react in anger. One second grader, for example, became assaultive when a favorite picture he had drawn was accidentally ruined. A mother described a situation where one morning she got up early and went outdoors to hang out laundry. Both of her children were sleeping, and normally would have continued sleeping for another hour. Unfortunately, however, her daughter, adopted at age three, woke-up and searched the house for her. She walked into the house to find her daughter in an uncontrollable rage. Even after she settled down, she had difficulty verbalizing and recognizing her emotion as fear rather than anger.

Parents who shared their stories for this book advised new adoptive parents of toddlers to expect periodic set-backs, especially in response to stressful events. Some parents mentioned that they felt their children continued to have a low threshold of stress, appeared to overreact to seemingly minor problems, and had major setbacks in response to real crisis. Absences were especially disconcerting for adopted children because prior absences were associated with permanent loss of a caretaker. One little girl had greeted her mom with the pronouncement, "You aren't my mommy anymore" when she returned from an extended hospital stay. It was months before she reconnected with mom and stopped becoming frantic if she was out of sight. Twins adopted internationally as toddlers who graduated this year from high school were included recently in the local newspaper's series on area graduates. They reported the most vivid memory of their young lives as being the tremendous grief and fear they felt when, as seven-years-olds, their mother was gone from home for four weeks to adopt a younger brother.

Many adopted children learned to be independent at an inappropriately early age. Good coping skills meant survival. These children often continue to be fiercely independent, fending for themselves even when they don't need to. While most children intuitively expect their parents to assist, reassure, and rescue them, especially in frightening or unfamiliar situations, many adopted children continue to rely on their own resources rather than asking for appropriate help or expecting us to intervene. When Natalie was in sixth grade, she read a true story about a young Native American who lived alone on an uninhabited island for ten years. As part of the assignment, she had to answer the question, "How long could you survive alone on an island?" Natalie ruefully responded, "To tell the truth, not long, perhaps a few days." I then asked Gustavo, who was following this conversation with interest, how long he thought he could survive alone on an island. Gustavo matter-of-factly responded, "As long as I need to." In the introduction to this chapter, I described five-year-old Juan's "stranger box," a shoe box filled with various survival and self-protection gear. When Juan's mother asked him who the "stranger" was, he replied, "A bad man that tries to get in my house." While it isn't unusual for children to engage in this type of fantasy, what is unusual is that Juan's mother was convinced that Juan would actually defend himself with whatever resources he had available if the occasion should arise and *not* turn to her first.

There is no magic formula which can be applied to determine the long term prognosis for any given child. Some children adopted as toddlers continue to display severe attachment problems well into their school years and beyond. Recently, parents of two sons who were birth siblings and adopted as toddlers described one son, now twenty-eight, as being firmly attached within five years following his adoption. The other son, however, now age twenty-seven, is still extremely resistant of attachment. Here were two people who shared the same genes, seemingly similar early life experiences, and seemingly similar parenting from their adoptive parents, yet each displayed extremely divergent adjustment.

Even though a few adopted toddlers discussed in this book displayed severe attachment problems for years following their adoption, the majority of the children displayed strong attachment to their parents within a few years after their adoption. Most of the children gradually acclimated to their new environment and eventually displayed attachment to their parents. Sometimes the children achieved major milestones within a short period of time, and other times their progress was indicated by tiny baby steps that only a parent would catch. A few parents reported that their children's progress was only obvious when viewed in retrospect. One mom remembered waking up one morning to the realization that for the first time since placement Mara had gone a week without a major temper tantrum. Sara's mother recalled that in contrast to last year's mother's day, when she was *persona non grata*, this year Sara showered her with affection!

Summary

As discussed throughout this book, factors affecting the attachment process included the child's and parent's preparation for adoption, individual temperament, the child's stage of development at placement, the child's preadoption circumstances, the number of disruptions, parental strategies and postadoption family circumstances. However, in spite of individual and family differences, every family that contributed information for this book reported that they had grown and benefited in many ways from their decision to adopt a toddler. Even those who were still struggling with attachment challenges were optimistic about the future. In the majority of cases, the adopted toddlers were functioning very well in their home and school environments.

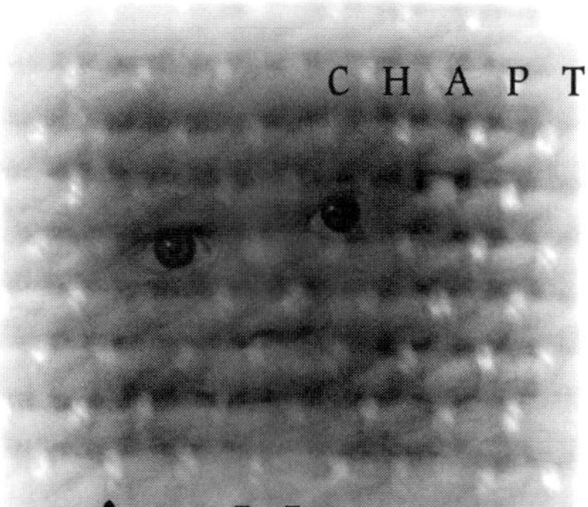

CHAPTER *Eight*

Behavior Management

"Carry me, carry me" wailed two-year-old Roberto. Beth, weighted down with three bags of groceries, responded, "You ll just have to walk if you want to get into the house." Roberto screamed in anger while rooted to the spot where he had stopped and demanded to be carried. Beth finally accepted the fact that Roberto wasn't going to acquiesce, in spite of the extreme cold.

Two-year-old Sara's parents were shocked by their new daughter's table manners. She ran around the table, grabbing food from plates and bowls.

Although his English language skills were slow in development, three-year-old Jamie could swear with abandon in his native language.

Where does a new parent begin? What style of behavior management works effectively with toddlers? Why are the strategies that work so effectively with other toddlers ineffective with newly adopted toddlers?

Discipline is one of the most challenging but essential aspects of parenting. While there is no foolproof system, parents can take steps to start their new toddler on the path to appropriate behavior. Children are reassured by knowing what is expected of them and count on their parents to respond in predictable ways. Children test their parents to find out if they will be consistent and trustworthy. Behavior management is about providing appropriate structure and guidance for children, not about punishing inappropriate behavior. Parents have the primary responsibility for providing the care, teaching and system of rules and expectations that children need to grow up emotionally healthy. These external structures are necessary for children to develop their own internal structure and guidance. Appropriate structure contributes to the development of children's attachment and self esteem and helps to make them feel loved and capable. Neglect and punishment, on the other hand, leads to feelings of being unlovable, unworthy, and incompetent. Unfortunately, many adopted toddlers have had little or no consistent guidance and structure from nurturing adults.

Management Style

There is no foolproof behavior management system. Just as children have individual personalities and temperaments, every adult brings his or her own unique experiences, aptitudes, and values to the parenting role. Finding the right management style depends on the environment, the individual characteristics and needs of the child, and the individual characteristics and needs of the parent. While children's needs should take precedence, parents' beliefs about children and discipline obviously influence their styles of management. Parents who spend time thinking and talking about their style of management before their child arrives usually feel better prepared to "hit the ground running." The following questionnaire was designed to help parents better understand their preferred style of behavior management. There are no right or wrong answers.

Personal Behavior Management Style Questionnaire

1. Which of the following statements best represents your belief about children's ability to make decisions?
   a. Children's decision-making processes must always be considered legitimate and valid.
   b. Children should be encouraged to make decisions within parameters established by their parents.
   c. It is the responsibility of parents to make appropriate decisions for their children.

2. Which of the following statements best represents your belief about children's temperaments.
   a. Children are born with an innate temperament, and parents have little ability to influence it.

b. A child's temperament is greatly determined by his family's behavior, their culture, neighborhood, schools, etc.
c. A child's temperament is influenced by her environment, but she is born with a predisposition to a particular temperament.

3. If the noise level of my children's play bothers me, I will most likely...
   a. discuss my discomfort with my children and attempt to reach some compromise, such as continuing boisterous play in another room.
   b. allow the noise to continue as long as the children are having fun.
   c. direct the children to "quiet down."

4. In regard to the selection of my young children's clothing, my role is to...
   a. select the appropriate outfit for my children to wear.
   b. encourage my children to select their own outfits.
   c. allow my children to select from a couple outfits which I have chosen.

5. If a younger child breaks an older sibling's favorite toy, I would respond by...
   a. scolding the younger child for breaking the toy and scolding the older child for not putting the toy in a safe place.
   b. not interfering unless the situation got out of hand.
   c. sending both children to "time out" together until they resolved the problem.

6. If my teenage children unanimously agreed that a family rule was unjust, I would respond by...
   a. dropping the rule.
   b. scheduling a family conference to try to arrive at a mutually agreeable compromise.
   c. informing the children that while I am sorry that they do not like the rule, parents make rules in the best interest of their children.

7. If my preschooler does not want to participate in a family activity, I would...
   a. explain the value of the activity and require participation.

b. try to find out why the child doesn't want to participate and try to find an alternative that is satisfactory to the child and the rest of the family.
c. respect the child's wishes and not apply any pressure to participate.

8. If my toddler tugs and whines at me when I am talking on the phone, I would...
   a. quickly ascertain if there is an emergency, and if there isn't, move the child or myself and continue the conversation.
   b. excuse myself briefly and explain to my child that I will attend to her needs when I am finished, then return to the caller.
   c. assume the child needs my attention and make arrangements to call the person back later.

9. If I anticipate that my toddler is going to resist putting on his pajamas at his regular bedtime, I would...
   a. play a strenuous activity and postpone bedtime until he's cooperative.
   b. remind him that it is pajama time in five minutes, and the consequences of not putting on his pajamas.
   c. at the regular time, pick him up and put his pajamas on in spite of any protests.

10. Babies learn to talk, walk, and other developmental skills because they...
    a. have an insatiable inner drive to learn.
    b. love the attention and praise they receive from their parents and significant others.
    c. have an inner need to become independent, but that inner drive is reinforced by praise and other external rewards.

11. If my preschooler complains when I tell her she can't have a treat before dinner, I would...
    a. ask her why it is so important to her, and try to come to some compromise, such as one bite of a treat if she promises to eat all her dinner.
    b. ignore the complaining and calmly stand my ground.
    c. let the child have the treat, so she experiences the natural consequence of not being hungry for dinner.

12. To acquire appropriate behaviors, children must learn...
   a. to respect their parent's judgment.
   b. inner control.
   c. to respect and follow their inner drives and needs.

13. A child misbehaves because...
   a. he has learned to misbehave.
   b. he has not been told that his behavior is inappropriate.
   c. he has a personal need that is not being met.

14. Which of the following best describes your philosophy of disciplining your children?
   a. Be strict, but warm and caring.
   b. Always put the child's feelings first.
   c. Be flexible, but establish parameters.

15. I believe my school age child will change her inappropriate behavior if...
   a. she believes it will help her be more accepted by others.
   b. she believes it will make her feel better about herself.
   c. she believes she will be rewarded.

16. If I am not feeling well, and I need my primary age children's cooperation, I will...
   a. tell my children how I feel, assuming they will be considerate by playing quietly.
   b. direct my children to watch TV, etc. while I rest
   c. arrange for a baby sitter or some other alternative care

Scoring Key:
Calculate the total number of responses in each of the following tables.

Table 1	Table 2	Table 3
1a 5b 9a 13c	1b 5c 9b 13b	1c 5a 9c 13a
2a 6a 10a 14b	2c 6b 10c 14c	2b 6c 10b 14a
3b 7c 11c 15b	3a 7b 11a 15a	3c 7a 11b 15c
4b 8c 12c 16a	4c 8b 12b 16b	4a 8a 12a 16c

Interpretation

The number of responses in each of the three tables provides an indication of a parent's style of behavior management. The responses in Table 1 are consistent with a child-centered discipline style, while the responses in Table 2 are consistent with the reactions of a parent who uses an interactive approach. Table 3 responses suggest a more parent-directed style of management.

If the majority of responses are in any of the three categories, the respondent probably feels quite strongly about being child-centered, parent-directed, or balancing the two (interactive.) People who have equal responses in each table, are either very flexible, or haven't developed a personal style of management.

Child-centered disciplinarians (Table 1) believe that rules inappropriately squelch a child's curiosity and desire to grow and develop. They prefer that children experience the natural consequences of their behaviors rather than arbitrary punishments. Active listening is used to show empathy and support. Child-centered discipline is illustrated by the following conversation between a newly adopted three-year-old and her mother:

Scene:	*At home.*
Mom:	"I can see that you're tired, Julie. I'd like to help you get your pajamas on."
Julie:	"No"
Mom:	"You don't want to go to bed?"
Julie:	"You don't do it right."
Mom:	"I don't get you ready for bed right?"
Julie:	"I miss my other mom."
Mom:	"You want Donna at bedtime."
Julie:	"Donna reads books to me."
Mom:	"Would you like me to read to you before bed?"
Julie:	"Ya, but I miss Donna."
Mom:	"You'd like to visit Donna soon?"
Julie:	"Ya"
Mom:	"I'll arrange that tomorrow. Now let's get ready for bed so that we can read together."

Interactive parents (Table 2) establish parameters of acceptable behavior, but are as flexible as possible within those boundaries. This is sometimes referred to as the authoritative style of management. Mutually acceptable solutions are sought when conflicts arise, but the parent is the final authority when consensus cannot be reached. A few, positively-stated rules are used which are appropriate to the child's developmental age and temperament. Logical consequences are imposed when children break the rules. The following scenario illustrates the interactive style of management.

Scene: *Parent and toddler at a restaurant. Prior to entering the restaurant, parent reviews family rule.*

Parent: "Remember that we sit down in the restaurant and we talk quietly. I've brought toys for you to play with until our food is ready."

Toddler begins to fuss, trying to climb down and run around the restaurant.

Parent: "Remember that you have to sit quietly. Would you like a different toy?" (If this doesn't work, parent continues.) "If you don't sit down you will need to leave. I'm going to count to three and if you are not sitting down, you will leave: One, two, three."

If it worked, great. If not, parent calmly continues.

Parent: "I'm sorry you didn't sit down. You've decided that you can't stay at the restaurant. You decided to leave." Parent informs the waitperson to cancel their order, then picks the child up and walks out.

Parent-directed disciplinarians (Table 3) believe in being restrictive and authoritarian. They typically use behavior modification techniques such as changing the environment and using rewards to change children's behaviors. Directive parents focus on a child's observed behavior, not on the underlying reasons for that behavior. While they prefer to reward good behavior, they do not hesitate to punish inappropriate behavior. The parent-directed style is illustrated by the following scenario.

Scene: *Toddler and parent back at the restaurant.*
Action: Toddler begins crawling down from the chair.

Parent: "Julie, sit down. You may play with these toys."
Julie: "Too full!"
Parent: "Julie, sit down. You may play with these toys but you cannot get down yet."

Julie quietly begins playing with her toys.

Parent: "I'm so happy to see you playing nicely. Would you like this cracker?"

Julie eats the cracker, but starts to climb down again after five minutes.

Parent: "Julie, sit down."
Julie: "No!"

Parent picks Julie up. After stopping at the cashier to pay the bill, parent and toddler leave.

The Newly Adopted Toddler...First Things First.

Toddlers often arrive home with a number of behaviors which their new parents would like to see changed. However, if parents try to change all of these behaviors right away, they will spend their entire time disciplining rather than enjoying their children. Many child development experts have recognized that the "best disciplined child is the least disciplined child." A child who is constantly being corrected quickly learns to tune-out the authority figure. It helps to establish priorities. When Gustavo arrived, for example, he would claw at our eyes when he was frightened or angry. This behavior became a quick priority for change and we tried to choose a strategy that would eliminate this hurtful behavior. First we tried the child-centered strategy of empathizing with his anger. When that didn't work, we tried telling him, "If you choose to hurt me I won't be able to play with you." This, too, was unsuccessful. It was only when we decided to firmly but gently restrain his hand that the undesirable behavior gradually stopped. Even the most experienced parents sometimes resort to the trial-and-error approach to behavior management. Still, it is comforting to know that there are some tried-and-true strategies consistently endorsed by parents of adopted toddlers.

Dealing with Power Struggles

Many adoptive parents I interviewed placed their children at the "strong-willed" end of the temperament continuum. Strong-willed children, especially those who are struggling with attachment problems, can easily recast the simplest interactions into power struggles. Just as unattached children have trouble trusting their new parents, so also do they resist conferring their new parents with authority over them. One mother provided a wonderful example of a typical power struggle with her newly adopted toddler. On a "10°F" day, her two-year-old decided that he wanted to be carried from the car to the house. Because Mom was already carrying two bags of groceries, she told him that he would have to walk. Assuming that he would quickly acquiesce due to the extreme cold, she stood at the door for ten minutes watching him scream while rooted to the spot where he had stopped and demanded to be carried. At that point she realized three things. First, he would stand there until he had frostbite or hypothermia. Next, a passerby was likely to report her for child abuse if she didn't go out and retrieve him. And finally, and most importantly, she had foolishly made an idle threat that she couldn't enforce. Once a conflict escalates into a power struggle no one wins. Parents often become quite defensive about conflicts, particularly when they perceive that their children are challenging their authority. New parents may feel insecure, questioning their right to parent or fearing that their children will walk all over them if they are too lenient.

The first line of defense should be to avoid power struggles whenever possible. Many toddlers, whether adopted or not, are prone to power struggles when they are tired, hungry or otherwise not feeling well. It takes two to tangle, so parents can divert many power struggles simply by refusing to participate in them. When toddlers give off warning signs of a pending explosion, parents should act quickly to redirect, diffuse, or minimize the confrontation. Redirecting a toddler's attention to some other pleasurable activity can sometimes diffuse a power struggle as well. Humor can be used effectively also, just as long as parents are laughing with their child, not at him. John's dad described a wonderful strategy that he discovered accidentally as a way of diffusing his son's anger. Their pet cat would growl menacingly as he stalked—and pounced on—his prey.

One day as John was revving up to pitch a major fit, his dad crouched down and growled like the family cat. At first John looked stunned, then broke out in hysterical laughter, and his rage was dispelled.

Toddlers who want to be in control feel important by being given responsibilities. Even a young toddler can handle simple chores such as carrying silverware to the table or putting clothes in the dryer. Pet care is also great for children who are not aggressive toward animals, as long as parents oversee the work. Parents sometimes unwittingly invite power struggles by their own words or actions. For example, it helps not to give commando type directives. Instead of saying, "Put your coat on right now young man," parents can say, "It's time for all of us to put on our coats so we can go to Grandma's." I've also learned not to ask a question unless I'm willing to accept "No" as an answer. For example, if I ask, "Are you ready to put on your coat now?" I have to be prepared for the answer to be, "NO." Gustavo will do almost anything to avoid what he perceives as "losing face." He can't stand being watched to see if he is following through on a directive. We have learned to say something such as, "You need to clean up the mess you've just made. I'm going to leave the room, and you can too, after you've cleaned up." We have also learned to avoid power struggles by giving Gustavo the space he needs to adjust to an expectation. For example, it is futile to expect him to get dressed immediately after he awakes. It's more effective to gently rouse him, then say, "I'll be back in a few minutes and I'll help you get dressed."

Newly-adopted toddlers are often sticklers about having their routines changed, especially when they are still adjusting to the changes related to a new home and family. While it is best to keep the toddler's routine as consistent as possible, that isn t always possible. There are a number of strategies that will help a toddler handle change constructively. Instead of saying, "Pick up your toys right now," parents can warn their child that "In five minutes it will be time to pick up the toys." To accommodate a toddler's limited time concept, parents might say, "As soon as the toys are picked up we will eat lunch." A clock can also be used to help manage activities. For example, you might alert your toddler that it will be time for his nap when the clock chimes. If Mom has to leave early for a meeting, she can tell her son the night before that when he wakes up, Daddy will be there, but Mommy will be gone.

Handling Aggression and Conflicts

Feelings of anger accompany many toddlers to their new homes. Positive conflict resolution is a skill many adults, as well as children, need to learn. Increasingly, schools are also recognizing the importance of team work and are incorporating conflict resolution skills into the regular curriculum at all grade levels. However, you can't wait until your children get to school to teach them how to handle conflicts in a positive way.

Important skills in resolving conflicts include acknowledging a difference of opinion, seeing the issue from the other person's perspective, respecting the other person's right to his point of view, controlling one's temper/behavior, showing willingness to seek a mutually satisfactory solution, identifying alternatives, compromising, and displaying commitment. With a parent's assistance, even toddlers can begin to acquire some of these skills.

Toddlers can be encouraged to suggest different ways they could have handled a conflict. For example, one morning three-year-old Gustavo lashed out at his father when the cat he was holding jumped off his lap. "You let Cloudy go," he shouted as he kicked his dad. When asked, "What could you have done instead of kicking dad," he appropriately suggested solemnly, "I should have asked Daddy to go and get Cloudy."

Toddlers can learn to verbalize and acknowledge conflict. Direct questioning invites the child to talk about her feelings. Ask, "How do you feel?" Claudia Jewett Jarratt recommends a strategy to begin helping children identify their emotions correctly in a technique called "The Five Faces." As described in *Helping Children Cope with Separation and Loss*, five cards with simple drawings of faces depicting sad, mad, happy, scared, and lonely are used to facilitate conversations about which feeling the person has. To learn the "game," the toddler might be asked, "Which face shows how you feel about having macaroni and cheese for lunch?" Gradually, the cards are used to talk about more important emotionally reactive situations. Even children whose language is not sophisticated enough to participate in the dialogue, but who seem stuck in the "angry" mode, can benefit from an exploration of emotions.

Toddlers can also learn to assume the perspective of someone else. When a child hurts another child, the adult in charge might ask, "How do you think Jamie feels? How would you feel if someone took your truck?" If a child throws something or hits a playmate, Mom can say, "I'm going to stop the playing now, because hitting is not fun.. When you've settled down we can play again."

Eventually children should be able to think of and suggest alternatives and negotiate resolutions to a conflict, but toddlers need help. For example, two three-year-old toddlers fighting over one tricycle could be told, "You can either take turns and each ride for five minutes, or we can put the tricycle away and play something else. However, you may not hit each other." Then follow through, verbalizing what is happening. If they share, say, "Ajay had the tricycle for five minutes; now it's Sheri's turn for five minutes. I'm so happy to see how nicely you're sharing." If they don't cooperate, remove the tricycle and say, "I'm sorry you weren't able to share today, so I will put the tricycle away. I know that you'll be able to share next time we take it out." By age four many children can start suggesting compromises. By that age, "Let's make a deal" was a regular part of Gustavo's vocabulary.

Alternatives to Time-Out

Isolating children for a period of time has become a popular discipline strategy advocated by many child psychologists and pediatricians. However, newly-adopted toddlers seem to be more upset than helped by time-outs. Time-outs are intended to provide an opportunity for both parents and children to calm down and change their behaviors, but it isn't effective for children who do not have self-calming strategies. Isolation can be traumatic for a toddler who is struggling with grief and/or attachment, and so perceives time-out as further rejection. If the child becomes angrier or more withdrawn as a result of being timed-out, try another strategy.

One alternative is for parents to impose a brief time-out on themselves by temporarily withdrawing their attention from their child. For example, the parent whose child is throwing toys stops playing, looks away, and firmly tells the child, "I can't continue playing until you stop throwing your toys." Sitting passively next to the child may be effective, especially if the child previously was engaged in an enjoyable activity with the parent.

Another alternative to parent enforced time-outs is self determined time-outs, where the child is provided the opportunity to withdraw from a conflict voluntarily or at least have some input into the time-out arrangement. The parent could say, "I understand that you got very upset when you had to go to your room yesterday after you hit Sara. Can you think of a different place you would like to go to calm down if you feel like getting in a fight?" If the child suggests going out on the porch, the next time a battle seems to be brewing, Mom or Dad can say, "Do you need to go outside to the porch and calm down before we talk more?" Some children eventually reach the level of self control where they remove themselves from a volatile situation without encouragement from Mom or Dad. These types of negotiations usually work better with older pre-schoolers or school-age children than they do with toddlers because of the reasoning skills involved.

Toddlers also can be timed-out effectively while in the safety of a parent's lap. Holding allows parents to talk to their child about why he's being removed from an activity. For example, the toddler who has thrown his truck at the cat could be picked up and held for a few minutes while being told, "I can't let you throw your toys at Misty. That hurts her, and in our family, we don't hurt animals." Objects which children are misusing should also be removed. For example, in the situation just discussed, the truck could be timed-out to a high shelf.

If parents still decide to physically remove their child for a time out, it should never be done in a way or place that frightens a toddler. Toddlers who have been frightened in the past by closed doors, dark rooms, or a particular room such as a bathroom should never be subjected to those settings. I know toddlers who, in their terror, have literally trashed the furniture and broken windows when they were locked in their rooms for a time-out. If parents feel a time-out is essential, it should be very brief, and in a location where the child can be supervised.

Understanding Where Behaviors Come From

Many of the so-called maladaptive behaviors displayed by newly-adopted toddlers are really quite adaptive given the child's past experiences. Sara's parents, for instance, were shocked by her table manners. She grabbed food from other people's plates and wouldn't stay seated–skills which she had acquired while living on the street. Jim watched in horror as his newly-adopted three-year-old grabbed the five-year-old neighbor's toy, and then pummeled him with it. Competing for attention and toys was the norm in the orphanage his son had lived in. Jamie, abused as an infant, recoiled from physical touch, and wouldn't make eye-contact. He was not avoiding loving touch, with which he was unfamiliar, but simply activating the early survival behaviors he had learned as a way to avoid further abuse.

Toddlers model their own behavior on what they see. Unfortunately, they have a knack for picking the worst time and place to show off their new skills.

At a formal banquet with my college associates, Natalie once blurted out, "Let's get the hell out of here!" The next day at preschool I found out that a playmate used that expression on a regular basis. Fortunately, a toddler's knack for modeling behavior has a positive side as well.

Toddlers who resist attaching to their parents may look to their older siblings or peers for cues to "acceptable" behavior. Stressing the importance and responsibility of being a role model is often an effective way to help an older sibling feel important during the adoption transition. Parenting style is frequently modeled by children when they play dolls or house. In fact, abuse and neglect can be revealed by a child's play with dolls as they act out their experiences. Attachment behaviors are more commonly shown when a toddler emulates parental nurturing behavior. It may take a long time before the adopted toddler is familiar enough and trusting enough to emulate his new parents behavior, but parents must nonetheless use language and behavior which they would want their children to model. Toddlers won't automatically adopt the behavioral expectations of their new parents. It takes understanding parents, time, and special help to unlearn old patterns of behavior and learn new ways of relating.

Many newly-adopted toddlers are overwhelmed by the size and composition of their new home. So many new things to see, to touch, to taste–irresistible electronic equipment, siblings' rooms filled with tempting objects, alluring kitchen appliances, and even an overabundance of toys can over-stimulate the new family member. Parents can eliminate a lot of behavioral problems by toddler-proofing the environment, and limiting the toddler's choice of toys and other manipulatives. Gates can be used to keep toddlers away from rooms that are off limits. Visible treats invite whining, demanding behavior. Feeding toddlers on breakable dishes is asking for trouble.

Positive Parenting

Toddlers need and deserve to hear a lot more praise than correction. Parents can find creative ways to maintain a high ratio of "yes's" to "no's." Children tend to do more of what they get attention for. Focusing on good behavior increases the likelihood of its continuing, therefore, parents will want to look for opportunities to give positive attention. For younger toddlers, simple statements such as, "Thank you for being such a good helper" while shopping, a hug for being cooperative while getting dressed, or an unexpected small treat as a reward for good behavior is often effective. Some children respond well to direct verbal praise, others prefer a hug.

Praise should be specific and concise. When it's necessary to correct a toddler's behavior, tell him what he is to do. "Put your feet on the chair," is better than, "Don't put your feet on the table." "I've told you a hundred times not to do that," or "How many times to I have to tell you to stop that," is criticism and instills fear and confusion rather than trust and self-confidence. It is more appropriate to say, "Stop throwing your carrots. Put them on your plate." Such corrective messages are clear, concise, and help the child learn how to do it better.

Parents can avoid having to correct toddlers by redirecting their attention before there is a need for discipline. For example, Sheri is toddling directly toward Aunt Sally's knickknack shelf (at home the knickknacks would have been placed out-of-reach). Rather than scold her for touching the knickknacks, Mom redirects her attention by quickly engaging her in play or leading her away from the breakables. Physical redirection is usually more effective with toddlers than are verbal distractions.

Sylvia Rimm, nationally syndicated columnist, refers to an effective strategy called *referential speaking*. Referential speaking involves speaking positively about a child within earshot of the child. For example, when Gustavo is playing a few feet away, I'll say to my husband, "Have you noticed how nicely Gustavo and Natalie have been playing together lately?" A child will immediately tune in on a conversation if he hears his name. This technique is especially effective for toddlers whose prior experiences have resulted in damaged self-esteem as well as for those who have difficulty accepting direct praise.

Physical action should accompany verbal directions whenever possible. Sometimes inappropriate behaviors are due to miscommunication. Toddlers, especially those whose first language was different than that of their parents, need simple and clear messages. Toddlers can only process one or two concepts at a time. Most toddlers can handle a maximum of only two sequential directions such as, "Put your cars away and come into the kitchen for your snack." Toddlers will tune out or focus only on part of long or complicated directions such as, "Put the cars in their case and put them in the cupboard before you put on your pajamas and come to the kitchen for a snack." The toddler who tunes out complicated directives may then be inappropriately chastised for "not listening" or "deliberately disobeying".

Another strategy is to simultaneously tell and show a toddler what do. For example, guide the toddler's hand over the cat while saying, "Pet the kitty gently, like this." Still another strategy to enhance understanding is to repeat a directive using slightly different words. For example, the toddler who does not respond to the directive to "Pet the kitty instead of hitting," could be told, "Put your hand on the kitty and rub her fur like this."

Summary

Parents have the responsibility and the privilege of guiding their toddler's behaviors. Newly adopted toddlers may not want parental guidance, but they need it. Whether parents use child-centered, interactive, or parent-directed discipline, they can incorporate effective communication, conflict resolution, and behavior management strategies to help their toddlers learn to behave in ways that are helpful to themselves and others.

CHAPTER *N*ine

Parents Have Needs, Too

Tom looked terrible and had fallen behind at work. His co-workers were getting impatient with missed deadlines and sloppy work. Finally Tom reluctantly admitted that his newly arrived two-year-old son was keeping the entire family awake with his frequent night terrors. Expecting compassion, Tom was completely unprepared for the reaction he got. "What did you expect when you adopted a child from that kind of background?" "Maybe you should rethink this adoption before it's too late," his co-workers demanded.

Molly's mom lamented, "She wouldn't ever sit still or let me touch her. I didn't even get the time to just hold her and study her face and get a sense of who is this person. How do they expect me to know what to do with her? How come everyone else seemed to know what to do and I didn't?"

Jim and Joan had friends who were also adoptive parents, and friends who had toddlers, but they knew no one else who had adopted a toddler. Their issues were very different, and they felt very alone.

Does life every feel *normal* again after a toddler adoption? Yes, but getting there is a journey in itself. By reaching out, and taking care of themselves, toddler adoptive parents can create a new and even more beautiful family tapestry then they had in the past.

Parenting can be the most rewarding experience of a person's lifetime—fulfilling, enriching, energizing. The day of arrival can be a time of exceptional joy—the culmination of a long struggle to become parents. However, parents fantasies can be shattered by a toddler who does doesn't share their enthusiasm for the new relationship. For a few adoptive parents, the challenges seem to outweigh the rewards, and the tasks can seem overwhelming. In particular, parenting children with attachment problems or who have other severe special needs can be frustrating, lonely, and demoralizing. This is the stuff few parents talk about in public. Some don't even talk about it in private.

Parents can't take care of their children unless they take care of themselves first. Parents need to acknowledge the stressors specifically associated with toddler adoption and develop strategies to cope with them.

Post-Adoption Stress.

Giving birth and placement day are similar milestones in a family's journey. Unfortunately, parents sometimes focus so much on the event itself that they forget to prepare also for the days, weeks, months and years of parenting which lie ahead. It is not uncommon to feel a sense of let-down following a child's arrival. This phenomenon, known as post-partum depression or "baby blues", is known to affect some birth parents. However, it is also such a common phenomenon with adoptive parents that Lois Gilman coined a phrase to describe it: post-adoption stress.[6]

Psychological and physiological changes can affect the birthmother, bringing on depression. For adoptive parents, it may be that the biochemical changes brought about by anticipation, anxiety, and the sense of relief associated with placement parallels some of the changes experienced in giving birth.

Post-adoption stress may be exacerbated by the physical appearance and arrival behavior of the adopted toddler. Some parents have told me that they were shocked and dismayed when they first saw their toddler in person. Some were hoping their toddler would look more like an infant. Others were unprepared for the reality of their child's physical disabilities, such as a cleft palate or orthopedic impairments. Some parents' dreams of a blissful first meeting were shattered by the grief or acting-out of an angry toddler.

Fatigue also plays a major role in post-adoption stress. Visitors show up at inconvenient times. Siblings and even pets jealously demand more attention. The

6 Gilman, Lois. (1987) *The Adoption Resource Book*. New York: Perennial Library. p. 211.

toddler doesn't sleep through the night as expected. Sleep deprivation and other challenges of daily living have led many new adoptive parents to wonder if they would ever feel refreshed again during those first months. Molly's mom lamented, "I was exhausted for at least three months. She was very active and into everything, and her tantrums and bedtime struggles really took their toll. On top of it all, my workplace was asking me to come back to work. I had no idea what to do!"

While most adults like to think of themselves as pretty adaptable, many have a hard time adjusting to the abrupt lifestyle changes that are part of the parenting package. While the infant requires round-the-clock care, she doesn't take over the entire house immediately. Many adopted toddlers' parents suddenly feel as if everything familiar to them is gone–an orderly house, quiet meals, and undisturbed nights. One mom lamented, "My house was no longer my home. He took over." Post-adoption stress is aggravated also by the lack of empathy from family or friends. Many new toddler parents feel guilty talking about anything negative they are experiencing, because, after all, they chose to adopt. One mother lamented that her friends wouldn't commiserate with her about sleepless nights, telling her, "You wanted this child so don't complain!" Another mother's plea for empathy from friends was greeted by a stony and unsympathetic stare and the response, "Well, what did you expect when you adopted an abused child?"

Even anticipated adoption costs drain many family budgets, but many toddler adoptions also involve unexpected costs. Some families are still trying to pay off their infertility diagnosis and treatment procedures. Sometimes a parent decides after an adoption not to return to work outside the home, requiring the family to adjust to the loss of that income.

Toddler adoptions can put other stressors on parents' careers. International adoption may involve unexpected delays in the child's country of origin or unplanned travel requirements. My husband's anticipated six weeks in Peru turned into ten weeks. He was fortunate that his management team and board of directors were incredibly understanding and supportive. His agency continued to operate without a hitch. But for many people, an unanticipated four week absence would result in the loss of a job. Having to return to work before you feel ready is extremely stressful. Unsympathetic or ignorant employers may feel that you need to spend less time at home with a new toddler than you would with an infant, erroneously assuming that because of a toddler's physical maturity, she doesn't require as much parental care as a newborn. Parents who choose not to return to work after the adoption of their toddler may struggle with their changing role. A important part of many adults' self concept is tied up in what they do.

Extended family, friends, pediatricians, nurses, and even perfect strangers are solicitous of the novice status of new parents of infants. In contrast, by the time a child reaches toddler age, her parents are expected to be experienced and competent. Parents of toddlers are expected to be able to manage their child's behavior, describe food preferences, recite all clothing sizes, provide medical histories, know their scheduling preferences, describe their sleeping and eating habits, and be intimately familiar with their temperament. Unfortunately, parents of newly adopted toddlers don't immediately and automatically acquire this repertoire of knowledge and skills! And unlike many older child adoptions, the toddler cannot provide any of this information to her new parents. New toddler parents don't want to be constantly explaining that their child has just arrived home, but unless they do, they are expected to be as competent as experienced parents. As one mom candidly commented, "Parents of infants are gently initiated into the expectations of parenthood, while we, as instant parents of toddlers, are constantly being expected to hit the ground running. No one comforts me when I don't have the slightest idea what to do with my child. When my son acts up in public, people ask me what's wrong with him. When I say I don't have the slightest idea, they give me the weirdest looks."

Another parent of two adopted toddlers reported, "The first time I freaked out because my son had a high temperature, the doctor wasn't very sympathetic because she assumed I'd been through this before. You find yourself always explaining that your child is newly arrived, but you get tired of doing this because you don't always want to have to explain the circumstances of your family's life."

Illse had lived in four different institutions before arriving home at age three. Efforts to establish an attachment to Mom were complicated by the fact that Illse has cystic fibrosis, a life threatening condition. Illse's mom's efforts to earn Illse's trust were severely undermined by the fact that Mom had to participate twice a day in painful medical procedures.

Many new parents of toddlers with challenging behaviors worry about how their children's behaviors reflect on their parenting skills, especially in public. Every parent who has been subjected to the incriminating stares of people who walk past their tantruming child and the thinly veiled whispers of diners at the next table who overhear a three-year-old loudly declaring his distaste for his food and his Mom and Dad, knows what I'm talking about. As a teacher, I encountered colleagues who conducted verbal autopsies on parental competence based on a child's behaviors in the classroom. Lonny and Karina's mom complained, "Children's behavior in our society is unfortunately considered a reflection of parenting ability. There is little you can do to console a crying, grieving two-year-old with many angry temper tantrums. It eventually passes, but if you don't want others to pass judgment you just stay home!" Joey's mom described how he would yell, "Please don't kill me" when reprimanded in public places! Karina's parents were mortified when she screamed "feo!" (the Spanish word for "ugly") at her parents in stores and restaurants, but were relieved that most people in their community didn't speak Spanish!

People have trouble feeling entitled to parent their new toddler when family or friends question their choice to parent a toddler. Questions such as, "Weren't there any infants available?" or "What kind of parents would have their child taken away after two years?" are difficult to handle. The toddler who physically and/or verbally rejects his parents further challenges their sense of entitlement. In fact, some parents worry that their child's rejection may be interpreted by social workers or others to mean that they really are incompetent to parent. Adoptive parents are acutely aware that guardianship rights can be terminated.

Lisa's mom recalled, "In hindsight, I think I expected too much too soon in the beginning. I remember sitting at the kitchen table with my mom and holding my head in my hands. I kept saying I couldn't remember why I had wanted to adopt this child. What was I thinking? My mother told me to be patient, that everything would be all right." Lisa's mom reported that things did finally work out, but that it took much longer than she'd anticipated.

Symptoms of stress reported by parents included feelings of anxiety, anger, tiredness, loss of appetite, frequent crying, and physical symptoms such as elevated blood pressure or hyperventilation. Most parents experienced the occasional "blues" but a few needed to be treated for depression.

Feeling Lonely

Many new adoptive parents of toddlers feel isolated both from new parents of infants and from other parents of toddlers. In the days following placement, Noel refused to eat. Mom and Dad were frantic. The information received from the orphanage indicated that he had been a good eater, and he wasn't seriously underweight. They wondered what was wrong, so they asked good friends who had parented three children through the toddler years what they would do. Their friends responded, "Relax, this (refusing to eat) is just another phase he (your son) will soon outgrow. You know how kids are." No, they didn't know how kids are. They felt patronized, incompetent, and lonely. Noel did start eating by the fourth day, but he continued to be apathetic about food for many months.

In retrospect, Noel's parents believe that their son was depressed. Molly's mom complained, "All my friends and family kept saying that her tantrums and hostile behaviors were normal toddler behaviors, but what they didn't seem to understand was that I didn't know her, I didn't know what was normal, but I just sensed that there was more to it. I kept feeling like other people were discrediting my feelings." It wasn't until Mom attended a post-adoption workshop sponsored by her adoption agency for adoptive parents of older children that she learned about the connection between attachment problems and rage.

Joan and Jim had a strong waiting-for-placement support network. Waiting families regularly called each other and met periodically to compare notes and provide encouragement. However, they were the only couple of the five waiting families who accepted a toddler referral. Three families adopted infants, and one family was still waiting for an infant referral at the time they provided information. Even though they stayed in contact with the other parents, they reported soon feeling like outsiders. Their issues were very different, while the other families seemed to have even more in common after their adoptions than they had had before.

Extended family may, but don't always, provide a support network. Mara's parents reported feeling isolated because family and friends didn't believe how difficult their situation was at home. Mara, like other unattached children, was charming and well-behaved in the presence of others, but she was rejecting and physically aggressive toward her own family. Mom and Dad hesitated to talk to anyone about their difficulties because they didn't want their daughter and family labeled as "troubled." After finally receiving professional help and learning to communicate their needs to close family members, the extended family become much more supportive.

Reaching Out.

Personal and professional networking is an important way to develop relationships. Parent mentors can both support and assist parents in their new role. Parents can join an adoptive parent support group, or those who are not group types can generate a relationship with a small number of other parents. Social service agencies are a great source of information about toddler-focused post-adoption support groups in the area. Post-adoption services often include training and support groups. Parents can ask their social worker for a referral to a parent partner, someone who will be matched specifically to their needs. Parents can also network on a larger level through the World Wide Web or national support groups.

Unfortunately, some families isolate themselves from the benefits of support systems. They may be so tired of dealing with others during the adoption process (home study coordinator, birth families, social workers, lawyers, immigration officials, well meaning friends who ask endless questions, etc.), that they just want to be left alone with their new child. Other parents may deliberately isolate themselves if they are struggling, feeling too embarrassed to seek help, or feeling committed to try to tough it out alone. Unfortunately, self imposed isolation may divorce parents from potential sources of help and advice when problems emerge. The longer parents delay, the more difficult it is to reconnect with helping professionals. Disrupted adoptions and/or marriages can be a result of never being willing to seek help. Parents usually have to take the initiative to create a support network and let people know what their needs are. They can't wait for someone to come to them and offer their services and support. Parents have to reach out.

Parenting an adopted toddler is an act of courage and commitment which may sometimes need to be supplemented by professional support services for the children and/or the entire family. Just as parents needed the help of trained professionals to adopt, they may need professional help transitioning and adjusting to their parental role. Justin's mom knew it was time to get counseling when she realized that her constant migraines were related to the fact that she had been so angry during Justin's first six months at home that her teeth were constantly clenched. Professional counseling can often strengthen and sustain the adoptive family.

Taking Care of Yourself

Parents are their own best resource, but only if their minds and bodies are working well and working together. Adults can't think clearly or act rationally when they're exhausted. They must devise strategies for getting more or better rest. New parents need to maintain their own health through an appropriate diet and exercise. Stress management strategies are essential. Meditate, journal, read, take a bubble bath, listen to music, get out alone once in awhile. Sometimes the best way to relax is to simplify your life by paying someone else to clean the house or dropping some committee work.

A strategy that helped many parents retain their optimism and sense of stability was to spend time every day focusing on the positives in their lives. One mother described her pleasure in seeing her new daughter dressed in the outfits she had so lovingly selected, while another took great joy in watching her four boys playing together. Mila's dad enjoyed watching his malnourished daughter relishing her food.

One of the most important resiliencies for adoptive parents of toddlers is nurturing their own sense of humor and playfulness. Laughter is medicine for the soul; it serves a restorative function; it helps people keep their perspective; and it even enhances attachment. One of my most prized possessions is a poem my daughter wrote for Mother's Day when she was eleven. In her poem, titled, "Why I Love My Mother," she describes me as having "laughing eyes filled with love." I can't think of a better compliment.

Parents don't have to assume responsibility for all of their child's difficulties. Likewise, they aren't responsible for fixing everything, for everybody, right now. Feelings of ambivalence or even anger don't make a person a bad parent. These feelings are "occupational hazards" of parenting toddlers, especially when parenting children with special needs. However, adoptive parents may need to talk openly with someone–a spouse, friend, relative, agency personnel, or therapist–to help them separate the bad experience from their feelings for their child. Mothers often have more difficulty disengaging than do fathers, especially if they do not work outside the home, or if they are working with family systems therapists who believe that moms bear the major burden of responsibility for their children's mental health.

Just as rituals are important to toddlers, parents feel grounded by keeping the traditions that give them a sense of well-being, such as having pizza delivered on housecleaning day. Most new parents enjoy building new family traditions too, such as having everyone cuddle together in Mom and Dad's bed on Sunday mornings.

Summary

People who adopt are entitled to parent their children through law and through love. We are not perfect parents, but we are the right parents for our children. We can never convince everyone we meet that toddler adoption is a first rate route to parenthood, but what we believe in our hearts is more important than what others believe. Parent's belief in the rightness of their decision to parent is the foundation upon which they build their families. In the National Adoption Clearinghouse publication titled *Explaining Adoption to Your Child*, Christine Adamec provides the following reassuring insight into adoptive parenting: "Assuming that you adopted your child lawfully, there is no reason to feel guilty. Perfectionism is burdensome and self-defeating. Try to accept imperfection in yourself, and you won't burden yourself (and perhaps your child) with unrealistic expectations. No parent is perfect, and your best should be good enough. If you have made a mistake, in almost all cases it can be corrected."

Little by little, new toddlers become an integral part of the family. One day their parents wake up and realize that they can't imagine their lives without their new son or daughter. Than they know that love has grown, and that the tapestry of their lives is forever changed.

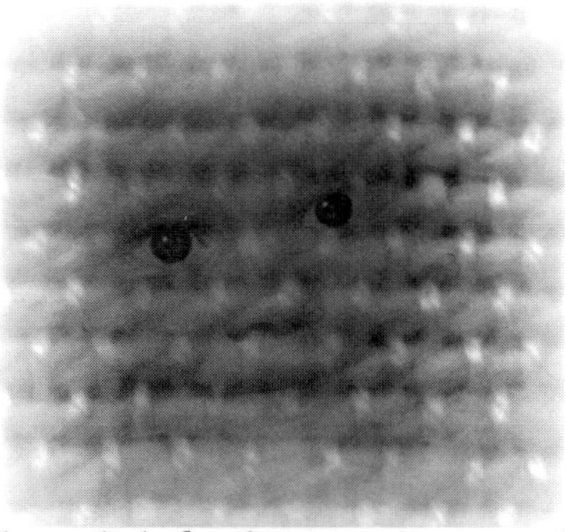

Epilogue

As I finish this book, my little family is growing up, and each day continues to bring new challenges and joys. The pattern of our individual lives and our family tapestry is rich, strong, and varied.

Natalie is growing into a beautiful young lady before our eyes and is thriving in middle school. On the threshold of becoming a teen, she continues to be loving and self-confident.

Gustavo is now seven years old and is a healthy and bright second grader. He starts each day by crawling into bed with Dick and me for a snuggle. His days are filled with friends, family time, piano practice, 4-H activities, and sports. His chocolate eyes sparkle with mischief and joy. Each stage of his life involves different understandings about his first year and a half of life. We are eagerly looking forward to an extended trip to Peru so Gustavo can meet the people of the village where he was born and walk the Inca trail.

The other children and families discussed in this book are changing and growing, too, adapting the past into their lives and moving forward. Katie, who was diagnosed as severely developmentally delayed shortly after her arrival at age two, is now an avid soccer player. The little girl who stopped talking after her arrival home at age three has recently moved again, this time across the country with her family. Even though she misses her old neighborhood and home, she is making new friends and doing well in second grade.

As we all look ahead to our children's school age, teenage, and adult years we know that we will face more challenges, but we have gained strength and confidence from surviving and growing during the toddler years. We are learning more every day about how to best meet the needs associated with each stage of our children's development. We will not hesitate to get help when we need it and we will celebrate every victory. We have grown in ways we never dreamed of, and the miracle of our children constantly reaffirms our belief in the value of life and the choices we've made. Our family tapestry is still incomplete, but each day the pattern becomes more evident, and the fabric becomes stronger.

At the end of my time on earth I will reflect on my life: my trials and my accomplishments. The most precious memories of my life will play out before my eyes. I will think of my family, and my memory of love will be of them.

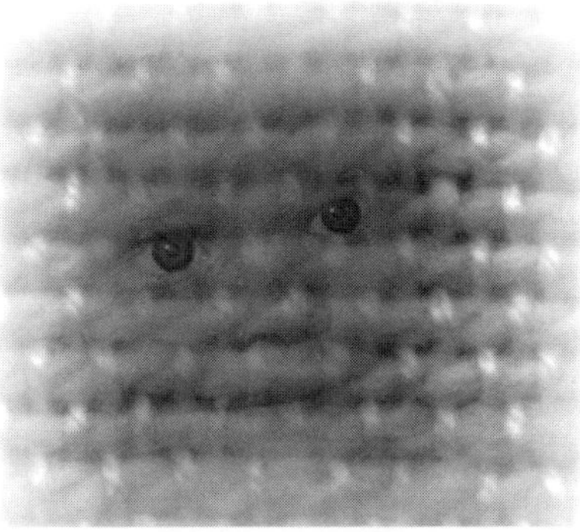

Appendix

Demographic Information on Questionnaire Respondents

Four of the children were adopted from the United States, while the remaining children were adopted internationally from Korea, Peru, India, Columbia, El Salvador, Guatemala, Honduras, Hong Kong, Romania, Brazil, and the Ukraine. Sixteen of the children were between twelve and twenty-three-months old at the time of placement, seven were between twenty-four and thirty-five months, and three were close to their third birthday. At the time the book was written one child was two years old, four children were three years old, seven children were four years old, five children were five years old, four children were six years old, and five children were older than seven years of age. At the time the book was written seven of the children were "onlies," while the others had from one to four siblings. The average family size was two children. In most of the families the adopted toddler was the youngest child at the time the book was written.

Four children arrived with diagnosed physiological, sensory and/or cognitive disabilities. Five others were subsequently diagnosed as having specific learning, emotional, and/or attention deficit exceptional needs.

Parental guardianship termination resulted in four of the children becoming available for adoption, while the others were either voluntarily relinquished by parents or abandoned. Approximately half of the children had experienced two preadoption placements (birth parent and one other) while the others experienced from three to an unknown number of disruptions. Three appeared to be the average number of disruptions prior to adoption.

At the time of adoption, parents ranged in age from twenty to forty-eight and averaged thirty-nine years of age. The vast majority had experienced primary or secondary infertility. Approximately one third of the parents had adopted other children, while four families adopted two toddlers. Approximately one-fourth of the families included birth children. Four parents were single at the time they provided information. The majority of the parents had completed between two and four years of post-secondary education.

Resources

Adopt INFO (Electronic Resource Collection and Network) contact: Lori Bock
The Children, Youth, and Family Consortium
University of Minnesota
12 McNeal Hall
1985 Buford Ave.
St. Paul, MN, 55108
(612) 625-7251
cyfcec@maroon.tc.umn.edu

Adoptive Families of America
2309 Como Ave.
St. Paul, MN, 55108
(612) 645-9955
www.adoptivefam.org

Adoptive Families
A Publication of Adoptive Families of America

Roots and Wings
Published by Roots and Wings Publications
P.O. Box 638
Chester, NJ, 07930

Attachment Disorder Parents Network
P.O. Box 18475
Boulder, CO, 80308

National Adoption Center
1500 Walnut St., Suite 701
Philadelphia, PA 19102
(800) TO-ADOPT

National Adoption Information Clearinghouse
10530 Rosehaven, Suite 400
Fairfax, VA, 22030
(703) 246-9095

National Resource Center on Special Needs Adoption
Suite 120
16250 Northland Dr.
Southfield, MI, 48075
(810) 443-7080

North American Council on Adoptable Children
Suite 106
970 Raymond Ave.
St. Paul, MN, 55114-1149
(612) 644-3036

Parent Network for the Post-Institutionalized Child
P.O. Box 613,
Meadow Lands, PA, 15347

The Developmental Delay Registry
7801 Norfolk Ave., Suite 102
Bethesda, MD, 20814

The Attachment Center at Evergreen
27618 Fireweed Dr.
Evergreen, CO, 890439

The Theraplay Institute
1137 Central Ave.
Wilmette, ILL, 60091
(708) 256-7334

Center for Attachment Therapy, Training, and Education
101 Hawk Point Ct.
Folsom, CA, 95630
(916) 988-6233

Adoption References

Adamec, Christine. (1993). *Explaining Adoption to Your Child.* National Adoption Information Clearinghouse. Rockville, MD.

Benson, P., Sharma, Anu and Roehlkepartain, E. (1994) *Growing Up Adopted.* Minnesota: Search Institute.

Borders, DiAnne. (1995). "The Passing of Innocence." *Adoptive Families,* Vol. 28. 26-28.

Fahlberg, Vera I. (1991). *A Child's Journey Through Placement.* Indianapolis, IN: Perspectives Press.

Fahlberg, Vera I. (1995). "Behavior Management and Reunification of The Child in Placement." Workshop presented on June 7th in Hayward, WI: Wisconsin Family Based Services Association.

Gilman, Lois. (1987). *The Adoption Resource Book.* New York: Perennial Library.

Hage, Deborah. (1995). "Building Self Esteem in Adoptive Families." Workshop presented at the 1995 Adoptive Families of America annual convention, Dallas, TX.

Hochman, Gloria and Anna Huston.(1994). "Providing Background Information to Adoptive Parents." Rockville, MD: National Adoption Information Clearinghouse.

Illsley-Clark, Jean. (1989). *Growing Up Again: Parenting Ourselves, Parenting Our Children*. Center City, MN: Hazelden.

Jarratt, Claudia Jewett. (1994). *Helping Children Cope with Separation and Loss*. Boston, MA: The Harvard Common Press.

Johnston, Patricia Irwin. (1992). *Adopting after Infertility*. Indianapolis, IN: Perspectives Press

Johnston, Patricia Irwin. (1995). "Talking with Children about Adoption." Workshop presented at the 1995 Adoptive Families of America annual convention, Dallas, TX.

Kirk, David. (1995). *Looking Back, Looking Forward, An Adoptive Father s Sociological Testament*. Indianapolis, IN: Perspectives Press.

Kirk, David. (1984). *Shared Fate: A Theory and Method of Adoptive Relationships.* Port Angeles, WA: Ben Simon.

Laws, Rita. (1995). "Between the Lines." *Adoptive Families*. Vol. 28, No. 4, pp. 34- 35.

Lockhart, Beth. (1994). "Talking about Difficult Adoption Information." *Ours*, 27(2).

Miller, Margi and Ward, Nancy. (1996). *With Eyes Wide Open: A Workbook for Parents Adopting International Children over Age One*. Minneapolis, MN: LN Press, Incorporated.

Mason, Mary Martin. (1995). *Designing Rituals of Adoption for the Religious and Secular Community*. Minneapolis: Resources for Adoptive Parents.

Reitz, Miriam. and Kenneth Watson. (1992). *Adoption and the Family System: Strategies for Treatment*. New York: The Guilford Press.

Rosenthal, James and Victor Groze. (1992). *Special-Needs Adoption.* New York: Praeger Publishers.

Roszia, Susan Kaplan. (1995). "Choosing an Adoption Therapist." Workshop presented at the 1995 Adoptive Families of America annual convention, Dallas, TX.

Schaffer, Judith and Christina Lindstrom. (1989). *How to Raise an Adopted Child*. New York: Crown Publishers Inc.

Smith, Debra. (1993). *Adoption and School Issues*. National Adoption Information Clearinghouse. Rockville, MD.

Van Gulden, Holly and Lisa Bartels-Rabb. (1994). *Real Parents, Real Children*. New York: Crossroad.

Attachment References

Belsky, Jay and Tresea Nezworski. (1988). *Clinical Implications of Attachment*. Hillsdale, New Jersey: Lawrence Erlbaum Associates.

Bowlby, John. (1973). *Attachment and Loss, Volume II: Separation, Anxiety and Anger*. New York: Basic Books.

Bowlby, John. (1980). *Attachment and Loss, Volume III: Sadness and Depression.* New York: Basic Books.

Bowlby, John. (1982). *Attachment (2nd ed.)* New York: Basic Books.

Bowlby, John. (1988). *A Secure Base: Parent-Child Attachment and Healthy Human Development*. New York: Basic Books.

Bowlby, John. (1989). *The Making and Breaking of Affectional Bonds*. London: Routledge.

Bradshaw, John. (1988). *Healing the Shame that Binds You*. Deerfield Beach FL: Health Communications.

Cline, Foster W. (1992). *Hope for High Risk and Rage Filled Children*. Evergreen, CO: Evergreen Consultants in Human Behavior.

Delaney, Rick and Frank Kunstal. (1993) *Troubled Transplants: Unconventional Strategies for Helping Disturbed Foster and Adoptive Children*. Portland, ME: National Child Welfare Resource Center for Management and Administration.

Jernberg, A. (1979). *Theraplay: A New Treatment Program Using Structured Play for Problem Children and Their Families*. San Francisco: Jossey-Bass.

Magid, Ken and Carole McKelvey. (1988). *High Risk: Children without a Conscience.* New York: Bantam Books.

Mansfield, Linda Gianforte and Christopher Waldmann. (1994). *Don't Touch My Heart: Healing the Pain of the Unattached Child.* Foreword by Foster W. Cline. Colorado Springs CO: Pinon Press.

McNamara, Joan. (1993) "Choosing a Therapist." *OURS. Vol. 26.*

Meisels, Samual and Jack Shonkoff. (1990). *Handbook of Early Childhood Intervention.* New York: Cambridge Press.

Watkins, Kathleen Pullan. (1987). *Parent-Child Attachment.* New York: Garland Publishing.

Welch, Martha. (1988). *Holding Time.* New York: Simon and Schuster Publishers.

Parenting References

Begley, Sharon. "Your Child's Brain." *Newsweek.* Vol. CXXVII, No. 8., pp. 54-61.

Blechman, Elaine. (1985). *Solving Child Behavior Problems at Home and at School.* Champaign, Ill.: Research Press.

Brazelton, T. Berry. (1989). *Toddlers and Parents.* New York: Bantam Doubleday Dell Publications.

Brazelton, T. Berry. (1995). *Touchpoints: Your Child's Emotional and Behavioral Development.* London: Penguin.

Brown, Lourene. (1990). *Toddler Time.* Boston: Little and Co.

Campbell, Susan B. (1990). *Behavior Problems in Preschool Children: Clinical and Developmental Issues.* New York: Guilford Press.

Children's Social Development: Information for Teachers and Parents. (1987). Urbana, IL: ERIC Clearinghouse on Elementary and Early Childhood Education.

Cline, Foster W. and Jim Fay. (1990). *Parenting with Love and Logic.* Colorado Springs, CO: Pinon Press.

Dinkmeyer, Don. (1989). *Parenting Young Children.* Circle Pines, MN: American Guidance Services.

Eisenberg, Arlene and Heidi Murkoff and Sandee Hathaway. (1994). *What to Expect: The Toddler Years.* New York: Workman Publishing.

Erikson, Eric. (1964). *Childhood and Society.* New York: Norton.

Kegan, Jerome. (1981). *The Second Year: The Emergence of Self-Awareness.* Cambridge, MA: Harvard University Press.

Herr, Judy. (1990). *Working with Young Children.* South Holland, IL: The Goodheart-Wilcox Company, Inc.

Kurcinka, Mary. (1991). *Raising Your Spirited Child: A Guide for Parents Whose Child is More Intense, Sensitive, Perceptive, Persistent, Energetic.* New York: Harper Collins.

Lieberman, Alicia. (1993). *The Emotional Life of the Toddler.* San Francisco, CA: University of California.

Lief, Nina. (1991). *The Third Year of Life.* New York: Walker Pub.

Linder, Toni. (1993). *Transdisciplinary Play-based Assessment.* Baltimore, MD: Paul Brookes Publishing.

Lindsay, Jeanne W. (1991). *The Challenge of Toddlers: Parenting Your Child from One to Three.* Buena Park, CA.: Morning Glory Press.

Miller, Karen. (1985). *Ages and Stages: Developmental Descriptions and Activities, Birth Through Eight Years.* Marshfield, MA: Telshare Publishing. Co.

Seifert, Kevin and Robert Hoffnung. (1991). *Child and Adolescent Development.* Boston: Houghton Mifflin Company.

White, Burton. (1990). *The First Three Years of Life.* New York: Prentice Hall.

Wolin, Steven and Sybil Wolin. (1993). *The Resilient Self: How Survivors of Troubled Families Rise above Adversity.* New York: Villard Books.

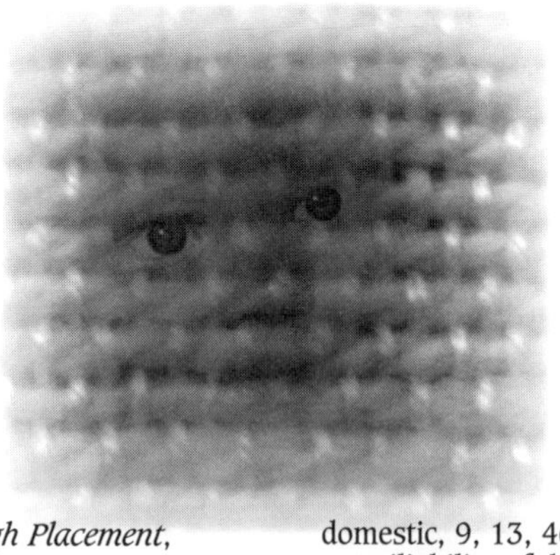

Index

Perspectives Press
The Adoption and Infertility Publisher
http://www.perspectivespress.com

Since 1982 Perspectives Press has focused exclusively on infertility, adoption, and related reproductive and child welfare issues. Our purpose is to promote understanding of these issues and to educate and sensitize those personally experiencing these life situations, professionals who work in these fields and the public at large. Our titles are never duplicative or competitive with material already available through other publishers. We seek to find and fill only niches which are empty. In addition to this book, our current titles include:

For Adults

Perspectives on a Grafted Tree
Understanding Infertility: Insights for Family and Friends
Sweet Grapes: How to Stop Being Infertile and Start Living Again
A Child's Journey Through Placement
Adopting after Infertility
Flight of the Stork: What Children Think (and when) about Sex and Family Building
Taking Charge of Infertility
Looking Back, Looking Forward
Launching a Baby's Adoption: Practical Strategies for Parents and Professionals
Choosing Assisted Reproduction: Social, Emotional and Ethical Considerations
Toddler Adoption: The Weaver's Craft

For Children

The Mulberry Bird: An Adoption Story (Revised)
Filling in the Blanks: A Guided Look at Growing Up Adopted
Lucy's Feet
Two Birthdays for Beth
Let Me Explain: A Story about Donor Insemination

About the Author

Mary Hopkins-Best is a mom. She and her husband Richard are parents of a daughter born to them on 12/25/83, and a son born on 5/27/89 who was adopted from Peru at seventeen months and arrived home at nineteen months. She has been a special educator, teacher educator, and college administrator for eighteen years and holds degrees in special and regular education, rehabilitation, and a Doctorate in education. She is the author of numerous publications about people with special needs, including "Bonding with a Toddler," *OURS*, November 1992, and has conducted workshops for UW-Extension and various adoption agencies. Dr. Hopkins-Best is a member of the Adoptive Families of America, Parents of Peruvian Adoptees, and Peruvian Adoptive Families; is a partner parent for Western Wisconsin Postadoption Project; and is a member of the Board of Directors for HOPE, International.